The Fractious Nation?

*Unity and Division
in Contemporary American Life*

Edited by
Jonathan Rieder

Stephen Steinlight
Associate Editor

UNIVERSITY OF CALIFORNIA PRESS
Berkeley · Los Angeles · London

University of California Press
Berkeley and Los Angeles, California

University of California Press, Ltd.
London, England

Library of Congress Cataloging-in-Publication Data

The fractious nation? : unity and division in contemporary American life.
   / Jonathan Rieder, editor ; Steven Steinlight,
associate editor.
        p.   cm.
   Includes bibliographical references and index.
   ISBN 0-520-23662-9 (alk. paper)—ISBN 0-520-
23663-7 (pbk. : alk. paper)
      1. National characteristics, American.
2. United States—Politics and government—
1989-.   3. Political culture—United States.
4. Citizenship—Social aspects—United States.
5. United States—Moral conditions.   6. United
States—Social conditions—1980-.   7. Social
conflict—United States.   8. Pluralism (Social
sciences)—United States.   I. Rieder, Jonathan.
II. Steinlight, Steven.

E169.12   F69 2003
973.931—dc21   2003001858

Manufactured in Canada
11   10   09   08   07   06   05   04   03
10   9   8   7   6   5   4   3   2   1

Contents

Acknowledgments

Numerous people and institutions made *The Fractious Nation?* possible. The American Jewish Committee (AJC) understood the urgency of the theme of fragmentation in American life and secured financial support for the original conference at Princeton University from which this volume evolved. This assistance is in keeping with its long history of safeguarding the rights of Jews, protecting the rights of all minorities, and affirming the ideals of respect and recognition that are crucial to liberal democracy. I also thank the W. K. Kellogg Foundation, most concretely for its generosity in providing the major funding for the Princeton Conference and more grandly for its broader concern for tolerance and equality. In addition, Princeton's Woodrow Wilson School of Government, as well as the Princeton Center for the Study of Human Values, offered intellectual, logistical, and financial support. Finally, when he was at the AJC as director of national affairs and later as director of publications, Stephen Steinlight played a role in the larger project and contributed to the book.

Jonathan Rieder

The Fractious Nation?

Jonathan Rieder

Throughout the last decades of the twentieth century, Americans recurrently worried about the conflicts that divided the nation. On the right and the left, mulling bitter struggles over abortion, politics, and race, people voiced concern that a certain testiness, and beyond, even fragmentation, had come to afflict our national life. *The Fractious Nation?* seeks to illuminate the schisms, the often anxious debates they inspired, and the powerful forces that continue to generate unity in the United States.

On the surface such political, racial, and cultural rancor seems starkly out of kilter with the feelings of shared purpose and molten outrage that appeared after September 11, 2001. That everything changed in the United States on that frightful day quickly became a great cliché, and like most clichés this one contains a kernel of truth. A book on unity and division in recent American history has to acknowledge the reverberating fact of brutal attack. Even though it has dimmed in memory, September 11 marked a break in our sense of time. Just as Pearl Harbor projected American might into the global arena and altered American politics and culture, the Al Qaeda attack has had a powerful, if not as drastic, impact on national solidarity, on perceptions of domestic and foreign enemies, on the balance of civil liberties and national security, on the debate over America's role as a global leader, on the congressional agenda, and on fiscal priorities.

Despite such undeniable changes, as well as the media's penchant for dramatic frames, everything did not change on that fateful day. No matter how successfully President Bush has exploited the anxieties of the moment, no matter how fecklessly Democrats have tried to articulate a rival message, the same ideological and cultural divisions that clove the electoral map into red and blue zones on election night 2000 were at work in the 2002 midterm elections. More critically, even if the kind of normality to which the United States has slowly returned after September 11 is not precisely the same normality we knew before, the nation's efforts to deal with threats are being shaped by forces that were forming right up to the moment when the two planes slammed into the World Trade Center. External threat may have mobilized feelings of internal unity, but unity did not appear out of nowhere. In short, the contrast between the time of fracture and the time of cohesion is not so stark after all.

Because *The Fractious Nation?* covers so much ground, it may help to preview what is to come. In the first chapter I offer a methodological prelude to the entire volume that recommends skepticism about the polemic on breakdown, in both its left and right versions. I have organized the essays that follow into three somewhat arbitrary parts that overlap in various ways: cultural clash, ethnic and racial division, and political conflict. The first part, Moral Unity, Moral Division, examines some of the moral and philosophical disputes that have divided Americans over matters of sexuality, multiculturalism, religion, family, and morality. Richard Bernstein muses on the proper balance between love of one's own ethnic or religious identity and loyalty to the larger public American identity. Shifting the discussion from nervousness about the loss of shared values, Martha Minow identifies other factors that bind Americans together, even in an age of so-called identity politics. Paul DiMaggio provides a chastening caution to fearsome scenarios of fragmentation by seeking a more precise definition of *fragmentation* than is common in the popular discussion. He also proposes a solution radical in its clarifying simplicity: look at the survey data to see if the evidence actually sustains the image of warring tribes, each hunkering down in its own cultural world. Jack Wertheimer reminds us that we do not come to the culture wars as abstract Americans but as carriers of distinctive religious and ethnic traditions; the split between secular modernist Jews and their Orthodox brethren, even as it participates in the broader dynamic of cultural contention, has its own distinctive accents.

The essays in the second part, Refiguring the Boundaries of Citizenship, explore how changing patterns of race and immigration have scrambled the boundaries of our national community. Actually, as both the Wertheimer and Bernstein essays suggest, the so-called culture war issues are not easily separated from the tensions generated by American racial, ethnic, and religious pluralism. Recent immigration, with its infusion of brown, olive, mahogany, yellow, and countless other colorations into the American mix, has radically challenged the black-white axis that has given American cleavages their shape for so long. Giving a more sociological twist to the popular query, Mary C. Waters questions whether the new immigrants are really so different from the lionized immigrants of yore. She argues that differences between them may lie in the social circumstances that shape their absorption into American life. Cecilia Muñoz documents a source of fragmentation at least as crucial as immigrants' refusal to embrace American culture: restrictions on classical American notions of citizenship, due process, and rights that characterized congressional immigration initiatives in the late 1990s. And Douglas S. Massey counters the parochialism of so much of the American discussion by placing migration decisions in their larger global context.

Black Americans, of course, remain at the center of the American Dilemma; race hasn't simply faded away, even as the new immigrants have complicated it. Jennifer Hochschild demonstrates that no matter how much they differ, ordinary whites and blacks overlap in many respects, suggesting rich areas of convergence no less than separatism and separation. Blacks, Kevin Gaines shows, continue to provoke white fears of the unassimilable black fragment, and the special history of blacks in this country complicates the efforts of black intellectuals to find the right balance of particularism and universalism.

Finally, part 3, Unity and Division in the Political Realm, analyzes political order and fragmentation. Theda Skocpol, rebutting the conservative attack on liberalism for its fragmenting tendencies, underlines the integrative functions of federal social policy and programs over the last century. Paul Starr, John J. DiIulio Jr., and E. J. Dionne Jr. examine more recent aspects of fragmentation in electoral politics. For Starr the 1996 election, and especially Clinton's victory following the 1994 Republican electoral surge, epitomizes the power of a vital popular center. DiIulio, mindful of the control that the more individualistic and heartless strains of right-wing ideology exert within the Republican Party, sketches the moral contours of a compassionate conservatism that is equally in key with the practical requirements of an American middle that hovers close to the center. Dionne's chronicle, which takes us up through the 2002 midterm elections, identifies new lines of division and disputation that over-

lap without entirely displacing the older liberal-conservative cleavages—
a center-left "Third Way" that Clinton and Tony Blair crafted in the 1990s
and a center-right "Fourth Way" that Bush offered, at least rhetorically,
in the 2000 presidential election. In the epilogue I consider how these
various forces are likely to play out in the near and somewhat more distant future, especially given the events of September 11.

Clearly, the articles vary by approach, as well as by subject. They range
from spirited confession of moral commitment to dispassionate analysis
of surveys. Some look at a long trend developing over decades, whereas
others hone in on a more circumscribed topic or moment. But all aim to
transcend the presentism that deforms so much social analysis, and all
aim to place some of our most important social, cultural, and political
divisions in historical and social organizational perspective. More, however, is at stake here than the abstract generalities of setting the record
straight and intellectual clarity: nothing less than the character of the
American nation and the resilience of its democratic culture.

FISSURES AND FRACTURES

To place the essays in context, I want to mention some of the contentious
events and fractious tendencies that have raised concern about whether
the center of American life is holding—and even whether there is such a
thing as an American center. Surely the signs of symbolic violence have
been plentiful enough. In the 1980s certain new right preachers called
for stoning homosexuals to death, and white supremacists, off the Web
and on, have fumed and declaimed. For a time the vituperation on talk
shows and video games gave rise to fears that there was something cor-
rosively amiss in our national life.

Verbal violence at times has spilled over into nasty political campaigns
in which candidates demonize their opponents. This tendency may have
reached a zenith at the 1992 Republican convention, when Pat Buchanan
issued his famous call for culture war. The Clinton impeachment hear-
ings, with their subtext of attempted coup, continued the ideological
vendetta, only by other means. Once again, in the midst of the Florida
electoral brouhaha in 2000, some Republicans whispered darkly about
judicial usurpation by liberals on the Florida State Supreme Court, not
to mention the perfidy of disloyal un-Americans who mocked the true
grit of the American military, all because the Democrats challenged the
military ballots from Duvall County.

On Michael Hannady's drive-time talk show on New York City's conservative WABC radio, a marine raised the specter of junta: he would take to the streets, machine gun in hand, before heeding the orders of an ersatz commander in chief like Gore. Liberals, responding to such ominous hints, warned of the dangers to constitutionalism. And when a right-wing Republican faction of the U.S. Supreme Court seemed to seize the reins of government, handing the election to Bush on constitutionally dubious grounds, liberals, too, muttered about judicial usurpation.

The violence in recent decades has not always been verbal, and race has been at the heart of some of the nation's nastiest skirmishes. In Crown Heights, Brooklyn, in the early 1990s a mob of blacks chanting "Get the Jew" ran down Yankel Rosenbaum and fatally stabbed him. This was only one of a series of racial dramaturgies in New York City that tore at the city's social fabric—including the racial murder of Yusuf Hawkins by a gang of white toughs in Bensonhurst, Brooklyn, and the "wilding" incident in Central Park, in which a gang of black youths were wrongly convicted of raping a white woman. The Los Angeles riots gave us the searing picture of Korean shopkeepers staring down black rioters with their AK-47s, as plumes of smoke and fire curled into the sky. In baroque permutation of alliance a Latino rioter cried, "This one's for Latisha"—he was referring to Latisha Harlins, the black teen slain by a Korean shopkeeper—before heaving his Molotov cocktail through the air. But violence was never confined to the realm of race. The entire debate swirling about the causes of the school massacre in Columbine, with its rival versions of causality and blame, further reinforced fears of fratricide. Echoing feminist cries about the violence of imagery, conservatives saw the violence of video games, rock lyrics, and movies as triggers for murder.

Less ostentatious forms of fragmentation have been even more prominent features of the social landscape. As Theda Skocpol argues (chap. 11), the long successful formula for generous public provision that bridged gaps of class, region, and religion and tied diverse Americans into shared networks of obligation and caring yielded to divisive rivalries among the races and generations. Meanwhile, observes Martha Minow, "Class divisions find expression in spatial separation, as privileged whites wall themselves off from others, huddling in suburbs and gated communities with their own security, garbage collection, and after-school entertainment" (chap. 3). And neonativists, convinced the new immigrants are fragmenting the nation, have done a bit of fragmenting themselves with queries like Pat Buchanan's: "If we had to take a million immigrants in, say, Zulus, next year or Englishmen and put them in Virginia, what group would be easier to assimilate and would cause less problems for the people of Virginia?"

Even our institutions of higher learning have not been immune to such mean-spirited and suspicious tribalism. For many critics the campuses have emerged as incubators of a broader retreat from democratic universalism. At the end of the last millennium the evidence was pervasive: anti-Semitic speakers such as Khallid Muhammad stirred black campuses, aroused students, shut down newspapers in the name of political correctness, and threatened a free press. The more common expression of the worst aspects of identity politics have been subtler but also disheartening: the refusal to engage, the timidity that masquerades as belligerent assertion of one's own kind, as the emergence of the word *Twinkie* among Asian-American students indicates: yellow on the outside, white on the inside. *Twinkie* has the same restrictive twist that is evident when blacks challenge the authenticity of other blacks by saying they are not black enough. This narrowness can take exquisitely Talmudic form, as when a convert to Orthodox Judaism at Brandeis University is rejected by the arbiters of Orthodoxy as "a jean skirt girl," meaning she's not observant enough.[1] Such provincialism and the dismissive separations that go with it have sometimes been validated by "left" proponents of multiculturalism in ethnic, women's, and gay studies programs. The "belief in essential group differences" of these new fundamentalists, as Todd Gitlin points out, easily converts into "a belief in superiority."[2]

THE VAGARIES OF FRAGMENTATION

If evidence has abounded for the proposition that the United States has been vulnerable to fragmentation, a number of things suggest some restraint is in order before we rush to judgment. As we will see throughout this book, the strange career of some of these divisions—the so-called culture wars over religion and lifestyle, the great divide of race and anxieties and anger over the new immigration, and the use of divisive appeals in the political realm—defies such simplifications.

For one thing the very term is problematic. Like other charged words, *fragmentation,* with its ominous implications of shards flying, can easily become a form of incantation. I have adopted the term *fractious,* which better evokes the facts of our condition and the normality of conflict as a routine feature of social life. For another thing the very sensuousness of graphic conflict, its ability to transfix, should give caution. Typically, surface events mask the deeper currents swirling below them.

As a result it is not always easy to separate enduring reality from something as lambent as mood. All in all, a country obsessed with palm recorders and *Survivor*, Viagra and e-trading, the Internet and *Sex in the City* is not the same as a country convulsed by the frenzies of abortion wars, of nativist recoil against immigrant strangers in our midst, and of intense racial squabbling. And neither cluster of images captures a country nervous about anthrax and Afghanistan, Iraq and Enron, deficits and dirty bombs.

A few examples from all three realms of the culture wars, ethnic and racial pluralism, and political contention underscore the need for historical perspective. The high point of nativist declamation, seeping into the 1995 gubernatorial race in California, provoked cries of "Send them back," and gamier cries still. Yet that very process, through a recoil in the next electoral cycle, helped elect a Democratic governor in California. Even more amazingly, the surging immigrant vote helped defeat Congressman Robert Dornan in that sacred fount of paleoconservatism, Orange County. And this presidential time around, Bush made every effort to parade his brown-skinned Latino nephew, who became the affirmative-action equivalent of a trophy wife. What really upset him about failing public education, Bush kept insisting all through the 2000 election, was that Latinos and blacks were being left behind. The party that turned its back on basic democratic principles during the civil rights revolution in the name of property rights was now testifying to its zeal for that charged and hackneyed word—*diversity*. And still after the election Bush kept stalking the black electorate (at least he tried to signal Republican moderates through his stalking), showing up to worship in black churches, whose prophetic black preachers knew they were among the likely beneficiaries of faith-based initiatives.

Meanwhile, new right diatribes had given way to a velvet revolution, in which sundry reverends—and even Ralph Reed, former director of the Christian Coalition—were grinning and bearing it with Bush's stealth version of prolife. Such equivocation aimed to finesse, to avoid scaring the middle-class soccer moms. Like some latter-day Cato, Jerry Falwell had retired to the cloistered life of Liberty Baptist University. Even Lynne Cheney, the wife of Dick Cheney and onetime cultural warrior at the National Endowment for the Humanities, seemed subdued enough, primly behaving through the 2000 election, in the interest of a Cheney-Bush effort to distance itself from the most demonic, potentially destabilizing, factions within the Republican base. In February 2001 she was able to briefly reprise her old culture warrior role in an attack on that artful, but infantile, wordsmith from the lumpen land of white Detroit, the rapper Eminem. Only this time she did so under cover of a defense of gays and lesbians against the white rapper's lurid homophobic lyrics.

A similar evolution has been evident in the realm of ethnic and racial pluralism. Not even a decade has passed since Salim Muwakkil wrote of "the nationalist moment." Capturing the black political mood in the mid-1990s, he observed, "For the first time in thirty years, it appears that black Americans again are on their own in their quest for equality. Ignored by Republicans and taken for granted by Democrats, many blacks feel politically invisible to a white mainstream that seems oblivious to the misery in many of their communities. . . . Unsurprisingly, black nationalism is the mood of the moment in the African-American community."[3]

But here, as in the larger political environment, that seems ages ago, and it may be more precise to describe this period as "after the nationalist moment," at least in the sense of organized and angry political manifestations. Farrakhan, like yesterday's news, has been eerily in remission. The fading of the passions of the O. J. Simpson trial and the Los Angeles riots are further surface indicators of that shift. And there are still other signs of this turning inward toward communal self-help rather than outward toward politics and the state. In city after city prophetic black preachers like Eugene Rivers in Boston and Johnny Youngblood in East New York, Brooklyn, precociously anticipating the era of faith-based voluntarism, have set about the task of building institutions and expanding the role of civil society in the process.

The vagaries in the reputation of rap, which has often served as a primal indicator of white race panic, nicely track this dynamism. From the outset the bardic element that was part of old-school hip-hop aimed to chronicle an earthier, plebeian reality that was denied by the smooth middle-class crossover of 1970s fusion soul and disco. But such storytelling was always eclipsed in the imagination of whites by their fixation on cop killers and West Coast thuggishness, not to mention the juvenile, lewd antics of groups like 2 Live Crew. But over the course of the 1990s, rap music underwent cultural rehabilitation, purging itself of its sordid connotations by snuggling under the blanket of hip-hop and mutating into something more cuddly—and crossover too. *Time* magazine heralded Lauryn Hill on its cover as the latest American diva. Hip-hop not only lost the cache of "alternative" music; it's no longer a sign of black separatism, a depoliticized version of the street slogan that used to appear on black teenagers' T-shirts, "It's a black thing, you wouldn't understand." Symbolizing the complex and changing process of cultural exchange, hip-hop has become a transracial genre open to Korean-American, Gujarati-American, and Filipino MCs, not to mention the so-called "wiggers," or "white niggers," who can scratch a turntable or handle a mike.

The career of rap impresario Sean "Puff Daddy" Combs embodies this familiar trajectory and may stand for one integrative dynamic that is alive in black life. Despite his various encounters with the law, he has been refigured—has refigured himself—as a society celebrity who mingles with Martha Stewart in the Hamptons. Combs has even held up as his models the Jewish businessmen from DreamWorks—Steven Spielberg, Jeffrey Katzenberg, and David Geffen. Indeed, the paeans to "living large" featured in one strain of rap music, much like the celebration of the "thug life," not only evoke "What Makes Sammy Run" but place this generation of tough guys in a longer lineage of Irish, Italian, and Jewish gangsters. In a sense, the rap moguls may be analogous to the garment-industry entrepreneurs who amassed crude capital so that the next generation would accumulate more cultured—and cultural—forms of capital.

Like some haunted refrain, the mid-1990s rap cry of "It's all about the Benjamins" (Benjamin Franklins, or one-hundred-dollar bills) simply underscored the timelessness of the American fascination with success, as does that department of MTV, "Cribs," that parades the palatial estates and chichi kitchens, with their honed marble and granite backsplash and stainless steel—to say nothing of the occasional Victorian chintz—of all manner of NBA and rap stars. And so, oddly enough, Combs becomes just another instance of a (Robert) Mertonian moment of anomic innovation, fiddling and finagling the hip-hop means toward a shared pecuniary end.

The outcome could have emerged from the fondest fantasies in the playbook of the Whigs in the nineteenth century, as they sought to get rid of the self-destructive image of aristocrats and to appeal to the common classes with the phantasm of pecuniary success achieved the Alger way: Puff Daddy, it seems, has joined the day traders, Web virtuosos, and Silicon Valley hotshots. They really are all Lockeans now. At least they were until the Dow began to plummet, worries about the transparency of financial institutions spread from the Third World to the United States, and savings bonds suddenly became a seductive alternative to mutual funds.

All in all, then, it is a good time to step back from the unfolding pag-
eantry of events to reach for the clarity of detachment. As we do so, we
discover this much: Even as they play out in the most intricate, sometimes idiosyncratic, incarnations, two sets of common themes course
through these ruminations on our current state. The first is methodological: simply put, our efforts to appraise the moral fiber and social
cohesiveness of a society, especially one as complex and multifarious as
the United States, are an especially dicey enterprise, inevitably subject to
a number of estimating errors and distortions.

The second point is more substantive. Although this volume is a testimony, at least modestly, to disagreements over the meaning, intensity,
and import of these battles, on balance a counterpicture emerges. In important respects American society has shown a striking resilience, a classic ability to absorb change without sacrificing its basic sense of identity.
Surely, conflicts of all stripes continue to divide Americans and threaten
democracy. But like the other slogans adduced to sum up change—
narcissism, culture war, backlash—the master imagery of "fragmentation" may be handier for expressing personal and cultural anxieties about
change than for illuminating them.

We have become in many respects, both in private life and public culture, a more tolerant, democratic, and cohesive society than we once were.
More fractions and sectors have been incorporated under the banner of
civic society. In a sometimes volatile, but ultimately creative, dynamic of
incorporation, essential notions of rights have been extended to broader
constituencies—not just to those "suspect classifications" like race but
also to children, wives, and the disabled. Rights of cultural recognition,
albeit trivialized in public-school celebrations of ethnic holidays and distorted by mythic third-grade histories of the Aztecs and Taino Indians,
have disseminated widely, if not always deeply, in vernacular forms. Perhaps most counterintuitively, the right wing is a more genteel, less ethnocentric right than it used to be. And in countless domains, including
the feistily contested ones of family and sexuality and race, divides of
opinion have been closing.

This analysis is not quite a swerve back to some ancient faith in American exceptionalism or the identity of redeemer nation. Such notions too
often displayed a blithe confidence in American institutions, heralding the
nation's successes at the expense of our failings. But neither is the cumulative wisdom of *The Fractious Nation?* quite a refutation of that progressive faith. It's more a chastened twist on the theme of democratic nationalism that recognizes both the vitality of the American liberal tradition

and the tough work of litigation and moral critique, protest and politics, that is needed to ensure the fulfillment of democratic ideals. There is nothing pristine or guaranteed about those ideals; to acquire suasive power, they often need to be reworked and revived and sometimes even remembered. As a result their energy—and the sense of collective "we" those values can inspire—has often been most evident when turned like a weapon against various forces of particularism—white, Puritanical, Anglo-Nordic, antigay, Christian, anti-Catholic—that reject inclusive universalism. Even claims for narrow forms of identity, as proponents of queer and hip-hop nations tacitly grasp, have managed to find in the universalism of the tradition a haven for their own tribal huddling.

None of this should be cause for smug celebration. In one of those ironic twists that recurs throughout this book, this relative cohesiveness—and one must emphasize that qualifier *relative*—is not entirely good news. For starters there's the problem of a baseline; if the starting point of racism is extraordinarily high, as it surely was in the United States, these two vexingly rival things can still be simultaneously true: racism of the most virulent sort has diminished mightily, and there remains a core of people who dislike blacks intensely, as much, perhaps, as one-fifth of the nation.[4] This latter bunch, it turns out, tends to comprise the same individuals who hate Jews, and they are not so fond of other kinds of difference either. There remains, then, a dangerous, if shrinking source of authoritarianism in the land.

Moreover, if the nation had truly become a good deal more cohesive even before September 11, it is not self-evident that harmony is the most noble ideal for societies to strive for. The absence of manifest conflict may simply mean accommodation to injustice, indifference to inequality, or the exhausted inability to imagine striking back. Quiet riots, as Roger Wilkins once deemed them, are utterly compatible with a lack of surface indications of "fragmentation," and they can be as damaging as less tranquil ones. Poverty, the diminished life chances that go with it, poor health, the excess political power that goes with money, and much more besides fragmentation—or these particular forms of fragmentation—threaten the fabric of society. The Enron scandal provided a timely reminder of David A. Hollinger's warning that a "business elite with a transnational focus will find certain uses for the American state, but it has little need for the nation. . . . Those who worry about the fragmenting of America would do well to attend more closely to this variety of separatism."[5]

Ironically, such relative convergence as has emerged in recent decades may not even be good news for partisans of order. After all, agreement in certain spheres has the uncanny ability to generate discord in others. To take only one example, the declining primacy of racism, anti-Semitism, and ethnocentrism among traditionalist Christians—one mark of diminishing incivility in a democratic society—helped quicken the tempo of ideological and cultural warfare, if only by creating a panreligious alliance devoted to moral restoration. We could even say the diminution of fragmentation made for, even was a necessary condition for, the heightening of fractiousness. The current state of affairs is replete with other contradictions that remind us that conflict and harmony, fragmentation and integration, are hardly polar oppositions, but that is not even the most ironic turn that emerges from the chapters ahead.

NOTES

1. Jonathan Rieder, "Jewish Women in Search of Themselves," *CommonQuest,* vol. 3, no. 3/vol. 4, no. 1: 6.

2. Todd Gitlin, *The Twilight of Common Dreams: Why America Is Wracked by Culture Wars* (New York: Henry Holt, 1995), 164.

3. Salim Muwakkil, "The Nationalist Moment," *CommonQuest,* vol. 1, no. 2: 18.

4. See Paul M. Sniderman and Thomas Piazza, *The Scar of Race* (Cambridge, Mass.: Harvard University Press, 1993), 35–65.

5. David A. Hollinger, *Postethnic America: Beyond Multiculturalism* (New York: Basic Books, 1995), 149.

CHAPTER I

Getting a Fix on Fragmentation

"Breakdown" as Estimation Error, Rhetorical Strategy, and Organizational Accomplishment

Jonathan Rieder

It is not easy to get a fix on "fragmentation." There is something too primal about social conflict and the passions it stirs to encourage calm appraisal. It is common to say that change can be "dizzying"; naturally enough, people become unnerved by the ominously open character of uncertainty. By upsetting familiar expectations, as Durkheim famously argued, even moments of good fortune may plunge its beneficiaries into the abyss of anomie. And cognitive psychologists have observed how the fallibility of human beings, who aspire to rationality but often fall short of attaining it, leaves them vulnerable to distorted judgment as they try to make sense of the world. Meanwhile, a key existential dilemma can deform our response to change: even as human beings yearn for a changeless state of tension-free satiation, we also have a more curious, restless disposition that nudges us forward to engage the world. This tension between embeddedness and emergence can provoke volatile, ambivalent reactions in times of social upheaval.[1]

The vertigo of change, the difficulty of construing the fractious events that provoke the label *fragmentation,* the ever-present danger of error and illusion—this chapter takes up these elemental themes and pursues them in their intricate variations. And although there are countless ways to succumb to misreading, three kinds of interpretive mistakes in particular provide the focus of this analysis. Once we take such mistakes into account, it becomes clear that the verdict of fragmentation is the outcome not just of major fractures in the foundation of social life but also of estimation error, rhetorical strategy, and organizational dynamics.

The first set of errors, the subject of section 1, involves dynamics both of mind and the senses. Transfixed by the flamboyant, if ofttimes rare, case, people—imperfect in their cognitive abilities, overwhelmed by a glut of equally imperfect information, yet resolved to fashion the semblance of a process of reasoning—often move from the skimpiest of evidence to grand verdicts. Such inferential leaping is only one of the ways the distractions of attention yield bad conclusions. Sometimes the convulsions of the moment simply envelop the observer in the haze of the present. In the process the ground of the past—and the comparative vantage it permits—vanishes from view.

The second category of errors, the subject of section 2, originates at some remove from sensuous experience and involves the dangerous trap of language. To some extent the way we construe the signs of fragmentation reflects our received rhetorics, which channel our judgments in ways that suspiciously sustain our ideological passions. In our time conservatives have resorted to the narrative of fragmentation more than have so-called progressives. At least the right has favored specific versions of the narrative, especially the theme of cultural war, whose effect, if not intent, tends to displace accounts that place economic injustice, social inequality, and racist exclusion at the core of social discussion.

The final set of interpretive errors, the subject of sections 3, 4, and 5, derives from the absence of what might be called an "institutionalist heuristic," a set of ad-hoc decision rules that guide human attention to the pragmatic institutional and organizational forces that often account, if not for the fact of conflicts of interest and identity, then at least for the precise form they achieve at a particular historical moment. Institutional dynamics shape both the choreography of conflict and the production of false impression and wrongheaded theorizing.

It may seem rarified to begin a volume on the frenzies of fragmentation with the abstracted concerns of interpretive methodology, but I hope to temper that sense of abstraction in two ways. First, as the essay progresses, without departing from the methodological emphasis I will gradually shift to the substantive question of what cumulative impression of divisions in the United States can be discerned in the various essays in this volume. The second point is more cosmic and moral. Surely there is a long literature in comparative history, sociology, and political science that warns of the danger of divisive conflicts to democratic life. Yet it is axiomatic that we can't buttress democracy by flailing at phantoms; we need a sober-minded, empirical sense of the magnitude and causal flow of the dynamics that threaten it.

SEDUCTION OF THE SENSES

The metaphor of fragmentation evokes the fragility of democratic pluralism. Seymour Martin Lipset captured the demonic power of xenophobic movements of the middle classes in his concept of "center extremism," in which a frustrated petite bourgeoisie turns to movements of populism, Caesarism, and fascism.[2] Mindful of such unnerving precedents, Kevin Phillips began to worry at an early point in the Reagan Revolution about the populist conservatism he himself had heralded only a few years earlier. Invoking the aphorism of alarm—"kindred causes, congruent psychologies . . . suggest a potential for turmoil"[3]—Phillips discerned four striking parallels with Weimar Germany: inflation, the collapse of faith in political institutions, the nihilism of a libertine and decadent culture of excess, and nationalist frustration in the aftermath of military humiliation.

Although one can spot in recent conflicts glimmers of such parallels, one has to be careful not to casually invoke them (as indeed Phillips did). Whether choosing metaphors or historic parallels, the trick involves making the apt comparison, and dangers emerge all along the way. The key challenges to clear-eyed understanding lie with a host of methodological difficulties that involve the ways we go about knowing, the ways we make inferences, the ways in which our attention is drawn to objects of fascination.

Perhaps the most daunting of these obstacles unfolds at the elemental level of the senses, and it involves the intrusive power of visual experience. What is more vivid than the pulverized body of James Byrd, after he was roped like a rodeo calf by white racist goons and dragged from the back of a pickup truck; the crucified body of Matthew Sheppard, strung up on a barbed-wire fence as testimony to homophobic mania; the almost balletic dance of the black thugs over the felled body of the white truck driver whose head they smashed with a concrete block in the midst of the Los Angeles riots; or the bodies of the kids strewn about the lunchroom in Columbine, Colorado.

Such evidence makes it easy to glide from the small moment to vast pronouncements in liquid elisions. Yet it's not always clear whether such fragments yield evidence or incantation. And if the former, what sort of evidence? The problem here is one of metonymic reduction combined with media-generated panic: the part may not stand for the whole. Worse, the flamboyantly vivid part can wield a power to transfix that easily leads one astray.

Such faulty estimates have been especially vivid in the realm of race, in which the media fit complex events into their own narrative form of racial spectacle. The Crown Heights riots, for example, were undeniably one of the most violent moments of "black-Jewish" conflict in U.S. history. They also served for many as a symbol of the murderous tribal passions that always threaten to tear apart the urban order. But that was not all Crown Heights was. Gavin Cato, the little Guyanese boy run over and killed by a car in the procession of the Lubavitcher rabbi, played with Jewish boys on his block. In the riot aftermath there were black residents who went out of their way, through compensatory smiles and waves, to affirm sympathy for their Jewish neighbors and distance themselves from the rioters. A Haitian-American taxi driver told me poignantly of the Jewish wariness his approach provoked. "As I get close, I can tell, the Jews are thinking, 'What's he going to do to me? Is he one of the guys who broke my windows?'" And in other respects Crown Heights could be seen as a polyglot neighborhood in which most of the time klezmer and calypso, rasta dreadlocks and Yiddish *payess*, West Indian carnival and Purim parade manage to coexist in an uneasy truce.[4] Clearly, observers have a good deal of discretion in how to code such interactions.

Beyond the oddities of Crown Heights, much of the 1990s public discussion of "black-Jewish conflict" and the meaning of black support for Louis Farrakhan suffered from a similar fixation on vivid events. Farrakhan's reference to "synagogues of Satan" conjured up the anti-Judaic elements of the New Testament, and in the mid-1990s, Khallid Muhammad, who never stopped taunting "Jew York City," upped the ante of anti-Jewish vitriol in his Kean College speech, in which he targeted "hook-nosed, bagel-eating, lox-eating Jews" for controlling the slave trade and "sucking our blood in the black community." In response to such incidents Henry Louis Gates Jr. offered a version of the following argument on the *New York Times* op-ed page: "While anti-Semitism is generally on the wane in this country it has been on the rise among black Americans." And its very character, worried Gates, had transmuted into " 'top-down' anti-Semitism, [which is] in large part the province of the better-educated classes."[5]

But even while black anti-Semitism took new organizational forms and disputes over Farrakhan, the Million Man March, and the burning of a

Jewish-owned store in Harlem stoked black-Jewish tension, anti-Semitism fell among blacks at all levels of education, as a 1998 Anti-Defamation League study conceded. Moreover, the report added, "The current survey reaffirms the strong [inverse] correlation between education level and acceptance of anti-Jewish stereotypes."[6] A wonderful wrinkle on the old theme of black philo-Semitism emerged from other data as well; anti-Semitic blacks had more favorable impressions of Jews than of whites in general.[7] In an oft-repeated pattern wild racial dramas riveted awareness that did not, and perhaps had no way to, take heed of the deeper—and silent—alignment of opinion.

We are dealing in part with the dilemma psychologists refer to as the "availability heuristic," which refers to the propensity of human attention to alight on rare but highly flamboyant instances in the quest to demystify a murky reality. Dependence on such obvious signs of hatred, intolerance, and breakdown as clues is not irrational; it follows the same economizing logic of "statistical discrimination." In a less than perfect world suffused with ambiguity, it's a way of getting information on the cheap. But with information, no less than any other purchase, you often get what you pay for, which means the information may be no more perfect than the world it seeks to know. So the relation between vivid sign and general tendency, between organized conflict and the sentiments of the broader society, between a cramped and bounded rationality and the distorted verdict that issues forth from it is hardly self-evident or mechanically linear.

Indeed, organized manifestations of violence may actually follow from "liberalization"; in some white ethnic neighborhoods, only after a loosening of racial attitudes has enabled blacks to gain entry to the housing market does sufficient integration reach a threshold to call forth the virulent rejectionists. In short, the expressions of "fragmentation" do not track precisely with some underlying set of attitudes, feelings, and opinions. As a result the tendency to read such volatile episodes as reflections of something deeper and more pervasive is risky business.

Less dramatic aspects of visibility than the power of rare and spectacular events to guide perception also encourage misreadings of fragmentation. Consider the markers of difference that figure so prominently in post-1965 migration debates. Those who believe the new immigrants refuse to abandon their home culture and embrace that of the host often cite visual, linguistic, and auditory evidence—the funny perfumes of New York taxicabs, voting instructions in Spanish, the odd inflections of convenience-store cashiers, the huddles of dark men milling about the mod-

ern shape-ups on the suburban "waterfront" across America who wait
for contractors and gardeners to whisk them away to their work sites.

As countless studies have established, the new Americans are not destabilizing the land with their separatist identities. On the contrary, the children of these latest travelers look more and more like previous older generations of newcomers to America. But how, then, to explain this gap
between actuality and perception without resorting to tired versions of
a frustrated lower-middle class repulsed by "otherness." Mary C. Waters (chap. 6) offers a more nuanced explanation of the misperception
of this aspect of fragmentation: the new immigrants differ from the old
ones less in their quotient of virtue than in the circumstances of their incorporation into America. (Those virtuous and "melted" immigrants of
yore—the Irish and Italians, Jews and Poles—were not so happily embraced as virtuous and melted at the time.) After neonativist restrictions
on immigration in the 1920s cut off the infusion of new ethnic colleagues,
greenhorns no longer dominated the immigrant population. By contrast,
for many of today's immigrants, such as the Mexicans, a constant influx
of newcomers continually replenishes the ranks of the visibly strange,
generating public markers of difference and thereby obscuring the underlying glacial movement toward linguistic, political, and cultural acculturation. This continuous flow has a powerful impact on immigrants' presentation of collective self to external audiences. As Waters observes,
"Simply put, the visible aspects of the ethnic group—speaking a language
other than English, occupational specialization, residential concentration—
will not be diluted, and it will strike the average American that the new
immigrants are not assimilating."

A similar instance of this choreography of illusion can be seen at times
in that most-bandied-about example of ethnic separatism, "the black
table." The specter of black students huddling together generates the impression of tribal huddling, and indeed it often reflects precisely such a
sentiment. But as Inge-Lise Ameer has shown in one of the few empirical studies of such tables, the impression may hide the reality that many
black, Latino, and Asian students have diverse and branching networks.
Like code switchers fluent in multiple codes, they shift between ethnic
and mixed tables in complex permutations; the constancy of the impression of black huddling is belied by the underlying rotation of members at any particular moment.[8]

The flip side of this affliction of the senses is an affliction of time: the
danger of immersion in immediate experience. To return to our starting
point: fragmented, to be sure, full of tribal animosities, but compared to

what? And compared to when? The 1960s, another period of "fragmentation," surely rival—and surpass—more recent decades for graphic
conflict that tore the social fabric. Take any number of vantage points in
the late 1960s and early 1970s: the mean streets of Washington, D.C.,
after Martin Luther King Jr.'s assassination, the mean streets of Chicago
during the police riot of 1968. As Godfrey Hodgson reported from the
front lines, "The schism went deeper than mere political disagreement.
It was as if, from 1967 on, for several years, two different tribes of Americans experienced the same outward events but experienced them as two
quite different realities."[9]

These were portentous signs, full of ominous promise. This may be
merely another way of stating the obvious: when hasn't the United States
been full of divisive tensions of one sort or another? Even if the United
States has enjoyed relative unity, as consensus historians used to argue,
consensus on certain points only intensified the likelihood of bickering
on others. Despite the entire legacy of "exceptionalism," struggles of class
and religion and ethnicity have always tugged and pulled.

Part of the comparative problem involves this matter of a baseline.
Take the people who complain about the Afrocentric passions of blacks
or the new immigrants who refuse to adopt the language of the host land.
They forget that for decades German-American, Irish-American, and
Italian-American politics were afflicted with "the politics of revenge," as
Samuel Lubell dubbed them—an isolationism that was payback for their
ethnic humiliation in wars against their homelands. Catholics were long
lambasted as practitioners of popish identity politics, and they built their
own equivalent of Afrocentric academies—they called them Catholic
schools. The Irish, like those of "Hebraic persuasion," were seen for a
time as members of alien, unassimilable races. Today nobody thinks the
Irish threaten American civic culture, and the Jews have long since "become" whites.

The moments of communal abrasion have varied in their intensity,
which adds a certain institutional context to the cycle of volatility. It
may be, as Albert Hirschman argued, that there is a certain endogenous
logic to the rhythm of engaged mobilization and quiescent withdrawal
into private consumption. But if we look comparatively, advanced societies vary a good deal in their susceptibility to such emotive swings,
and the United States has followed the rhythmic alternation of idealistic effusion and crude materialism, of public engagement and private
enrichment.

Students of party realignment have been especially keen on thirty-two-

or thirty-six-year intervals: 1828, 1860, 1896, 1932, 1968 (things get a bit tricky afterward). Or perhaps progressive movement and conservative rejoinder—thus the 1920s, the 1950s, and the 1980s bear a striking similarity, at least in their smug self-congratulations, only to be retracted a decade later. However you reckon it, this fact of alternation implies a problem of practical epistemology: From the limited standpoint of amplitude in a wave in the cycle, the United States can look very different: we can seem, say, like grubby materialists or noble idealists, devotees of civic entanglement or lonely bowlers, fans of property or Jeffersonians in pursuit of self-fulfillment.

The truth of the matter is that the United States, like other complex societies, is hardly one, unambivalent thing. Even individualism, our much-trumpeted signature, implodes into rival strains: a Jeffersonian tendency of self-expression and rights, a utilitarian one of economic striving and self-making. Garry Wills, taking a knock at Louis Hartz's emphasis on the single-minded fixity of the liberal tradition, once complained that "Hartz did not see the connection of the Horatio Alger ethic with religious fundamentalism, with Methodist morals and Baptist fervor and Puritan rhetoric. Hartz views his Locke in a cool secular light which does not reach to the dark things, the self-punishment, behind Americans' abject devotion to success."[10] All of this warns against seeing universal law at work when only a historically particular element in a broader cultural repertoire has been given decisive, visible expression.

THE TRAP OF LANGUAGE: FRAGMENTATION AS RHETORIC

It could be argued that Americans are less divided than they used to be, at least in certain respects. "The pattern of social cleavages," cautions Paul Starr, "may be neither as new nor as threatening" as recent worries suggest (chap. 12). Paul DiMaggio makes a similar point in underscoring the sloppy way people talk about polarization, which can mean at least two different things: "a shift in opinions of the whole population from moderate centrist views toward more extreme positions, leaving a yawning gap in the middle of the ideological spectrum," or "disagreement between specific kinds of people thought to be at odds with one another, such as men and women, blacks and whites, or Republicans and Democrats." "On virtually every other issue [save abortion]," DiMaggio concludes, "polarization either remained constant or actually declined. The public actually has become *more unified* in its attitudes toward race, gender, and crime since the 1970s" (chap. 4).

Alan Wolfe's powerful eight-community study of "what middle-class Americans really think about God, country, family, racism, welfare, immigration, homosexuality" adds force to the essentially centrist portrait of Americans. Wolfe ranged widely, from liberal, Jewish Brookline, Massachusetts, to heavily black Dekalb County, Georgia; from prosperous Broken Arrow, Oklahoma, home to one of the nation's largest charismatic Pentecostal megachurches, to the working-class suburb of Eastlake, California, with its large numbers of Asian and Mexican first-time homeowners; from the gated retirement community of Rancho Bernardo, California, to many other places, too. And wherever he went, Wolfe found not a yawning chasm of moral disagreement and inflamed cultural resentment but people who "long for a sensible center and distrust ideological thinking." All in all, Americans are "reluctant to pass judgment, they are tolerant to a fault."[11]

If this diagnosis is right, why is there such an eager audience for dire predictions? Part of the problem is that we rarely approach such heated moments with the benefit of Olympian distance. It may be there is something in the human psyche that is perversely drawn to dramatic idioms of crisis and breakdown, the same logic that attracts us to horror films and other popular genres of horrific fantasy. In both these cases, as the line between drama and melodrama collapses, there is a danger that the trope of crisis may become a tropism, a virtually autonomic response that reflects our sense of vertigo.

Social scientists have hardly been immune to such imagery. Their love affair with the rhetoric of crisis, rooted in a fearful fascination with modernity, has a long history. Not so long ago the left was busy embracing all manner of "fiscal crises of the state," "legitimation crises" and other versions as well, as if to compensate for the primal God that failed and the main big-bang economic crisis—and the convulsive class conflict it would trigger—that never materialized. More often conservative proponents of order of various stripes, from Burkeans to homeostatic functionalists, have been drawn to the beauty of equilibrium, and they have fretted more often about crises of values and morale.

Here is not the place to rehearse the complex careers of these idioms of breakdown, but it is worth noting that they often confuse or conflate breakdown and conflict, demonizing the first and delegitimating the second. They also tend to overestimate the importance of moral solidarity in holding societies together, as if there were not other forces that produce common ground besides shared norms and beliefs. And they support a basically ahistorical perspective that dispenses with the tricky work of specifying comparative baselines. Moreover, they often reflect the partisan passions of those who dispense them.

It wouldn't be worth slamming home this last point so relentlessly if the matter was merely academic. But neither our love of the apocalypse nor the idioms we choose to express it are purely innocent of politics. Another obstacle to knowing involves this organized character of our public debate, the fact that, to use William Gamson's apt phrasing, our idioms are sponsored—carried forth, advocated, and mocked by specific political interests and institutions. It thus makes sense that in the contest of rhetoric, some are more drawn to the rhetoric of breakdown—and to specific versions of the idiom of breakdown—than others.

In the decades after the New Deal enshrined itself and realigned the nation's electoral channels, the right has had a vested interest in blurring economic tension with crosscutting issues of foreign policy, internal subversion, and the like.[12] As the instability of the post-1968 coalition, based on a "marriage of the classes," became evident, conservatives and Republicans plied the "social issues" as a way of shifting the axis of debate and abrasion. More recently, Theda Skocpol observes, conservatives have targeted liberalism as "the enemy of community and an agent of fragmentation, turning young against old, class against class, and black against white" (chap. 11).

Idioms, like individuals, have biographies, and the right didn't come to its particular version of the fragmentation narrative overnight. The aristocratic right of the 1950s recoiled from what it diagnosed as "civilizational malaise." This was pretty rarified, the anxious musings of esoteric elites—southern agrarians, Straussians, Christian triumphalists, neo-Burkeans, even sentimental monarchists. But soon the broader environment began to expand the market for restorationist appeals beyond cerebral reactionaries.[13]

Starting in the 1960s, the right-wing diagnosis of breakdown began to diffuse and take a more popular—and pseudopopulist—form. Increasingly, the average person on the street who couldn't have cared less about "civilizational malaise" was becoming disquieted by social breakdown. After Miranda warnings, other controversial Supreme Court decisions, and a burgeoning crime rate began to deepen popular fears of lawlessness, right-wing cries against the "usurpations" of judicial activism—rather obscure stuff by any reckoning—began to resonate at a more popular level. In a pattern repeatedly evident the state, in the form of the judiciary, played a crucial role in politicizing, and thus mobilizing, right-wing populist conservatism.

This crossing over of the idiom of breakdown coincided with, and was energized by, the white backlash that helped foment the rhetoric of crisis. At the same time, the youth rebellion, sexual high jinks, and crisis of authority that originally seemed an affliction of the well heeled began to diffuse and flourish in the more plebeian reaches of the nation. This was the broader environment in which Nixon, Agnew, and Wallace refined their respective versions of the fragmentation narrative. As James Sundquist observed in the 1970s, "In the public's perception, all these things merged. Ghetto riots, campus riots, street crime, anti-Vietnam marches, poor people's marches, drugs, pornography, welfarism, rising taxes, all had a common thread: the breakdown of family and social discipline, of order, of concepts of duty, of respect for law, of public and private morality." [14] Long before the phrase "culture wars" gained popular parlance, the attack on the McGovernite wing of the Democratic Party as the party of "Acid, Amnesty, and Abortion" crystallized the theme of moral disarray. The fragmentation narrative, then, is a weapon in the rhetorical assault that is inseparable from a larger political struggle.

Of course what constitutes "breakdown" or "disequilibrium" is not always clear, as Martin Luther King Jr.'s rejoinder to the arguments for order suggests. King's answer was based on a set of reversals: suffering could be redemptive; conflict was the creative condition of a more just harmony. In this inversion the presence of fragmentation was transformed, lifted from the realm of the "dysfunctional" into a healthy signal of painful inequality and oppression. And the containment of conflict, the surface appearance of harmony at the expense of justice, was transfigured into the dysfunctional—to individuals, sectors, and classes who suffered from oppressive life conditions.

The same definitional scuffling erupted around the riots of the 1960s, which looked quite different to liberal and conservative analysts: one person's breakdown is another one's insurgency. None of this was purely a matter of "social construction," one narrative being equivalent to the other in some relativist standoff. There were good data to suggest the rioters were not unhinged members of an anomic underclass, flailing about in frustrated rage. On the contrary, in general rioters bore many of the signs of political rationality. They were politically knowledgeable and boasted a strong belief that they could control their fate. More critically, they embraced a vernacular theory of justice that found the system normatively wanting, which led to their withdrawal of moral legitimacy from the state. [15]

As the right's increasingly antielitist rhetoric indicates, the narrative battle between left and right settled in heated debates over the character of the vaunted "middle classes." Since de Tocqueville, and even before, defining the American has been a national pastime. For decades both the right and left have energized that timeless effort, and it is only natural that in this quintessentially bourgeois nation, they have often focused on the middle class—as an object of disappointment, celebration, or mockery. In the right's "populist" telling the moral common sense of the virtuous middle has been under attack by a decadent media and libertine mandarins who, with their loose morals and fancy notions of therapy, excuse badness and disdain square values. Such judgments have been offered up by Doctor Laura and Pat Robertson and by William Bennett and Gary Bauer. This analysis locates fragmentation in the moral failures of dangerous voluptuaries and the anomic anarchy that followed from their disregard for moral regulation and the needs of the collective conscience.

Bill Clinton proved an irresistible projective screen for such a demonology. From his wanton love of cheeseburgers to his sexual gluttony to his fickle regard for truth, he seemed to embody the moral failures encoded in the cry of "acid, abortion, and amnesty": feral immersion in the compulsions of pleasure, an inability to discipline himself and his appetites. Who besides Clinton could achieve this interpretive triumph: taking some 1950s cartoon of Freudian exegesis that understood cigars as phallic symbols and desublimating them into a sex toy? Here was a man clearly guilty of the fallacy—one is tempted to say the phallacy—of misplaced concreteness. And who can forget the famous fellatio of misplaced concreteness too?

If the fragmentation narrative has been more attractive to the right than to the left, some portions of the left, at least of liberalism, have proffered their own version of the idiom of fragmentation. Paradoxically, since the social democratic impulse of New Deal liberalism gave way to something different—what the right used to attack as "limousine liberalism"—the liberal left has been in sway to a less majoritarian vision: alienated from the middle, it has often conjured up a land full of racist beasts, religious maniacs, and mean misogynists.

This redepiction of the middle, whatever its partial basis in empirical reality, was accompanied by a shift in the institutional domain in which liberalism achieved many of its victories. As Michael Walzer once pointed out, throughout the 1950s and 1960s a disproportionate share of liberal victories—on reapportionment, separation of church and state, individual rights of speech, abortion, and birth control—came not through popular assemblies but through the courts, the Supreme Court in particular.

Part of Clinton's genius was to rescue the middle from its ignominy. Jimmy Carter's biracial populism, especially notable through the South outside the classic Black Belt electoral districts, which in 1948 bolted from the Democrats, had already pointed the way beyond George Wallace's courting of "forgotten Americans," a phrase that resounded with echoes of Franklin Roosevelt. Clinton's faith in the progressive possibilities of the center jibed perfectly with his adviser Stanley Greenberg's larger academic diagnosis: "In the wake of the civil rights struggle, it was difficult to contemplate policies that would encompass the aspirations of both impoverished blacks and working-class whites."[16] The remedy was to find policies that would move the middle from populist conservatism back to some variant of populist progressivism. Writing from a different perspective, William Schneider concluded, "It will not be easy to get Democrats to think in universal terms. Most voters have no problem with the Democratic Party's speaking out for the interests of women, blacks, and working people; that is its traditional role as advocate for the disadvantaged and victims of discrimination. But speaking out for the interests of feminists, labor unions, and civil rights organizations is something else. That is not populism. That is interest-group liberalism."[17]

Fragmentation here was thus located not in liberal indiscipline or merely in the mean-spirited and racist dispositions of vulnerable whites but in the failure to implement policies that might transcend racial, economic, and generational differences. As Theda Skocpol points out in this volume, fragmentation is not just a matter of "irreconcilable conflicts of identity and interest." It is, at least in part, a contingent product of broader historical choices and institutional strategies that vary in their potential to promote alliance or altercation. "Politics and the state are not helpless witnesses to those divisions. Government efforts—especially social policies—can either exacerbate conflict or diminish it" (chap. 11). Over the long haul, progressive social policies, far from fragmenting the nation, have achieved precisely the opposite. Part of the problem with the contemporary political situation is that liberals, not always mindful of their own triumphant history, began to disavow universalistic policies that might bind the races and classes together.

THE FRACTIOUS (BUT NOT FRACTIONATED) CULTURE: CHANGING ATTITUDES VS. ORGANIZING IDENTITIES

Clearly, the narratives circulating among activists, members of the political class, the intelligentsia, and the punditry do not precisely reproduce the distribution of opinion in the communities for which they presume to speak. Underscoring the potential for considerable divisions between elites and rank and file within the same cultural communities, James Hunter, a key scholar of culture war battles, writes, "Public culture is largely constituted by the activities and pronouncements of elites."[18] The verdicts emanating from such special agents of cultural production often reflect the skewed vantage point from which they look out at the world, the distinctiveness of their worldviews, and the unique lore that courses through their coiled networks.

In emphasizing the idiosyncrasies of activists we confront not just the danger of reading quirky signs as reflections of the whole or the accident of happening upon randomly produced images. The likelihood of perceptual mistakes is also a product of socially organized processes involving activists on both the supply and demand sides, the subject and object sides, of the availability heuristic. The first set of factors generates susceptibility to misimpressions or partial impressions generated by organized groups. As the previous example of Jewish scrutiny of anti-Semitic speakers suggests, individuals are not randomly positioned or attentive vis-à-vis such florid signs; Jewish organizations have created a vast apparatus, including specialized departments of reporting and research, to monitor the larger environment for anti-Semitic and populist authoritarian dangers. The second set of factors generates the production of episodes that serve as the evidentiary basis for perceptual errors. The most common form of this institutionally generated gap between appearance and reality involves confusing opinion that is highly organized—and thus vividly available for all to see—for opinion that is popular and pervasive. Our concern in the three final sections of this essay is with the institutional and organizational dynamics that irretrievably shape the expression and perception of fragmentation in each of the realms of culture clash, ethnic and racial difference, and politics.[19]

An exploration of select features of Christian right mobilization underscores the power of an institutionalist account to illuminate integrative dynamics that are obscured by the surface production of "fragmenting" evidence. The visibility of evangelical and fundamentalist Christians, the telegenesis of televangelists, and the general upsurge of groups like the Moral Majority in the early 1980s conspired to produce a disturbingly alien picture of traditionalist Christians. To some observers they seemed to betoken a frightening current of authoritarianism coursing through the land; they were, in Molly Ivins's resonant phrase, "Shiite Baptists," stirred up by the fundamentalist mullahs.[20] The fund-raising missives of liberal groups like People for the American Way reinforced the idea that the new right was flirting with a homegrown American fascism. Alan Crawford, in his *Thunder on the Right,* was only one of those who invoked Vachel Lindsay's "Bryan"—"Prairie avenger, mountain lion, / Bryan, Bryan, Bryan, Bryan, / Smashing Plymouth Rock with his boulders from the West"[21]—to convey the danger of heartland *ressentiment* turned against the guardians of effete seaboard culture.

Those who nursed such fears were not entirely wrong. In the early 1980s, stray local Moral Majority leaders, imagining AIDS as the ultimate in God's vengeance, actually called not for extending the embrace of agape to gays but for their death. In a 1980 Moral Majority letter that warned, "We're losing the War against Homosexuality!" the Reverend Jerry Falwell, noting that gays had just gained permission to lay a wreath on the Tomb of the Unknown Soldier "to honor any sexual deviants who served in the military," virtually shuddered, "That's right . . . The Tomb of the Unknown Sodomite!"[22]

This popular imagery of crazed Christians fit neatly with a dominant academic view of traditionalists and a radical cultural schism between tradition and modernity. It echoed Richard Hofstadter's depiction of a "paranoid tendency in American politics," to which religious fundamentalists were said to be especially susceptible. Symbolized by the title of Seymour Martin Lipset and Earl Raab's *Politics of Unreason,* the imagery of psychic "strain" was used by many academics to explain the aggrievement of right-wing fundamentalism as a frenzied flight by displaced groups into a clarifying past. "People or groups who are the objects of change," argued Lipset and Raab, "seek a general 'fundamentalism' in order, as Paul Tillich put it, 'to have a principle which transcends their whole disintegrated existence in individual and social life.'"[23]

As an elemental matter of shrewdly sizing up traditionalists, this diagnosis had problems. It did not really seem as if Jerry Falwell, Pat Robertson, and Ralph Reed suffered from "disintegrated existence." All three appeared to operate in the modern world quite effectively. There was the related problem of the rhetoric of unreason: in replacing the moralistic idiom of sin and salvation with the therapeutic one of health and sickness, the cosmopolitan classes seemed to be in sway to the same kind of either-or thinking they attributed to the provincial classes.[24]

The clinical verdict of mania also could not square the kinetic sensationalism of some religious rightists with the empirical nuances of contemporary born-again Christians, whose moral and political diversity was striking. There were progressive evangelicals, middle-of-the-road ones, and many other kinds, too; the right-wing portion of Christians who mobilized thus did not represent Christians as a whole and may have numbered barely 20 percent.[25] Where evangelicals as a whole differed from other Americans—all things being equal—was on a small number of issues dear to them—homosexuality, prayer in school, and tax-exempt status for Christian academies.[26] Even so-called profamily evangelical and fundamentalist Protestants rarely made political decisions simply on the basis of such issues as gay rights and abortion. In the early 1990s, pointing to the urgency of everyday concerns with taxes, health care, and economic security among evangelical voters, one Christian right activist conceded what the survey data had shown for some time: "Even more startling, only 22 percent of self-identified born-again evangelicals . . . listed abortion as an important issue."[27]

Against the reality of complexity, liberal denigration begins to look a bit, to borrow that loaded word, know-nothing. And to continue this flipping, the "culture war" appears not just as a revolt of the hidebound periphery against a cosmopolitan center but also as the provincial animus of the cosmopolitan classes against their traditional enemies. One can discern a suspiciously functionalist twist in this story: decrying the fanaticism of self-righteous Christians served to reflect back to cosmopolitans their own civility. Or, taken more innocently than the liberals' need for distinction, such decrials could reflect the fact of cosmopolitans' circumscribed social networks, and all that followed from that closure: distance from other cultural sectors of American life, provincial assumptions about those "others," lack of experience in the social regions of K-Mart and NASCAR racing, Home Depot and the Grand Ole Opry.

More was in play than the liberal confusion of the part with the whole; the liberal theory did not precisely apply to even that part comprising politically conservative fundamentalists, let alone the hidebound segment of evangelicals. Among citizens who favored the religious right, roughly three-quarters expressed comfort with the idea of blacks, Jews, Hispanics, Catholics, and Asians as neighbors. In Tom Smith's rendering, "If one moves beyond the small groups of the right-wing fringe, religious intolerance in general and anti-Semitism in particular do . . . [not] penetrate into the much larger and more centrist conservative political and religious movement."[28]

Nor did the most hidebound segments of traditionalist Christians seem entirely backward-looking in recent decades. As early as 1942 the founding of the National Association of Evangelicals marked what James Hunter has deemed "a more conciliatory" response to modernity.[29] The recent political visibility of pious Christians followed their structural integration in the post–World War II period, as millions of conservative Christians, no longer shielded from the ravaging intrusions of secularism, were pulled into the orbit of new forms of social relations—the market, national organizations of entertainment and communication, the life of the metropolis. Meanwhile, their economic and educational status was rising apace. Hardly a disoriented protest of declining sectors, born-again Christianity was very much the ideology of rising economic and social sectors across the Sun Belt.

More thematically, the "past" that moral restoration sought to reinstate was a dynamically moving line of "modernized" traditionalism that had absorbed much of the culture around it. Restorationists who once declaimed against fornication now sought to hold the line at gay marriage while reading Christian sexual manuals that advised on the importance of female orgasm. Meanwhile, the fusion of religious and therapeutic ideals in Christian counseling, the emergence of the hybrid genre of Christian rock, and the blending of marketing, entertainment, and spirituality in so-called megachurches embodied the permeability of the boundaries between separatist subculture and secular society. And most notably in the decline among traditionalist Christians of anti-Semitism, anti-Catholicism, and racism one could see a continuing movement of right-wing Christianity beyond ethnocentric provincialism.

What was shifting was less the vast attitudes of the overwhelming tens of millions of ordinary Christians than the political self-conception of a segment of right-wing evangelicals and fundamentalists who were no longer content to dwell in quiescent contemplation of the anticipated Kingdom. Members of the religious right were distinguished from other citizens primarily by their ideology of Christian nationalism, "the idea that America's political troubles can be alleviated by bringing Christianity into the government."[30] In Paul DiMaggio's judicious parsing (chap. 4) this was not fragmentation in the form of a widening moral chasm between secular and observant sectors but a change in the way a specific segment of pious Christians—and the political forces seeking to appeal to them—began to organize their political identities.

That specialized cadre of right-wing Christians was beginning to glimpse new connections between religion and politics, a shift in self-conception that facilitated and was facilitated by their increasing links to one another in organizations that leveraged their power. The process of linking dated back to at least the Carter years, which represented a powerful moment of coming out for evangelicals. The evangelicals' sense of betrayal over Carter's tightening of the rules governing Christian academies' tax-exempt status further politicized evangelical citizens. Meanwhile, conservative Republican strategists had identified evangelical and fundamentalist Christians as ripe for mobilizing and had begun to target their communal identity as a way to accomplish just that.[31] And interlocking groups such as the Kingston Group began to link secular portions of the right—the gun lobby, the antitax troops—with the more religious groups, which created new efficiencies for Republican efforts to coordinate the various elements and integrate them into the electoral and legislative process. All the while, organizers disseminating booklets like the one the Moral Majority entitled "A Program for Political Participation of Church-Going Christians" underlined both the collective political identity of "those individuals who believe in the Bible and attend church regularly" and the organizational resources the Christian right could draw on ("The Christian community has the advantage of physically gathering together on a regular basis").

In his autobiography, *Strength for the Journey,* the Reverend Jerry Falwell recalls his opposition to Martin Luther King Jr.'s activism and to the civil rights movement more generally. Following the participation of hundreds of clergy in the Selma, Alabama, protest, Falwell reminded his flock in his "Ministers and Marches" sermon, "The Christian's citizenship is in heaven. . . . Preachers are not called to be politicians but to be soul winners."[32] By the 1980s Falwell had adopted a more this-worldly translation of his faith and a new vision of Christian citizenship. In the process he closed some of the distance between King and himself.

The early 1990s writings of Ralph Reed, that quintessential new-style promoter of Christian values and the onetime director of the Christian Coalition, epitomize this growing rhetoric of identity, rights, and pluralism among Christian conservatives. Reed became the traditional Christian's point man. He perfected an evangelical version of "modern [Jewish] Orthodoxy." His boyish looks, salesman's instincts, and modern-looking suits suggested neither Cromwellian fervor nor Elmer Gantry but Bible Belt conservatism with a human face. Reed's exultantly entitled *Politically Incorrect,* with its talk of Christian victims and group identity, echoed the secular humanists he targets.

Conceding the "dark stain" of racism that is still upon evangelicals— "George Wallace may have stood in the schoolhouse door, but evangelical clergy provided the moral framework for his actions"—Reed calls for "repenting of the racist past, making amends by building a biracial future." Meanwhile, the tables have turned. Christians, Reed argues, are no longer the purveyors of intolerance. "Today the victims are [pious] Roman Catholics, Jews, fundamentalists, and evangelicals." Faced with an imperious secularism that dominates established cultural institutions, traditionalist Protestants, Jews, and Catholics too can find no reflection of themselves in popular imagery. On the contrary, they are mocked and humiliated, dismissed as fanatical practitioners of holy war. As a result the "patchwork quilt of American democracy is less beautiful, less attractive, and less colorful because one of its boldest and brightest fabrics— its religious faith—has been torn away from public display." In countless ways Reed was witnessing to a pluralism if only it would include his people in the aura of hallowed difference.[33]

FRACTIOUS (BUT NOT FRACTIONATED) PLURALISM: PERFORMING ETHNIC AND RACIAL IDENTITIES

Liberal fears of fragmentation have tended to focus on the divisive tendencies of an ethnocentric cultural right or a racist Middle America. By contrast, conservative fears of fragmentation have focused on threats of ethnic and racial particularism to American values and social solidarity. At the core of these arguments has been the complaint that Afrocentric blacks and recent immigrants are Balkanizing the nation by their defiant refusal to assimilate. Also targeted have been the academic high theorists who, from their perch in ethnic and gay studies departments, give formal warrant to less scholastic forms of tribalism. By no means confined to the right, such appraisals have spanned visceral and cerebral, democratic and racist, incarnations. In his famous jeremiad Arthur Schlesinger Jr., the avatar of classical New Deal liberalism, complained about the disuniting of America. And democratic leftists have sometimes joined them in their nervousness over identity politics, as when Todd Gitlin laments "the twilight of common dreams" in his book of that title.

Although not baseless, much of the overwrought debate on identity

politics has suffered from the same estimation errors that figured in appraisals of the Christian right. Analysts have read fractious moments as
signs of deep fault lines in the society rather than as the outcome of more
precise organizational and institutional dynamics. This lack of an institutional heuristic has been most evident in the tendency to infer popular support for ethnic and racial separatism from highly visible, socially
organized expressions of identity.

Susceptibility to false impressions caused by the availability heuristic
has been intensified by the power of mobilized cadres to produce florid
instances of ethnic conflict—the fiery apocalypticism, say, of Nation of
Islam ministers Louis Farrakhan and Khallid Muhammad—which block
out less visible main tendencies—the movement of far greater numbers
of former members of the Nation of Islam toward universalistic classical Islam under Wallace Dean Muhammad, Elijah Muhammad's son.[34]
In the early 1990s, in front of a Korean-owned produce store, a small
network of black nationalist activists hurling racist taunts, most of them
African Americans in a heavily Haitian-American Brooklyn neighborhood, reinforced the media frame of black-Korean conflict, even though
divisions between Afro-Caribbean and African-American leadership
were intense.[35] Back in the 1960s, as white Americans recoiled from media images of activists like H. Rap Brown proclaiming, "Burn, Baby,
Burn," the majority of black Americans experienced Black Power as pride
in one's race and moral impatience over unfair treatment more than as
hatred of whites.[36]

In this section I concentrate on the misreading encouraged by narratives of fracture that lift moments of failed assimilation and separatist
anger out of their larger institutional field. That failure to deploy an institutional perspective has two major consequences: it downplays the tensions between particularism and universalism that have recurred through
American history, and it downplays the resilience of the American ability
to reconfigure its cultural boundaries and the vibrant pluralism—sexual,
ethnic, religious, and racial—that has emerged from it.

To highlight this context, I will return briefly to the parallels between
the growth of an activist sensibility among conservative white Christians
(as well as Orthodox Jews and charismatic Catholics) and the forces of
prophetic black Christianity during the civil rights movement. Like Ralph
Reed's appropriation of the rhetoric of cultural rights and recognition,
such commonalities highlight a broader shift in the social organization
of difference. Are indignant Christians in search of recognition really so
different from indignant blacks, gays, or women in search of recogni-

tion? Conservatives who bray that liberals are quick to certify certain groups as worthy of respect and not others have a point. The left has often parroted the decreasingly modish jargon of "transgressing boundaries" and of not "exoticizing" others. But these strictures have not always been applied across the board. There are good others—blacks and Latinos—and not-so-good others—evangelical Christians, white ethnics, and Orthodox Jews.[37]

Once black, gay, Christian, Jewish, and Latino identity politics are no longer separated from the broader milieu of mobilization, they take their place in this changing balance of particularism and universalism that has been eroding the old identity regime established in the postwar period. As much as any fundamental change in underlying values, there has been a shift in the institutional rules that govern the performance of identity in public.

Enshrined in a distinctive version of civil religion, that older settlement dictated the rules of politeness regulating the performance of ethnocultural loyalties and engagement with the larger plural society. As John Cuddihy chronicled in *No Offense,* during the post–World War II period the enlightened segment of each of America's major religions sought to tame the ferocious triumphalist forces within their ranks. For the no-longer-dominant Protestants this meant giving up the exclusivist distinction of those "saved by Jesus"; for the Catholics it entailed jettisoning the notion of the "One True Church." And Jews had to tiptoe gingerly around the notion of "The Chosen People."[38]

These battles were more than simple contests of ideas; they were fought out by specific organized sectors of each religion in specific institutional settings—within and between the respective communities. Such universalism could take the most paradoxical twists, as organizations like the American Jewish Congress entered amicus curiae briefs that reinforced the wall of separation between church and state. Here was a distinctively "particular" kind of universalism—Milton Himmelfarb once called Jewish liberalism the Jewish particularism that likes to call itself universalism.

His mention of "calling" underscores the rhetorical aspect of this dynamic: none of this was purely "civic religion" in Robert Bellah's terms, Americans' earnest acceptance of a set of moral values. It involved something savvier and more streetwise, tempering the gauzy idealism of the metaphor of redeemer nation with a wily Goffmanian sense of pragmatic entente. Civic religion defined a set of linguistic rules, a way the various components of a plural society learned to talk (and not to talk) about one another in public. Like etiquette more generally, this meant a differentiation of social realms into a formal, restrained front stage and an earthier, more tribal, back stage.

What proponents of shared culture miss, then, is not the fact of change but its character: not simply the growth of particularistic sentiments but also the erosion of restraints on consigning them to private life. Starting with the Black Power movement, there began an erosion of the civic culture vision that dictated, "Give no offense." In a spiral of mutual borrowing, groups became determined to parade their difference in the public realm.

One might argue that this institutional reading does not allay all anxiety about the divisive character of identity politics; it simply shifts the onus from the realm of free-floating values and personal attitudes. Nor do the parallels between prophetic black preachers and millennial white ones prove that identity politics is always benign. Proclamation of pride in one's religion or ethnicity, as certain versions of the fragmentation narrative argue, can slide easily into the rejection of the life lived in common, into provincial huddling with one's own kind, or even into mean baiting of others. Whatever its lofty rhetoric, multiculturalism has sometimes promoted what Richard Bernstein deems "a new orthodoxy exceedingly intolerant of disagreement. . . . [I]t invents . . . separate cultural worlds" and repudiates the idea of a "common cultural vocabulary" (chap. 2). There really are Afrocentric partisans who believe in the essential deficiency of white "ice people," queer theorists who laud the superiority of a unique gay sensibility, members of the Modern Language Association who view the American liberal tradition as mainly a fraud that masks white male domination, and deconstructionists who reject the idea of an American—or any other—tradition.

If identity regimes that hallow difference risk promoting fragmentation, overemphasizing such dangers carries risks of its own. Above all, it misses the fascinating paradox that characterizes American life as a whole in recent decades: the growth of organized expressions of particular identities has coincided with the growth of tolerance of difference, as well as of the respect and recognition that are crucial to liberal pluralism. Six related aspects of this seeming paradox temper fears of the fragmenting power of the current identity regime.

First, many assertions of ethnic and racial identities are reactive, less the result of coherent separatist values than a wounded response to the ethnocentrism of others. Long before people were worrying themselves about black tables, Latino tables, and gay tables, jocks, preppies, and fraternity boys were practicing their own forms of white identity politics, only no one called it that. This was more than simply a matter of labeling and language. The source of that distortion lay in a problem of practical phenomenology: the dominant groups, oblivious to their own dominant presence in the culture, were too much a part of the ground to feel themselves as figure; they simply did not experience their particularism as particular. They took it for granted.

It's instructive to remember that Governor George Wallace was one of the pioneers of identity politics. How else to think about the Confederate flag dwarfing the American over the Alabama state house or the unapologetic way he wore cracker ethnicity on his sleeve and in your face? Indeed, Wallace's notion of a southern nation-within-a-nation preceded the black nationalist mantra of "Nation Time"; the red, black, and green of African liberation flags; the rap community's vision of the "Hip-Hop Nation"; out gays insisting, "We're here and we're queer"; up-front yarmulke-bearing Jews; and assertive Christians who want creches back in the public sphere. To the extent that black nationalism has varied historically with the indifference and hostility of the larger society toward black suffering, one could say that Wallace was a prime generator of black identity politics. At the least we cannot say we have gone from a past untainted by fractious ethnic sentiments to one awash in communal vendettas.

A second flaw in the panic over the danger of identity politics, the focus on the centrifugal forces generated by particular identities, ignores the institutional forces that modulate the exaggeration of difference and generate superseding commonalities. Even as certain gays, women, blacks, Jews, and others have been cultivating unique aspects of their experience, other centripetal forces conjoin them. Rejecting the "unexamined and fallacious premise in the narrative of fragmentation: that elevating a singular, shared American identity . . . is the only way to unify the nation," Martha Minow emphasizes the institutional power of constitutional culture, crosscutting ties, and participation in a common culture of consumption to bind the nation (chap. 3).

Third, fearsome scenarios of ethnic and racial conflict often confuse particularism with hostility to universalism. But as the Jewish case suggests, even a love of one's own kind elaborated in a vast array of ethnic self-defense organizations that promote Jewish interests and identity can coexist quite well with attachment to the central values of the larger society. West Indians, even as they may distance themselves from African Americans, switch among multiple identities, including black, West Indian, island (Jamaican, Trinidadian), and American. And both the West Indian and the American components of that identity repertoire may intensify simultaneously.[39] The game of identity is not zero sum.

This dynamic is highly visible in the religious sphere, as R. Stephen Warner has elegantly documented. In recent decades the cohesiveness of a shared civil religion has given way to a decentralized religious order, and the observant often assert "badges of religious identity—from the Christian label to the crosses, yarmulkes, and *hijab* coverings worn by today's college students." Yet these badges can mean quite different things. They "are increasingly asserted to invite recognition from the like-minded, embolden comrades, confound enemies, and invite inquiries from those open to persuasion." The main emphases here, reproducing and redefining the meaning of one's own identity, in no way "require antagonism toward one's neighbor." On the contrary, Warner concludes from the revitalization of congregational life among Jews, African Americans, and recent immigrants, "The new religious particularism may also help repair our culture."[40]

It follows, fourth, that worries about generic "particularism" pitch the debate at too high a level of abstraction. Such fears commingle distinct phenomena such as passionate feelings about one's ethnic or religious identity, the willingness to exhibit that identity in the public realm, rejection of shared values of the larger society, hostility to white society, and class resentment. For example, two warring sensibilities have claimed the mantle of multiculturalism. One, as proponents of the fragmentation narrative rightly point out, is separatist, fabricates mythic history, and is hostile to empathy. But the other carries forth the ideals of tolerance, robust debate, and empathetic universalism. Current academic battles to expand the canon, Lawrence Levine reminds us, repeat older struggles over the curriculum that accompanied the incorporation of "new constituencies of students among the middle and working classes, women, immigrants, and minorities."[41] This opening up and making way parallels the timeless pattern in American life: group bids for incorporation—Germans, Catholics—coexist with the individualism of the formal ideology.

In this latter sense, rather than promoting anti-American values the current identity regime is compatible with vital American traditions of pluralism and mutual respect. Philosophers may quarrel about whether liberal states must be neutral toward the content of various cultures, as Quebec refuses. But even if such states bear no duty to ensure the survival of specific subcultures, liberal universalism is consonant with according equal dignity to diverse ethnic and racial groups no less than to individuals.[42]

"Consonant with" puts the matter too diffidently, which suggests still a fifth reason for calm in the debate on identity politics. Assertions of rights to cultural recognition also carry with them a certain universalizing momentum. A key dynamic of Jewish liberalism entailed the logic of what goes around comes around: affirming tolerance for all helped fashion tolerance for one's own kind and vice versa. Peter Steinfels captures this logic of reciprocity as it unfolded in the late 1990s at Georgetown University, a Jesuit institution, when students began to call for the restoration of crucifixes that had always hung in Georgetown classrooms. University officials, fearful of seeming to promote a medieval, uncivil Catholicism, demurred. Into the breach stepped Protestant, Muslim, and Jewish student organizations, which told the university chaplain, as Steinfels recounts, "The more Georgetown was specifically Catholic rather than striving for a generic religiosity—the more comfortable they felt being specifically Protestant, Muslim, and Jewish."[43]

The same kind of categorical imperative, an ethic of mutuality in which particular claims affirm the more universal right of other cultures to recognition, is playing itself out in delis across New York City, and elsewhere too, where Mexican employees come to greet their Korean bosses and cashiers with formal bows accessorized with Korean phrases and receive in turn the greeting, "Hola, Pepito."[44]

As this nod to heterogeneity indicates, all assertions of particularistic identities are not the same, and when we step back and look at the system as a whole, the dominant tendency has been toward expanding the boundaries of sexual, ethnic, and racial belonging, extending citizenship and rights to once-marginal communities, and blurring the sharp line between insiders and outsiders. This cumulative development is the sixth and most crucial rebuttal of the narratives of ethnic and racial fragmentation.

We can see this dynamic at work even in the realm of race, America's most troubled domain of difference. In truth racial life in the United States has long been too complex to conform to the frame of the "great divide between the races" favored during the Simpson trial, epitomized in columnist Scott McConnell's *New York Post* reflection, "The jury has spoken. Black America has done its celebratory end-zone dance; whites have gasped in astonishment. And the analysis has begun: 'Two nations'; 'different planet'; 'racist police'; 'jury nullification.'"[45] Ishmael Reed has wonderfully described this narrative frame "as Zebra journalism, where everything is seen in black-and-white."[46] No less than the earnest frame of "color blindness," "great divide" denies the grayed subtleties of race precisely at the moment our old binary system of black and white is giving way to something more fluid.

Ethnic and class differentiation among blacks; the infusion of yellow and brown, olive and ochre, mahogany and taupe immigrants into the black-and-white mix; the complex patterns of ethnic distance and conflict between and among blacks and other "people of color" are rescrambling boundaries between the races and their meaning. It is even possible that for many Asian Americans and South Asians racial designations are becoming "ethnicized" in the minds of whites. The same may even apply to some upwardly mobile Latinos and Caribbean blacks. Spiraling rates of intermarriage across religious and racial boundaries further mark the birth of a new racial regime. As the 2000 census revealed, a rising proportion of younger biracial people not only refuses to pigeonhole its identities in the old restrictive classifications but is actively taking advantage of new opportunities to declare its membership in multiple "races."

Moreover, notwithstanding racially charged conflicts over social policy, the most ferocious forms of antiblack racism have diminished among whites, who, write Paul Sniderman and Thomas Piazza, "no longer react uniformly to issues of race."[47] Black-white conflict has increasingly become shaped by class divisions and policy clashes rooted in ideological differences rather than racial animosity. Even as uttered in the racially resentful precincts of the white working and lower-middle classes, virulent language such as "niggers" and "black shit" is not always an unambiguous marker of racist hatred. As performed in the local context of vernacular speech codes, such terms—as distasteful as they may be—often reflect plebeian efforts to make intricate distinctions of class and character not readily apparent to cosmopolitan outsiders peering into such communities from a distance. More generally, the division between white lower-middle and upper-middle classes over issues of law and order originates not just in different levels of racial tolerance but also in class-based differences in language, in exposure to crime, in links to networks of acquaintanceship with victims of crime and police officers, and in conceptions of abstract rights and due process.[48]

The changing character of white identification with black crossover figures marks a similar erosion of racialism. It is true that even at the height of ideologies of unvarnished racism, plenty of whites enjoyed minstrelsy. Some cultural theorists interpret the current white adulation of figures such as Oprah Winfrey, Michael Jordan, and Will Smith—whom they view as "deracialized" beings—as modern equivalents to coon shows. But this view misses what is different in the dynamic of white identification. Whites are imagining black Americans, from Colin Powell to Denzel Washington, as moral sages, not simply as fun-loving children. Blacks have come to represent character, courage, and grace.

Nor does black opinion conform to the stark unity suggested by the theme of Great Divide. The nationalist sentiments of one interviewee cited by political scientist Michael Dawson—"I'm tired of that one-nation-under-God boogie-joogie. . . . We are our own nation"[49]—represent a powerful strain of black opinion, but Dawson is at pains to stress the neglected diversity in black ideological life. Moreover, the very label of nationalism misses the variety of strains—from democratic to ethnocentric, from pragmatic to millennialist—encompassed in its reach. In another, less-than-enthralling instance of narrowing the gulf between the races, a considerable proportion of blacks accepts the negative stereotypes of blacks voiced by whites.[50] Similarly, strong currents of support for law and order and cultural conservatism course through black working- and middle-class neighborhoods.

Even African-American opinion in the Simpson case was not single-minded. Undeniably, there were blacks whose desire for racial payback fused admission of Simpson's guilt and exultant pleasure in seeing the black man "get over" or "get away with it." Yet many blacks who rejected the ethic of racial loyalty embodied in the practice of jury nullification disagreed with whites on how to read the evidence that entered judgments of reasonable doubt and the plausibility of police malfeasance.[51] This latter gap between the realm of ought and the realm of is, between moral convergence and empirical disagreement, has been emphasized by Jennifer Hochschild, who argues that even as they divide on some issues, blacks and whites enjoy broad moral agreement on a whole host of issues. Vast majorities of both groups agree that America should promote equal opportunity rather than equal outcomes and that trying to get ahead is key to "making someone a true American." Against the master image of racial fragmentation, Hochschild identifies the "strong foundation of shared beliefs and values on which to build an ethos of task responsibility" (chap. 9).

Nor is it hard to detect assimilatory impulses among the new immigrants whom neonativists have dubbed defiant refusniks, standing aloof from American culture while exploiting its rich opportunities. Surely the new multiculturalism adds moral legitimacy to inchoate comfort with one's own kind, as do affirmative action programs, ethnic studies pro-

grams, and other institutional forces that promote collective categoriza-
tion. It is also true that the emergence of transnational ethnicity may entail a greater reluctance to abandon home-country ties, and the modern
world of fax machines and e-mail, cheap plane tickets and instant cash
transfers makes retaining ancient—and dual—loyalties easier than ever.
And encounters with American racism may sour immigrants on their hope
for acceptance. "I will always be a minority in Boston," one of Peggy
Levitt's informants told her. This man, an immigrant from the Dominican Republic, believed he could "make this my home" if he worked hard
and "kept his head down. . . . No matter how much money I make, I
will never be considered a full-fledged American. . . . I don't want to be
an American anymore. . . . In Miraflores, I will always belong." [52]

The presence of these forces makes even more impressive the "strong
assimilationist impulses [that are unfolding] alongside vivid expressions
of diasporic consciousness." [53] As the second generation forges its way
in America, it is becoming increasingly clear that its members really do
not look quite so different from previous second generations. Alejandro
Portes and Rubén Rumbaut, among others, have documented the linguistic assimilation that is taking place. [54] Philip Kasinitz writes, "The
out-marriage rate for second-generation Chinese Americans is already
higher than it was for Jews a generation ago. Across the country, second-
generation high school students prefer English to their parents' native
languages, even if they voice strong ethnic identities, and many are losing their parents' language altogether." [55]

Even the identities of *Asian American* and *West Indian* reflect an
oblique form of becoming American; crafted in the new land, responsive
to its concerns, *Latino* signifies the gradual erosion of the specific identities of Dominican, Puerto Rican, Mexican, and the like. Such invented
identities are a way station on the road to acculturation. It helps to recall that Italian immigrants didn't think of themselves as Italians at first
but as something homier, not far from the idea of "homies" or *lands-
man*. The scope of identification was intimate: one's *paisane* from
Abruzzi and Bari. Italians "became" Italians rather than Calabrese first
in the eyes of the Americans who could not, as the saying goes, "tell them
apart." Like every other word in the dance of identity, such American
locutions have the quality of a forged identity; it's a way one learns to
name oneself and be named by others.

As a result, just as immigration has long meant loss and yielding, it
remains a story of opening up and self-making. This is why those whites

who fumed at the Mexican flags waved by teenagers protesting California's Proposition 187 (which restricted benefits to illegal immigrants) got it wrong. Far from wanting to " 'remember the Alamo' in reverse,"[56] Roberto Suro shrewdly observes, they were attesting to their Americanism in the very act of claiming a place for Latino Los Angeles. And in fashioning a distinctive vision, they were paying homage to the new rhetoric of rights, thereby certifying themselves as honorees of deep American traditions.

This exuberant process of cultural creation is embodied for Suro in banda music, but it well stands for the experience of Asians, South Asians, West Indians, and countless others: banda is "the sound of immigrants who skip across national borders, picking up music—corridos, hip-hop, rock and roll—wherever they go."[57] The same processes of fusion, melding, and syncretism are unfolding across the land and reconfiguring the cultural boundaries of the next generation.

That is not to say that there is not a good deal of alienation among many blacks and members of the second generation of immigrants. In truth, this is the source, both actual and potential, for much fragmentation. But such alienation, even when it takes a culturally separatist form, is rarely a simple reflection of preexisting attitudes about identity. Despite the media focus on its black component, the Los Angeles riots involved a broad-based class coalition of the enraged, linking African Americans, second-generation Central American gang members, the progeny of Mexican immigrants, and others. In the Crown Heights riots African-American teenagers from the projects made common cause with alienated second- and third-generation Jamaicans, Trinidadians, Barbadians, and other West Indians; and all vented their rage against an array of targets.[58] And across the generation the sons and daughters of immigrants from many different lands are embracing rival visions of identity. In the case of immigrations from the Caribbean, an upwardly mobile, optimistic track clings to its West Indianness. A more alienated segment, generally less endowed with cultural capital and facing less attractive life changes, increasingly identifies as black.[59]

This pattern of splitting within the second generation underscores the embeddedness of identity formation in broader economic and demographic contexts. It also underscores the major failing of the conservative narrative of fragmentation, its tendency to separate the discussion of divisive tendencies and identities from the structural forces that give them shape and energy. Ultimately, whatever its complex causes, it is this class fragmentation—with all its human costs in violence, riven families, and drug addiction—that poses the greatest threat to our long-term coherence as a society.

IDEOLOGICAL FRAGMENTATION AFTER FLORIDA:
THE FRACTIOUS (BUT NOT FRACTIONATED) POLITY

Given that the eruption of cultural politics and anxiety over ethnic and racial discord have been hallmarks of American life in recent decades, it should not surprise us that we find in the electoral arena the same paradox evident in these other areas of American life: partisan vendetta and formal commonality, moral dispute and ideological convergence, liberalizing tendency plus conservative ascendancy. This mismatch between the flux of opinion and institutional design helps explain much of the volatility that has characterized the American political system over the recent electoral cycle.

The tendency to misread fundamental institutional shifts as marking shifts in popular opinion is natural enough. At the time, it seemed as if the 1980 Reagan victory marked a sea change in the basic cultural core of American life. To liberals, agape at the defeats of liberal stalwarts like Senator Frank Church, it felt like a radically unfamiliar moment had arrived. The entire postwar premise of a vital center that governed much political sociology was displaced by a frightening roar from some netherworld previously thought beyond the pale of post–World War II legitimation. Contributors to *The Radical Right,* the collection Daniel Bell edited in the late 1950s, may have recoiled from "the paranoid tendency" in American life, but they could rest easy that the paranoids were confined to a kooky fringe; they weren't knocking at the doors of government.

None of this assurance would endure. In an unwitting riff on the old theme of American exceptionalism, Jürgen Habermas's pronouncement in *Legitimation Crisis*—that quarreling about economic output, material rewards, and efficiency had replaced deeper questions of equality, moral values, and the character of the good society—seemed woefully anachronistic in the face of the invigorated ideological fervor.[60]

The liberal critique of Reagan's deflective Teflon coating and his bedazzlement through "smoke and mirrors" thus got it precisely wrong. Anticipating Clinton's formidable powers to marshal the resources of style, image making, and charm in the service of recrafting liberalism, Reagan artfully used his power to expand a constricted discourse beyond the consensus of a not-so-vital center. Reagan made an immense contribution to robust democratic debate. The facts of liberal disarray and failure of nerve should not detract from it.

The best evidence for a seismic shift was the realignment of social and economic policy, the restructuring of the judiciary and its spreading ideology of conservative judicial activism, the swerve in fiscal theory, and the revolution within administrative agencies that soon issued forth from the Reagan Revolution. These ideological currents found incarnation in symbolic totems like Rehnquist as the chief justice at the Supreme Court, Meese as attorney general, and Watt as secretary of the interior.

A natural folk form of reflection theory sustained the verdict of cataclysmic ideological change. How could there be such a reconstruction if not for a basic change in the hearts and minds of the voters, a plausible inference given credence by conservative and academic theories of realignment that had been swirling about ever since the rise of white backlash, the birth of the rubric of Middle America, and a discernable "emerging Republican majority"? (Indeed, an entire faction of the Democratic Party was prepared to junk much of the party's key ideological commitments in order to catch the wave of this new putatively popular consensus.) There was a naive democratic faith at work in this assumption, as if electoral demand mystically summoned an electoral supply to assuage it. The secular, much ballyhooed, trend of the collapse of 1960s liberalism, no longer obscured by the detour of Watergate and the Carter redemptive movement that countered it, had finally achieved electoral consolidation.

Such a faith operated with too neat a vision of harmony. The truth of advanced societies is that a good deal of slippage can occur among institutional sectors. And the institutional gauntlet—the configuration of elites, the rules governing primaries and the selection of convention delegates, other factors beyond popular opinion that determine the composition of party activists and their often disproportionate control over outcomes—tends to further weaken the direct relationship between a clear ideological signal of "the people" and the electoral outcome. As a result it is not surprising that the sphere of opinion—in this case a highly amorphous, pragmatic, and fluid "conservative" mood—could not claim the status of ideology. The Reagan years witnessed relatively little erosion in basic indicators of support for the welfare state. "The long-term trends in public opinion," Paul Starr concludes, "show a general rise in liberal attitudes and beliefs during the 1960s and 1970s that has since leveled off but has not been reversed" (chap. 12). "If American public opinion drifted anywhere over Reagan's first term," the authors of *Right Turn* concluded, "it was toward the left, not the right, just the opposite of the turn in public policy."[61] In short, the country witnessed a realignment in policy, perhaps an accompanying realignment of mood, but not necessarily a realignment in habits of the heart. None of this prevented Reagan from instigating a set of institutional arrangements that would soon be unhinged from the vague demand that gave them life.

In a pattern that would play itself out recurrently—most obviously during the 1994 surge of congressional Republicanism and the Contract with America but also throughout the impeachment crusade—conservatives continually misread the mood and overreached themselves, ignoring the fundamental pragmatism of the center, its eclectic populism that fused elements of conservatism and liberalism. This misconstruing of the popular meaning of the Republican victory was ironic (as well as self-serving). It was ironic because in heralding the popular mandate, the conservative theory gave short shrift to the organized grassroots campaign that produced it by rearranging the internal structure of primaries, displacing older regional elites in the party in favor of southern and Sun Belt ones, and generally creating a new organizational vehicle for populist conservatism.

Reagan was no fool in these matters; he knew the difference between majority and mandate, and he quickly learned to talk not about reducing government but about slowing its growth. And it is why the right's ancient language of "socialistic" Social Security, programs hungrily devoured by elderly Lockeans in Sun Belt strongholds like Phoenix and Jacksonville, suddenly vanished. Nor was Reagan taken by the forces of cultural restoration he exploited. On his occasional visits he'd give the National Association of Evangelicals a dollop of the idiom of evil.[62] But thanks to his own lukewarm feelings about the culture war and the survey data of Richard Wirthlin and his other pollsters, he realized that cultural polarization was not a viable national strategy, even if it helped convulse the Republican primary base. As early as January of 1982 major conservative leaders "warned President Reagan today that he was allowing 'the abandonment, reversal or blunting'" of the culture war issues dear to them.[63] By the summer *Conservative Digest* was asking on its cover, "Has Reagan Deserted the Conservatives?" and noted "the growing conservative disappointment with the president."[64] After what the *New York Times* described "as a string of defeats on his proposals to legalize school prayer and ban abortion" and failure "to enact any of his agenda of legislation on social issues," Republican senator Jesse Helms observed of the Senate, "Conservative it ain't, Republican it is."[65]

A telling sign of paradoxical convergence was the evolution Reagan effected within the very structure and sensibility of conservatism. In effect, he domesticated it by removing the animus of resentment that has infused so many of its disparate strands. Weaning the right of its racism, anti-Semitism, and anticonstitutionalism, Reagan disavowed what Rogin once deemed "the punitive consequences of frustrated optimism,"[66] replacing them with a sunny Lockeanism. In Louis Hartz's terms he dispensed with the terror (of red scares, of evil internal enemies) in favor of enchantment (the Alger invitation). His own grace and humor, whatever its stylistic origins, was a rebuttal of Nixon's frowning *ressentiment* of George Wallace's sneer.

To bring the point home, one need only compare any of the generic law-and-order speeches of Agnew or Nixon with the expansive rhetorical community Reagan crafted over the course of his presidential speech career. The litany of heroes who remind us "what it means to be an American" included Lenny Skutnik and Sargent Trujillo, and they were joined in his 1985 State of the Union Address by West Point cadet and Vietnamese refugee Jean Nguyen and the Harlem founder of a home for the infants of drug-addicted mothers, Clara Hale.[67]

In a sense the right was shucking off the baggage of ethnocentrism and nativism, the better to distill the essence of ideological and class warfare into its most pure, virtually philosophic, form. The shift in sensibility found structural expression in the blurring of ethnic, religious, and racial boundaries that marked the emergence of an inclusive movement of right-wing mobilization. This "right-wing pluralism" required the end of "the attacks on racial and religious minorities that had disfigured evangelical political crusades of the past."[68] Such restraint was a necessary condition for the emergence of an alliance of former enemies— Orthodox Jews, charismatic Catholics, and fundamentalist Christians. Anita Bryant's Miami coalition, with its happy family of Orthodox rabbis and fundamentalist ministers, anticipated the erosion of these traditional doctrinal and denominational boundaries. Falwell's outreach to the Jews, given added intensity by the philo-Semitism of various wings of fundamentalism, reinforced the dynamic. All sorts of mutual overtures between prolife Catholics and evangelical Protestants added force to conservative ecumenicism

In the midst of ideological polarization the uncivil right was being incorporated under the broader umbrella of civic culture. In a sense the right was finding its way toward its own brand of universalism, which nicely contrasted with the vulnerability of liberals and the left to the charge that *they* were splitting the country into specific communal tribes. This reconfiguration is of a piece with the public display of conservative affirmative action at the 2000 Republican convention and George W. Bush's creation of a cabinet "that looks like America."

No matter how decorative and opportunistic, such a strategy of self-presentation honored an unspoken truth: liberals won the culture wars—just not on the perfect terms the most zealous longed to achieve, and with much of the loonyness removed, and with qualifications like "by and large." Most Middle American women might recoil at "those feminists," but notions of a right to equal treatment, comparable worth, and much more now pervade the heartland of the nation. Ashcroft's avowal before the Judiciary Committee during his confirmation hearing that *Roe v. Wade* was settled doctrine and his invocation of a woman's "right to an abortion" on Larry King in February of 2001 attested to a similar state of affairs. Notwithstanding the vigilante militia right and the wackiness of the Waco-obsessed, the reborn right was at once a more fractious and more liberal right.

E. J. Dionne Jr. put the matter as presciently as anybody at the time, and he updates his basic argument here (chap. 14). The proponents of wedge issues

> posed complex matters of moral and social conflict in race, in family life, and in sexuality as false polarities, in either-or terms that did not speak to the amorphous center where the majority of American voters dwells.
>
> In truth, America's cultural values are a rich but not necessarily contradictory mix of liberal instincts and conservative values. . . . Americans believe in social concern and self-reliance; they want to match rights and responsibilities; they think public moral standards should exist but are skeptical of too much meddling in the private affairs of others. (chap. 14)

This was why that notoriously dealigned electorate, decreasingly channeled by party loyalty and surging about the polity, could shift its allegiance so quickly from Reagan and Bush to Clinton in 1992.

For the diminishing band of aficionados the culture wars simmered through the dark years, especially on talk radio, given new intensity by the right's visceral hatred of the Clintons. The Christian right could still complain that "no administration in history has so blatantly been against God's moral values legislatively and misused them more personally."[69] Such sentiments fostered the near-vertiginous triumphalism that attended the Republican counteroffensive of the Contract with America. And Republicans in Congress promoted divisive tendencies under the guise of "immigration reform." As Cecilia Muñoz captures these moves (chap. 7), a series of legislative and policy enactments in the mid and late 1990s—especially provisions of the welfare and immigration bills of 1996—assaulted the old American immigration regime. Perhaps the most radical expression of that attack was a proposal floating around Congress to retract the timeless American commitment to birthright citizenship. In Muñoz's words, "They have made suspicious appearances—and thus biological criteria—a ground for withholding fundamental liberties. They have created new divisions within the national community, not just between immigrants and citizens but between citizens from dominant ethnic and racial groups and citizens who look 'different' or have Asian- and Latino-sounding names and between undocumented immigrants and their U.S.-citizen children. They have subjected large numbers of U.S. citizens and legal immigrants to the infringements and invasions of arbitrary state power."

Yet it is the fleeting quality of both, not the triumphs of the Contract and the war on immigrants, that endures. Clinton's comeback in the 1996 election unveiled the limits of the Republican use of wedge issues to fragment the nation; like Pat Buchanan's frenetic performance at the 1992 Republican convention, Republican support for immigration restriction both in California and nationally hurt the Republicans in 1996. The burgeoning power of the strategically located Latino vote in Texas, Florida, and California gave an added impetus toward empathy.

This pattern continued through the 2000 presidential election. The Florida sideshow cannot obscure it. The stylistic surface of the story offers one version of proletarian romance: Bush, no striped-pants patrician, expunges the effete Ivy demons through self-invention—born again as a wildcat oil man, as a real hell-of-a-fellah, and finally *really* born-again—as a Christian. The deeper story is the gravitational pull of a more liberal center, which played out in a series of inverted symmetries. The post-Clinton regime forced Republicans to play the onetime Democratic game of "taking back the center." Like 1970s and 1980s Democratic line-drawing between paleoliberals and neoliberals, all the Republican theorizing about compassionate conservatism reflected not some obsessive disorder but the changed political environment in which the party had to operate.

This was the import of Bush's denial of kinship with the congressional Republicans. It was as if Bush and his cronies had resolved to lock Tom

Delay, Trent Lott, Dick Armey, and Dan Burton in the attic until Bush was safely ensconced in the White House. Unfortunately, the Ashcroft nomination reminded everyone that once the election was over, they might want to come down out of the garret and claim their place in the sun. And as the weeks rolled by and conservatives gloated that Bush was more Reaganite than Reagan, it became clearer than ever that Bush had tucked away his true unvarnished conservative self in the attic as well.

Still, no matter how cloying or contrived, no matter how much it could serve as a marketing strategy, compassionate conservatism took heed of the larger reality: of soccer moms and independent voters and Latino voters. Suddenly, the party of toughness and testosterone was the one that had to convince voters of its ethos of care, its ability to feel the other guy's—and woman's—pain. This may be preferable to the harsher versions of conservatism analyzed by Muñoz. Yet no matter how noble, it's hard not to look on the rhetoric of compassion with a modicum of skepticism, unless it's seen as a supplement to something larger. After all, faith-based forms of action run counter to the tested formula Skocpol has sketched for integrating Americans in some larger national community. As Paul Starr argues, privatization and faith-based initiatives fragment after their own fashion, splitting the nation into smaller units of private household and provincial congregation, of homogenous religion and distinct ethnicity. In the process such "soft fragmentation" deprives us of some broader sense of national community or legitimating ethos (chap. 12).

As the nation moves beyond the faltering first steps into the millennium and absorbs the shocks of September 11, a powerful paradox will define the nation's cleavages and its efforts to modulate them. On the one hand, any current pattern of disputing always reflects underlying structural forces. And this much is clear: the vagaries of the global economy will create new winners and losers, distribute harm and largesse in not entirely foreseeable ways, and displace some groups and empower others. The radically shifting demography of the United States will similarly rearrange the character of our pluralism, the axis of our altercations. And the new geopolitical realities of a post–cold war world that includes demonic and perhaps less predictable threats of its own will further cut across familiar divides on foreign policy.

But this much is also clear: the narrative forms through which we seek to understand these changes have a kind of stubborn resilience, even if the meanings the forms convey are more fluid. For the moment, President Bush—hardly chastened by the murkiness of his "victory," but then further emboldened by his ordeal by fire as commander in chief, protecting the national community against the "axis of evil"—has resurrected the pristine language of Locke, dressed up with the right's cultural passions and populist invocations of community, to justify a decidedly non-populist program of redistribution. Where precisely "compassion" lies in this mix is not entirely clear.

But this amalgam, as the Reagan experience reminds us, is as inherently unstable as it is familiar. Exuberant Republicans, buoyed up by their recovery of the Senate in the 2002 elections, will forget this history only at their own peril. For one thing, the cultural selection process is governed by an unforgiving logic of practical success; an ambivalent, pluralistic citizenry can respond to a range of appeals, as long as the basic needs of family, sustenance, and security are satisfied by the regnant policies. Second, much like the distinct ingredients from which it has been culled, the cultural mix embodied by the Bush administration speaks to only some of the nation's powerful impulses and not to others. In the end the contest between the forms is no less enduring than the idioms themselves: the rhetoric of moral redemption and the calculus of cost, the apotheosis of private life and the imperatives of community, the pursuit of profit and the more expansive community of rights. The cultural strains that momentarily have been pushed aside will reassert themselves, inspiring new cries and frictions. In the end this inescapable fact of fractiousness may be the ultimate form of constancy in a mercurial world.

NOTES

I thank R. Stephen Warner for his typically astute critical reading of this chapter.

    1. The language of embeddedness and emergence comes from Ernest Schachtel's brilliant *Metamorphosis: On the Development of Affect, Perception, Attention, and Memory* (New York: Basic Books, 1959).

    2. Seymour Martin Lipset, *Political Man: The Social Bases of Politics* (1960; reprint, Baltimore: Johns Hopkins University Press, 1981).

    3. Kevin P. Phillips, *Post-Conservative America: People, Politics, and Ideology in a Time of Crisis* (New York: Random House, 1982), 157.

    4. See Jonathan Rieder, "Reflections on Crown Heights: Interpretive Dilemmas and Black-Jewish Relations," in *Antisemitism in America Today*, ed. Jerome A. Chanes (New York: Birch Lane Press, 1995), 348–84.

    5. Henry Louis Gates Jr., "The Uses of Anti-Semitism," in *Blacks and Jews: Alliances and Arguments*, ed. Paul Berman (New York: Delacorte Press, 1994), 217, 218.

    6. *Highlights from the November 1998 Anti-Defamation League Survey on*

Anti-Semitism and Prejudice in America (New York: Anti-Defamation League, 1998), 24.

7. Seymour Martin Lipset and Earl Raab, *Jews and the New American Scene* (Cambridge, Mass.: Harvard University Press, 1995), 104–5.

8. Inge-Lise Ameer, "The Daily Dance," *CommonQuest*, vol. 3, no. 4/vol. 4. no. 1: 36–39.

9. Godfrey Hodgson, *America in Our Time* (Garden City, N.Y.: Doubleday, 1976), 363.

10. Garry Wills, *Nixon Agonistes: The Crisis of the Self-Made Man* (Boston: Houghton Mifflin, 1970), 512.

11. Alan Wolfe, *One Nation After All* (New York: Viking, 1998), 283, 278.

12. See Michael W. Miles, *The Odyssey of the American Right* (New York: Oxford University Press, 1980).

13. See George H. Nash, *The Conservative Intellectual Movement in America, since 1945* (New York: Basic Books, 1976), esp. chap. 3, "The Recovery of Values and Tradition"; and Jonathan Rieder, "The Rise of the 'Silent Majority,'" in *The Rise and Fall of the New Deal Order, 1930–1980,* ed. Steve Fraser and Gary Gerstle (Princeton, N.J.: Princeton University Press, 1989), 243–68.

14. James Sundquist, *Dynamics of the Party System: Alignment and Realignment of Political Parties in the United States* (Washington, D.C.: Brookings Institution, 1973), 312.

15. See, e.g., Jeffery M. Paige, "Political Orientation and Riot Participation," *American Sociological Review* 36 (Oct. 1971): 810–20.

16. Stanley Greenberg, *Middle Class Dreams: The Politics and Power of the New American Majority,* rev. ed. (New Haven, Conn.: Yale University Press, 1996), 5.

17. William Schneider, "What the Democrats Must Do," *New Republic,* March 11, 1985, 17.

18. James Hunter, *Culture Wars: The Struggle to Define America* (New York: Basic Books, 1991), 338.

19. No inherent logic of functionalist unity perfectly aligns the dynamics within each sphere. The degree of alignment or friction is historically variable. Thus during the civil rights movement, racial tension created opportunities for racist demagogues, who intensified conflict within the polity. On the other hand, the centrist dynamic of a two-party electoral system may modulate ethnic and racial fragmentation. Still, as we scrutinize examples from each of the three realms, we will encounter notable formal parallels.

20. See Molly Ivins, *Nothin' but Good Times Ahead* (New York: Random House, 1993), 236.

21. The poem appears at the start of Peter Viereck's famous 1955 essay, "The Revolt against the Elite," reprinted in *The Radical Right,* ed. Daniel Bell (Garden City, N.Y.: Doubleday, 1964), 161.

22. Fund-raising letter from national Moral Majority headquarters, August 14, 1980.

23. Seymour Martin Lipset and Earl Raab, *The Politics of Unreason: Right-Wing Extremism in America, 1790–1977,* 2d ed. (Chicago: University of Chicago Press, 1978), 118.

24. For an early statement that dissects various paradigms of new right cultural mobilization, see Jonathan Rieder, "What Is the New Right?" in *What Is Pro-Family Policy? Proceedings of the Bush Center Symposium on Family Policy*, ed. Susan Munchow and Mary McFarland (New Haven, Conn.: Yale University Bush Center in Child Development and Social Policy, 1982); and Jonathan Rieder, "Crazes, Crusades, and Cockfights," lecture delivered at Emory University, March 1983.

25. For an evocative portrait of the internal diversity in evangelical life, see Randy Balmer, *Mine Eyes Have Seen the Glory: A Journey into the Evangelical Subculture in America* (New York: Oxford University Press, 1989).

26. See *Public Opinion* 4 (April/May 1981): 24–25. Although the summary reported that on "a limited set of social questions which touch directly upon family and home life and upon personal morality," evangelical Christians are more conservative than nonevangelical Americans, "in part, this difference reflects the regional and class makeup of the evangelical movement. Southerners and those of lower social and economic status (SES) are more conservative culturally, and are more inclined toward evangelical persuasions" (24).

27. Ralph Reed, *Politically Incorrect: The Emerging Faith Factor in American Politics* (Dallas, Tex.: Word Publishing, 1994), 225.

28. Tom W. Smith, *A Survey of the Religious Right: Views on Politics, Society, Jews, and Other Minorities* (New York: American Jewish Committee, 1996).

29. James Davison Hunter, "The Evangelical Worldview since 1890," in *Piety and Politics: Evangelicals and Fundamentalists Confront the World*, ed. Richard John Neuhaus and Michael Cromartie (Washington, D.C.: Ethics and Public Policy Center, 1987), 52.

30. Smith, *Survey of the Religious Right*, 31.

31. Key leaders of the secular new right were quite open in the opportunism of their stoking of culture war issues. As A. James Reichley recounts, " 'The New Right is looking for issues that people care about,' observed Paul Weyrich, director of the right-wing Committee for the Survival of a Free Congress. 'Social issues, at least for the present, fill the bill.' " Because neither Weyrich nor two other key players, Richard Viguerie and Howard Phillips, were Protestants, they began to cultivate friendships with important fundamentalists and evangelicals who might build a network of Republican Christian activists. See A. James Reichley, *Religion in American Public Life* (Washington, D.C.: Brookings Institution, 1985), 319–20.

32. Jerry Falwell, *Strength for the Journey* (New York: Pocket Books, 1987), 276.

33. Reed, *Politically Incorrect*, 237, 65. This Christian version of identity politics offered one final parallel with the larger society from which religious traditionalists were said to be alienated. Far from an earthy resignation to human fallibility, the Protestant cultural critique brimmed with the classical Armenian strain in America's dissenting religious tradition that rejected the dour pessimism of Calvinist predestination. Just as Freud's existential pessimism was transmuted into a sunny technology of mind-cure in the United States, the born-again ethos reflected not world-weary flight from the world but a faith in the possibilities of individual renewal and upward spiritual mobility. So the religious

version of perfectionism—with its resolve to eliminate sin—did not really look so out of key with its more secular forms—hygienic, sexual, and therapeutic, with their search for perfect everythings from abdomens to psyches. Increasingly suffused with therapeutic ideology, Christian protest converged with other forms of recovery and authenticity.

34. The best estimates suggest that after Wallace Dean Muhammad broke with the Nation of Islam and its apocalyptic brand of Muslim racialism, Farrakhan retained only ten to twenty thousand followers in the Nation of Islam, whereas one hundred thousand adherents followed Muhammad toward a more conventional, nonracist Sunni Islam. See C. Eric Lincoln and Lawrence H. Mamiya, *The Black Church in the African-American Experience* (Durham, N.C.: Duke University Press, 1990), 390. For Wallace Muhammad's invitation to white people to join the Nation of Islam, see Karl Evanzz, *The Messenger: The Rise and Fall of Elijah Muhammad* (New York: Pantheon, 1999), esp. chap. 19 and epilogue.

35. Jonathan Rieder, "Trouble in Store: Behind the Brooklyn Boycott," *New Republic,* July 2, 1990, 16–22.

36. Joel D. Aberbach and Jack L. Walker, "The Meanings of Black Power: A Comparison of White and Black Interpretations of a Political Slogan," *American Political Science Review* 64 (June 1970): 367–88.

37. One should not press the point too far. In a notable countervailing tendency the empathetic impulse can be glimpsed in a spate of studies of those supposedly decertified others—fundamentalist Christians, evangelicals, and Orthodox and Hasidic Jews—carried out by the very liberal, feminist, and even leftist social scientists who are supposed to be so eager to certify only their own kind. Lyn Davidman's *Tradition in a Rootless World: Women Turn to Orthodox Judaism* (Berkeley: University of California Press, 1991); Debra R. Kaufman's *Rachel's Daughters: Newly Orthodox Jewish Women* (New Brunswick, N.J.: Rutgers University Press, 1991); Faye Ginsburg's *Contested Lives: The Abortion Debate in an American Community* (Berkeley: University of California Press, 1989); and Judith Stacey's *Brave New Families: Stories of Domestic Upheaval in Late-Nineteenth-Century America* (New York: Basic Books, 1990) all seek to understand the rich nuances and spiritual integrity of "alien" cultures without the presuppositions that have often deformed liberal cosmopolitan takes on exotic "others."

38. John Cuddihy, *No Offense: Civil Religion and Protestant Taste* (New York: Seabury Press, 1978).

39. See Philip Kasinitz, *Caribbean New York: Black Immigrants and the Politics of Race* (Ithaca, N.Y.: Cornell University Press, 1992); Milton Vickerman, *Crosscurrents: West Indian Immigrants and Race* (New York: Oxford University Press, 1999), chaps. 3–5.

40. R. Stephen Warner, "Changes in the Civic Role of Religion," in *Diversity and Its Discontents,* ed. Neil J. Smelser and Jeffrey C. Alexander (Princeton, N.J.: Princeton University Press, 2000).

41. Lawrence W. Levine, *The Opening of the American Mind: Canons, Culture, and History* (Boston: Beacon Press, 1996), xiv.

42. Michael Walzer, "Comment [on Charles Taylor]," in *Multiculturalism: Examining the Politics of Recognition,* ed. Amy Gutmann (Princeton, N.J.: Princeton University Press, 1994), 99–103.

43. Peter Steinfels, "Renewing the Forest: Catholics in the Multicultural Mix," *CommonQuest,* vol. 3, no. 3/vol. 4, no. 1: 92.

44. See Hee-Jung Hwang, *Fresh Market: Mexicans, Koreans, and the Making of a New Pluralism* (unpublished undergraduate senior thesis, Department of Sociology, Barnard College, 2001). In this pattern of mutual recognition one can find a parallel in the realm of gender and sexuality. In the lamentations of the cultural right, American life has been fractured by moral relativism, antifamily feminism, and sexual promiscuity. At the same time, the ideals of comparable worth and a right to sexual gratification can be seen not as the legitimation of narcissistic pleasure but as an ethic of mutuality against a "fragmenting" masculinity that thinks only of its interests and pleasure.

45. Scott McConnell, "O. J. Fallout: Are We 'Two Nations'?" *New York Post,* Oct. 11, 1995, 19.

46. Quoted in Henry Louis Gates Jr., *Thirteen Ways of Looking at a Black Man* (New York: Random House, 1997), 119.

47. Paul Sniderman and Thomas Piazza, *The Scar of Race* (Cambridge, Mass.: Harvard University Press, 1993), 34.

48. For a more detailed exploration of these issues, especially of the diverse motives governing white backlash, see Jonathan Rieder, *Canarsie: The Jews and Italians of Brooklyn against Liberalism* (Cambridge, Mass.: Harvard University Press, 1985).

49. Cited in Michael C. Dawson, *Black Visions* (Chicago: University of Chicago Press, 2000), 90.

50. Sniderman and Piazza, *Scar of Race,* 44–45.

51. "Reasonable doubt has a history attached to it and a color," writes Marcia Ann Gillespie in "Reasonable Doubt," in *The Darden Dilemma: Twelve Black Writers on Justice, Race, and Conflicting Loyalties,* ed. Ellis Cose (New York: HarperCollins, 1997), 107.

52. Peggy Levitt, *The Transnational Villagers* (Berkeley: University of California Press, 2001), 111.

53. David A. Hollinger, quoted in Nancy Foner, *From Ellis Island to JFK: New York's Two Great Waves of Immigration* (New Haven, Conn., and New York: Yale University Press and Russell Sage Foundation, 2000), 185.

54. Alejandro Portes and Rubén G. Rumbaut, *Immigrant America,* 2d ed. (Berkeley: University of California Press, 1996).

55. Philip Kasinitz, "Children of America: The Second Generation Comes of Age," *CommonQuest* vol. 4, no. 3: 35.

56. Roberto Suro, *Strangers among Us: How Latino Immigrants Are Transforming America* (New York: Knopf, 1998), 116.

57. Ibid., 123.

58. See Jonathan Rieder, "Crown of Thorns: The Roots of the Black-Jewish Feud," *New Republic,* Oct. 14, 1991, 26–31; Peter Noel, "Crown Heights Burning," *Village Voice,* Sep. 3, 1991, 37–40.

59. Mary C. Waters gives a good account of this splitting in *Black Identities: West Indian Immigrant Dreams and American Realities* (Cambridge, Mass.: Harvard University Press, 1999), esp. chaps. 6 and 8.

60. Jürgen Habermas, *Legitimation Crisis* (Boston: Beacon Press, 1975).

61. Thomas Ferguson and Joel Rogers, *Right Turn: The Decline of the Democrats and the Future of American Politics* (New York: Hill and Wang, 1986), 28.

62. See, e.g., Reagan's remarks to the National Association of Evangelicals' Annual Convention, Orlando, Florida, March 8, 1983, reprinted in Paul D. Erickson, *Reagan Speaks: The Making of an American Myth* (New York: New York University Press, 1985), 155–66. After telling the audience of his belief in "intercessionary prayer" and condemning abortion and sexual promiscuity, Reagan added, "There is sin and evil in the world, and we're enjoined by Scripture and the Lord Jesus to oppose it with all our might" (161).

63. *New York Times,* Jan. 22, 1982, A20.

64. *Conservative Digest,* July 1982.

65. *New York Times,* Sep. 25, 1982, 9.

66. Michael Paul Rogin, *The Intellectuals and McCarthy: The Radical Specter* (Boston: MIT Press, 1967), 47.

67. See Kathleen Jamieson's discussion of this point in her *Eloquence in an Electronic Age: The Transformation of Political Speechmaking* (New York: Oxford University Press, 1988), chap. 6.

68. Kenneth Wald, *Religion and Politics in the United States* (New York: St. Martin's, 1987).

69. Dr. Tim LaHaye, "The Clintonistas' War against God," *Family Life Seminars' Capital Report* 8 (Oct. 1994): 1.

PART I

Moral Unity, Moral Division

CHAPTER 2

The Fetish of Difference

Richard Bernstein

In his biography of Meyer Amschel Rothschild, the founder of the international banking dynasty, the Israeli writer Amos Elon talks about the creation of the first modern Jewish school in the city of Frankfurt, where the Rothschilds lived in the narrow, overcrowded ghetto known as the Judengasse. The school was the brainchild of Seligmann Geisenheimer, an "Enlightenment" Jew whom Rothschild had hired to be his bookkeeper. Geisenheimer is an important figure. Until he arrived on the scene very early in the nineteenth century, the Jews of the Frankfurt Judengasse were educated strictly along religious lines, with no instruction in the local majority language, much less in classical secular subjects like Plato or mathematics. But the school that Geisenheimer set up under Rothschild's auspices, known as Philantropin, or "School for the Poor Children of the Jewish Nation," taught Torah as well as Voltaire, Rousseau, Lessing, and Herder. Its guiding principle, writes Elon, was "Torah and Derekh-Eretz,"[1] Torah and the customs of the land.

Among the many interesting things about Philantropin, looked at from the perspective of multicultural America, is that the school aroused the ire of an odd collection of political bedfellows. The Orthodox rabbinate was opposed to its inclusion of secular subjects. And many of Frankfurt's Christians disliked that idea as well. As one writer of the time put it: "It seems as though the Christian gentlemen begrudge Jews the light of knowledge and are downright eager to keep them in their ignorance."[2]

This episode of two hundred years ago offers an ironic, inverse echo of the debate about multiculturalism and identity politics in the United States today. From college English reading lists to corporate sensitivity training workshops a new vision of American identity has been taking shape. It is a "multiculturalist" identity in which "diversity" is pursued as an end in itself. The current idea is that we will be held together by a frank recognition of our differences, by celebrating the variety of America's equal cultural components and stressing, above all, tolerance and acceptance of each of them.

It is a beautiful vision. And it seems quite different from the one of those Frankfurt Christians who were alarmed at the prospect that Jews would not stay as separate as they wanted them to stay. After all, the Christians were more concerned about preserving the subordination of Jews than the richness of Jewish culture. Yet in their way—a way that stressed the separate cultural and religious identity of Jews—the Christians were the multiculturalists of their epoch, whereas for those like Geisenheimer, who wanted to encourage Jewish worldly success and engagement, "multiculturalism" was an obstacle.

I recognize that the multiculturalism of today aims, at least in rhetoric, at something different—inclusion and success, not separation and subordination for those who are different. At its best it is a moral call to the American nation to live closer to its values than it has lived in the past. It is precisely this moral grounding, and the high-flown motivations behind it, that gives multiculturalism its special power and appeal.

But that, alas, is all too often the theory. In practice, whatever the claims that are made on behalf of it, multiculturalism has proved to be far less an avenue toward inclusiveness and tolerance than a new orthodoxy exceedingly intolerant of disagreement. At the same time, its emphasis is on what makes various American groups different rather than on what brings them together. In the guise of bringing about a fairer society, it invents and then sustains separate cultural worlds, especially in our educational institutions, which are so respectful of "diversity" that they have lost sight of the simple fact that everybody needs to master a certain common cultural vocabulary in order to get on the ladder of upward mobility in American life. And, by denying the very existence of a common American identity, multiculturalism foments a narrow orthodoxy as the sole moral truth that endangers the very liberal values that are the genius of American life.

This multicultural vision is no fringe phenomenon. It is pervasive and entrenched. As the title of a 1997 book by Nathan Glazer puts it, with wistful resignation, "We are all multiculturalists now."[3] Almost every campus boasts what are euphemistically called "theme dorms" in universities—a euphemism that serves to cover up the fact that the dorms are a new form of segregation—blacks living in one set of houses, whites in another. (I somehow doubt that university administrators will proclaim their success in creating black- and white-only housing on campuses, even if that is what "theme" dorms actually are.) There are now minors and majors in black studies, women's studies, Hispanic studies, and gay and lesbian studies. Six credits in "multicultural courses" are now required in something like half of the nation's three thousand colleges and universities for undergraduates to get their degrees. A very popular idea, one that has become near gospel in many professional organizations of educators, is that different groups have different "ways of learning," different "learning styles," these "ways" and "styles" corresponding to racial and sexual and ethnic differences. The logical conclusion of this philosophy is that everybody needs to be helped, not because we need to share a common culture but because different groups will be advantaged by learning different things. Is this not the perfect realization of the vision held by the Orthodox rabbinate and the Christian anti-Semites of early-nineteenth-century Frankfurt?

Despite the differences between then and now, the irreducible feature of multiculturalism holds that the very notion of a common culture is an imposition on cultural minorities, and an unfair imposition at that. Rather than wanting everybody to master the same culture, the multiculturalists want society as a whole to recognize the worth and equality of each separate culture. Its stress is not on the things that each person must know in order to succeed in American life. Its stress is on changing the rules so that the ladder will be available to all, whether they master the majority culture or not. The educational idea is for children to see themselves "reflected in the curriculum," as the common saying goes, so they will feel better about themselves and do better in life.

But think about it. Before Geisenheimer the philosophy of the Jewish schools of the Frankfurt Judengasse was to privilege the Jewish culture, to enable Jewish children, especially poor Jewish children, to see themselves reflected in the curriculum of Talmud Torah. It was not to read the works of the hegemonic, anti-Semitic culture of the dead white *goyische* males. The benign Jewish motive in this was primarily to encourage religious observance; secondarily it was to perpetuate the values and the identity of the Jewish people. The Christian motive was not so benign.

It was to perpetuate Jewish noncompetitiveness forever. The multiculturalist motive of today, of course, is different. But it is fair to ask whether
the results will be the same.

My assessment of the meaning of multiculturalism emerged from more
than cranky ideological recoil. When I was traveling the country doing
research for my book *Dictatorship of Virtue,* I visited numerous institutions of American life to see what actually was being done in the name
of the new American value of diversity. I visited elementary schools and
universities, corporate "diversity training" seminars, newspapers striving for "diversity" in their coverage, curriculum development commit-
tees, and meetings and conventions from Massachusetts to California.

I confess that some of what I witnessed surprised me, as in the almost
entirely black schools of Milwaukee's inner city, where Afrocentrism had
become the reigning doctrine. I have opposed Afrocentrism, in part because it is the weaving of an entire broad fabric of supremacist myth—
a mirror image of the myths of white and Christian supremacy that
reigned in Europe for so long. But I also felt uneasy about Afrocentrism
because it purveyed, I thought, wrong ideas about how children get ahead
and how they get self-esteem. Children, I believed, feel good about themselves not by seeing themselves reflected in the curriculum but by expe-
riencing the thrill and satisfaction of acquiring knowledge, mastering material, achieving things—not by being fed propaganda about how the
"hegemonic culture" is biased against them, how it eradicates their identity and alienates them from their true natures.

Despite those misgivings I came away from the schools in Milwaukee
thinking that Afrocentrism could actually be a good thing after all. Or
maybe it wasn't the Afrocentrism. The schools I saw were hopeful places.
There was a vibrancy to them. Expectations were high. The children were
well behaved. They wore uniforms, an indication that school was a special place, like church, and that you don't go there in just any old clothing. In other words, under the guise of Afrocentrism the children were
given the message that education is important and serious, a matter of
hard work and discipline. If a few false myths get thrown into the picture, that seemed a price worth paying if the inner-city children of Milwaukee and many other places were to be served better by the public
schools.

Unfortunately, it turned out, the Milwaukee case was rather excep-
tional. More typical was another school I visited, this one in Minneapolis,
where the board of education had created the Hans Christian Anderson
Schools of Many Voices to further the multiculturalist approach to ed-

ucation for the future. Here, as in Milwaukee, I was impressed with the spirit of enterprise, the liveliness of the school, the dedication of the teachers, the obvious energy and commitment that was going into things. But when you looked at the curriculum of the school, at the message conveyed to the pupils there, things seemed less bright. The school was a realm for the practice of the victim cult, with white males set up as the victimizers of all of the nonwhite peoples, who represented the good. The underlying message of the place (actually it wasn't all that underlying; it was pretty overt) was that we are all different rather than all the same and that we have to stress that difference, to identify with it in almost everything we do.

The philosophy of the school was summed up in a series of not-very-easy-to-remember initials—MCGFDA pedagogy, for Multi-Cultural, Gender-Fair, Disability-Aware pedagogy. When I first heard that phrase, I admit to feeling just a twinge of suspicion that the Hans Christian Anderson Schools of Many Voices were going to be places of High Virtue, that everybody was going to be made to attend the compulsory chapel of political morality in education. And so it was. I attended a poetry-reading class for one of the lower elementary grades (the school went from kindergarten to fifth grade). After each poem was recited, the teacher would ask the students to identify the poem by its ethnic origins. So after the poem the children would shout out "Langston Hughes—African American." They sang in unison "European American" after the name of another poet, "American Indian, Zuni," after another, "Asian, China," for yet another. The feeling pervaded the school that recognizing the diversity of American life was not just a goal created in the service of tolerance but that it was the ultimate objective of the entire educational experience, the single-issue campaign to be waged through the six years that children would spend there. A banner displayed in the school saying "I Learn Through Diversity" summed up this idea. But that seemed to me an empty slogan, a phrase utterly without real meaning. How does one learn through diversity? Does it help with addition? Can you master a foreign language with it? Does it teach correct English usage? Could there be another banner reading "I Learn Through Homogeneity"?

On a bulletin board I saw a display of children's essays in which they expressed their ideas on making the world a better place. At the bottom of each little essay the pupils had written their names and their ethnic identity, along the lines of "My name is John Smith and my culture is European American" or "My name is Elisa Jones and my culture is African American." There was, in other words, no American culture, no com-

mon culture at the school. There were just separate cultures, which, on
further scrutiny, were actually divided into only two cultures: the victim cultures and the hegemonic cultures (although the children themselves were not actually taught this trendy vocabulary; this is more a
matter of the language used at big educational congresses these days,
like the conference of NAME, the National Association for Multicultural
Education, that I attended in Los Angeles shortly before my introduction to MCGFDA pedagogy in Minneapolis).

When I asked a series of social studies teachers what they actually
taught, however, the notion of the victim cultures and the victimizers became clear. "Whom do the students admire after they have finished at
the school?" I asked one teacher. Her reply: "The sentiment in my room
is that they don't like Christians and they don't like white people, because they saw what has been done in the name of Christianity and what
the white people did to the Indians and the Africans."

"What about George Washington?" I asked, wondering if there was
at least one admirable white person for American children to admire.
"What do you teach about him?" "That he was the first president, that
he was a slave owner, that he was rich—not much," she replied. This
teacher (who, it must be stressed, was a dedicated person who gave the
strong impression of caring deeply about her pupils) told me that her
pupils did learn about Eli Whitney, the cotton gin inventor, in her social
studies class. The children learn, she said, "that he stole his invention
from a woman who didn't patent it," she said, spoiling my illusion that
at least some whites could be portrayed in a generous and positive way
under the strict rules of MCGFDA pedagogy.

Actually, my visit to Minneapolis indicated an important truth: multiculturalism has almost nothing to do with culture, and it isn't very multi
either. Draping itself in the language of respect, tolerance, and diversity,
multiculturalism does not respect difference, and its idea of diversity is
extremely truncated. Diversity to a multiculturalist means a group of
people who look different and who have different sexual practices, religious beliefs, and ethnic origins but who think pretty much alike.

If you want multiculturalism, real multiculturalism, get on an airplane
and go someplace else. Out there in that great region of the world called
"Abroad" there are practices like female circumcision, amputation of the
hands of thieves, head-to-foot veils for women. That place called Abroad,
by the way, is not the place where tolerance for homosexuality was invented, or equal rights for women, or where the phrase about all men
being born equal and endowed by their creator with certain inalienable

rights was struck. Try getting on the bus in China and you will see what multiculturalism is all about. I am a great enthusiast for Chinese culture, but the notion of women and children first, or even of standing in line, is not among its more practiced attributes, although putting people in prison for the crime of criticizing the government is.

There is a supreme irony here. Multiculturalism is at best a misnomer, a well-intended but inaccurate synonym for a set of values that is Western in origin and that makes up a key part of the American culture to which we all actually belong. Yet multiculturalism denies that there is such a thing as a common American culture. The funny thing is that in all of my travels among the multiculturalists I almost never encountered one who had actually bothered to undertake the serious study of another culture. It might have something to do with the fact that it's a lot easier and emotionally gratifying to substitute a few honeyed and heartwarming clichés for in-depth knowledge. It might have something to do with the inherent difficulty and the consumption of time involved, say, in learning three thousand ideograms so that you can read the newspaper. Because it's impossible to take a few years off from your regular life to do that—the only way you can become literate in the Chinese culture, literacy being, it seems to me, a kind of prerequisite for cultural understanding— you can learn a few boilerplate phrases about the yin and the yang instead, or you can be fed a couple of prefabricated notions about how the native peoples of America have always valued spiritual wholeness over competitiveness—never mind that the Indians waged wars against each other every bit as vicious and unsparing as the wars waged between the Indians and the U.S. cavalry.

If you did really learn the Chinese culture, of course, you would discover what ought to be obvious: that it is made up of some combination of admirable and not-so-admirable features. Or you are likely to see as admirable those features of the Chinese culture that seem similar to your own values and practices. The Chinese culture puts a very strong value on the family, which has, from our point of view, the admirable consequence of stability and security; but, again from our point of view, it also has the less desirable consequence of patriarchal authoritarianism. The great poets of the Tang and Sung Dynasties are an unmitigated cultural good, but you're going to have to expand your list of ideograms from three thousand to five thousand or so if you are ever going to read them in the original.

The truth is we are better off in the United States of America with our own culture, not with the Chinese culture. Our own culture has produced the greatest degree of upward social mobility and the greatest cultural, religious, and political freedom in human history. Moreover, its very notions of liberal democracy have provided the moral and political weapons that have helped to attack our own society's violations of those cherished truths, as with slavery, sexual inequality, and segregation. For the members of my subgroup, the Jews, the gradual realization in practice of American values has led to the greatest prosperity for the most people in conditions of the greatest political freedom and the fullest participation than at any time in Jewish history since the destruction of the Second Temple. There is, in other words, something more to this culture than the pupils are learning at the Hans Christian Anderson Schools of Many Voices.

I, for one, prefer to be a member of the culture that we share as Americans. I don't want the pre-Geisenheimer Jewish culture of the Judengasse. I don't want my children to have to write on the bulletin board that their name is Bernstein and their culture is Jewish American, whatever that might mean to the faceless bureaucrats of some school system who, with their relentless good intentions, reduce the real and ineffable complexity of human life to a few simple concepts that they, in their ignorance, think they understand. I would want my children in their public institutions to be considered irrespective of their private identities, not to have those identities hung on their breasts like badges of merit. I am a Jew. I am an American. I am not a Jewish American. Why not? Because the concept Jewish American entails a public identity that erases one of the most important distinctions in American life, a distinction unrecognized by the rising ethic of multiculturalism. Since the first great waves of immigration the United States has been a country of qualified assimilation. New arrivals who were put under pressure to shed all of the cultural trappings of past life refused to do so completely. In becoming Americans they retained a degree of private separateness, linguistic, cultural, or religious, even as they became public members of the common American culture, that complex blend derived mostly from England but mixed with influences from numerous other places of origin from Angola to the shtetl.

They did that out of patriotic duty perhaps, given that in decades past most immigrants arrived in the United States without any intention of reproducing in every detail the lives they had abandoned in the old country. But even if they did not feel patriotic love for the new country, they did it because they had no choice. Americanization was, as Norman Podhoretz famously put it, a brutal bargain. It was freedom and opportunity in exchange for a substantial measure of cultural homogenization, which meant a substantial measure of cultural eradication. In John Higham's classic book *Strangers in the Land* we read how the members of the first great wave of immigration from southern and eastern Europe were met in America with an intense campaign for what was called 100 percent Americanization, which was a well-intentioned effort by progressive thinkers to try to ensure a place for the new arrivals—the opposite, in its way, from the Christian opposition to Geisenheimer's school in Frankfurt. There was also a thought, still common in virtually all countries but the United States, that anybody who wanted membership in the club ought to be willing to pay the cultural price of admission. But there was something more than mere nativist defensiveness in its creation. Above all, 100 percent Americanization involved instruction in English, in American history, and in American civic life, and it brought with it the underlying message that anybody could become an American. As Lilian Wald, a social worker who was among the pioneers of 100 percent Americanization, put it, the challenge consisted of "fusing these people who come to us from the Old World civilization into . . . a real brotherhood among men."[4]

There's no point in idealizing the approach to immigration and cultural assimilation of yesteryear. Its welcome was limited to white people from Europe, who were seen as culturally very different from the majority in place. People of color were not included in the brutal embrace. It involved rites of initiation that seem in retrospect disrespectful and unduly harsh. Higham describes the ceremony that took place in the Ford English School, set up by the automobile manufacturer with attendance required for foreign workers. There was a great melting pot in the middle of the stage. "A long column of immigrant students descended into the pot from backstage, clad in outlandish garb and flaunting signs proclaiming their fatherlands. Simultaneously from the other side of the pot another stream of men emerged, each prosperously dressed in identical suits of clothes and each carrying a little American flag."[5]

Like I say, some of this was brutal. But it was also a commonsensical approach to the realities of nation building, and it was aimed at inclusion, at Lilian Wald's "brotherhood of men." (She would, of course, have to find some gender-neutral language to express that idea now, the words *brotherhood* and *men* having been banned by the language police.) But the truth was that the new arrivals never all wore identical cultural or religious clothing. The melting pot, as Nathan Glazer and Daniel Patrick Moynihan found in *Beyond the Melting Pot,* was never wholly successful. The genius of Americanization lay in the respect it retained for the distinction between public and private life. The cost of entry involved public homogeneity, but it allowed for a wide latitude in private difference. One could become an American and not experience identity eradication at the same time. Americans could be individuals in the public sphere and members of identity groups at the same time—often, in their latter capacity, fighting for the right not to be taken as the member of a group in the public sphere but to be deemed an individual without any determining group affiliation.

Multiculturalism would upset that delicate balance between public and private, between individuality and group affiliation. If it had its way, rather than presenting ourselves as members of the common culture with private identities, we would present ourselves as the bearers of private identities who also share elements of the common culture. Such a shift would be more than a subtle change of emphasis. It would diminish something precious in our liberal democracy, a heritage worth affirming, not out of smug self-congratulations but because it has proven resilient enough to give us moral courage to confront our own society when it has failed to realize those worthy ideals.

NOTES

1. Amos Elon, *Founder: A Portrait of the First Rothschild and His Time* (New York: Viking, 1996), 124.

2. Ibid.

3. Nathan Glazer, *We Are All Multiculturalists Now* (Cambridge, Mass.: Harvard University Press, 1997).

4. Quoted in John Higham, *Strangers in the Land: Patterns of American Nativism, 1860–1928* (New Brunswick, N.J.: Rutgers University Press, 1955), 238–39.

5. Ibid., 247–48.

CHAPTER 3

Fragments or Ties?

The Defense of Difference

Martha Minow

There is a school of thought that holds that ours is a time of unusually high conflict between groups. Generations square off against each other as senior citizens support cutting funds for schools and children's services while maintaining support for themselves. Fiscal warfare is intensified by a lack of compassion across ethnic and racial lines. New regionalisms arise even as global communications surge. Class divisions find expression in spatial separation, as privileged whites wall themselves off from others, huddling in suburbs and gated communities with their own security, garbage collection, and after-school entertainment.

Even more dangerous, some argue, are the divisions created by "identity politics," the allegiances that gays, blacks, immigrants, Latinos, and others show to their own kind. Whether embodied in group claims for recognition; battles to transform white, Euro-American-dominated curricula; or the demonizing language of separatist demagogues, such instances have provoked widespread fear that assertions of group identity threaten national unity. They also raise the question as to what does, or could, bind Americans together. As we will see, the answers to that query have not always been entirely satisfactory.

IDENTITY POLITICS AND ITS CRITICS

Those who worry that group conflicts are fragmenting American society often cite "the division of society into fixed ethnicities," as Arthur

M. Schlesinger Jr. put it in *The Disuniting of America.* "When a vocal and visible minority pledges primary allegiance to their groups, . . . it presents a threat to the brittle bonds of national identity that hold this diverse and fractious society together."[1]

In the waning years of the twentieth century these charges took various forms, but the basic elements remain relatively constant as we move into the new millennium. They include a defense of the values of Western civilization against critics who condemn it as racist, sexist, imperialist, and otherwise oppressive; opposition to sentiments of ethnic or linguistic separatism and to the demagogic hucksters and mass media that stir them; and a rejection of new "feel good" histories that nurture group pride and self-esteem for the children of minority groups. Against such fragmenting tendencies the critics often invoke an American national identity, as reality or aspiration, that unites the diverse residents of the United States.

These charges are not entirely unfounded. Even a thoughtful historian like Eric Foner, who admires how the new histories give increased attention to previously neglected groups such as women, blacks, and Latinos, nonetheless observes, "When history moves from recognition of the irrefutable fact that different peoples have had different historical experiences to an effort to locate supposedly primordial characteristics shared with other members of one's group and no one else, it negates the study of change that is the essence of the discipline itself" and ignores the influences of different cultures on one another to shape America.[2] Too much emphasis on what divides rather than unites Americans risks undermining true depiction of the past and actual practices of national cohesiveness.

Unfortunately, most of those who anguish about ethnic fragmentation lack Foner's sense of historical nuance. Their diagnoses of identity politics suffer from several weaknesses. For one, they miss the needs to which identity politics responds. Identity politics offers those who embrace it a life raft in the turbulent search for meaning, a sense of home, acknowledgment, and redress. Joining with others to seek recognition may be easier than going it alone.

Second, the critics tend to miss the logic, as well as the predictability, of identity politics. When citizens injure others because of their race, gender, sexual orientation, religion, or disability, it makes sense that the injured parties will resist along those very lines. Demanding recognition or restitution on the grounds of group membership is also a way to deny that such membership is a natural or legitimate ground for injury. Efforts to resist mistreatment on the basis of a shared trait naturally evolve into celebrating of the trait and seeking recognition and redress on its basis.

Communal injuries include present harms and the memories of past ones. African Americans remember the laws that prevented them from voting and the violent white resistance to their efforts to gain justice.[3] In 1990 young blacks and young whites with equivalent résumés were trained to behave identically to test the job market; whites did substantially better.[4] Hispanics have continually risked loss of jobs, land, and language.[5] Japanese Americans—many of whom were citizens—lost property, homes, dignity, and health when they were corralled into internment camps during World War II.[6] American Indians endured ethnic cleansing and massive killing; implicit and explicit policies deprived them of land, children, self-government, and language.[7] Women of all backgrounds could be denied participation in juries in some parts of the country until 1975 and refused admission to private schools and clubs up through the present; women still face risks of domestic violence, bias in the courts, and sexual harassment in the workplace.[8] Gays and lesbians encounter job and housing discrimination with little protection. Persons with disabilities have been denied education, employment, and housing and also have been confined in often brutal and disgusting institutions.

Third, the critique of identity politics overstates the risks of divisiveness, thereby missing a more urgent problem: the danger of restrictive notions of group loyalty. We do not need fancy theories to recognize that members of excluded groups may embrace new stereotypes to define themselves even as they reject the stigmatizing ones inflicted by outsiders. But reducing the complexity of a person or a group to a single trait, even for ostensibly self-affirming reasons, misses much of what matters to individuals and invites demands for conformity. Moreover, no single trait can convey the richness of experience and identity individuals draw from belonging simultaneously to multiple groups—such as the special experiences of being Chinese American and female, or African American and Baptist, or Muslim and second-generation New Yorker, or male and gay and Catholic. Mobilizing around identities forces people to choose sides when the lines are themselves often arbitrary, shifting, mythical, or nonexistent.

The San Francisco public schools adopted a rule permitting a parent to change the racial identification of a child only twice, and the U.S. census now allows individuals to claim multiple racial identities. What acknowledgments that the lines of identity do not work! As individuals increasingly marry into races different from their own, more and more children have multiple lines of racial ancestry, and many of them actually claim them.

Communal injuries encompass more than exclusion, economic hardship, and humiliation. Injured groups suffer less tangible injuries to the self from the "web of narratives . . . [developed to] legitimize those exclusions by constructing an identity of the excluded group."[9] Such symbolic assaults may not only inspire those who denigrate the excluded; the targets of denigration may themselves come to believe they possess inherent defects of competence and character.

To some extent, then, the identity politics of the excluded can be viewed as a way of rejecting not some unifying national identity but rather the identity politics of those who have excluded them. As Foner notes, the effort to turn history into psychological uplift and to emphasize innate and immutable group differences better characterizes the political right than the political left. "[W]itness, for example, *The Bell Curve,* or *Alien Nation,* Peter Brimelow's recent screed against nonwhite immigration as destroying America's 'ethno-cultural community,' grounded, according to him, in a shared European ancestry." The strongest advocate of "feelgood" history designed to promote self-esteem, according to Foner, is "Lynne Cheney, former head of the [National Endowment for the Humanities], who condemns the new history standards for neglecting the greatness of the Western tradition and offering a 'depressing' portrait of our nation's past."[10]

BEYOND IDENTITY

The obsession with identity politics reflects deep anxiety about the fragility of the ties that bind a nation of diverse and mutually suspicious people. Because of this, many critics of identity politics embrace assimilation to an existing, although gradually evolving, American identity.

Underlying all of this is a largely unexamined and fallacious premise in the narrative of fragmentation: that elevating a singular, shared American identity—if one could be invented—is the only way to unify the nation. Indeed, there are at least three other forces that bind Americans to one another: American civic culture, consumer culture, and crosscutting affiliations. Taken collectively, these dynamics remind us of the institutional sources of order in pluralistic societies.

In the view of those who herald the power of civic culture, to be American a person need embrace neither a general American identity nor any particular national, linguistic, religious, or ethnic identity. The threshold for belonging is a commitment "to the political ideology centered on the abstract ideals of liberty, equality, and republicanism."[11] The ideals of civic culture include political participation and representation offered to all *and* freedom for religious pluralism and other private pursuits. Amish parents seeking to exempt their children from compulsory schooling and Satmar Hasidic Jews seeking to gain public special education benefits for their children could subscribe to these ideals sufficiently to work through the political and judicial systems to achieve their goals. Some people may subscribe to the civic culture only for short-term or even long-term reasons of self-interest, but that is sufficient, so long as their behavior comports with the principles at stake.

This vision of a workable and inclusive civic culture does not fully describe our nation's past or present. Even defenders of the ideals of civic culture acknowledge such historical lapses as the exclusion of blacks, Indians, and Chinese and Japanese immigrants from its moral protection.[12] Yet these failures do not disprove its power—periodically in the past and potentially in the future—to hold together the diverse residents of this nation. The United States can claim pluralism as one of its defining values. The United States *is* "a nation of immigrants," whereas "France is a nation that attracts and incorporates immigrants."[13] Constitutionalism affords resources to redress the gap between rhetoric and practice; when criticized by the aggrieved or their spokespeople, the gap itself may serve as a moral tool for persuading the larger nation to live up to its claims.

Attachment to constitutional law does not imply unanimity or even a high level of consensus. It may indicate the prevalence of conflict requiring adjudication. Nor does venerating the Constitution necessitate agreement about its meanings. Sanford Levinson, who puts the Constitution at the heart of American civil religion, argues that such interpretive fights have been as great a source of disunity as have fights over the Bible's meaning.[14] Such conflicts, much like our constant resort and imaginative references to litigation, reflect shared respect for the Constitution and the legal resolution of disputes. We can fight hard within the ideological and institutional framework that we take for granted and reaffirm by regular use. Allegiance to the framework, if not to the content of specific decisions, is a unifying force.

It might seem as if the emphasis on rights in our civic culture would exacerbate group conflict. The pervasiveness of winner-take-all litigation and the stress on individual or group entitlements at the expense of the public good suggest as much. But even Mary Anne Glendon, an eloquent critic of the excessive devotion to rights in American culture, recognizes, "The very heterogeneity that drives us to seek an excessively abstract common language may indeed be one of our most promising resources for enriching it."[15] If the constitutional culture tilts toward individualism and liberty rather than toward community and responsibility, it nonetheless affords a common starting point for debate.

Americans' consciousness of their Constitution is not restricted to a limited band of elites. Trends in this area are not easy to establish, but popular discussions about rights burgeoned during the bicentennials for the Constitution and the Bill of Rights and may play some role in reanimating commitment to those legal documents. Curricular programs for high school and even elementary school students increasingly model judicial action and focus on contemporary legal issues. If only as a point of departure, the language of law and constitutionalism can provide a common set of civic reference points for Americans who otherwise feel little in common.

A second source of national unity may be found in the integrative functions of consumer culture. Whether one celebrates or bemoans them, the marketing strategies of leading advertisers and merchants increasingly appeal to images of respect for diversity. Sociologist Todd Gitlin observes, "Today it remains true that immigrants want to assimilate, but the America into which they hope to do so is not the America of white bread. It is an America where the supermarket shelves groan beneath the varieties of bagels, sourdough rye, seven grain, and other mass-produced loaves. One belongs by being slightly different, though in a predictable way."[16] The United Colors of Benetton advertising campaign of several years ago that showcased multiethnic individuals in Benetton clothing appealed to the ideal of pluralistic mixture.

Malls across the country replace restaurants with "food courts" that array mass-produced fast food with distinctive ethnic presentations, and customers then sit down in a common eating area; those at one table may be eating Mexican food while those at another consume Japanese fish; at another table individual family members each relish different ethnic foods. When General Mills decided to replace the picture of Betty Crocker on its syrup and cereal packages, it substituted a computer-generated composite of seventy-five American women of various racial and ethnic backgrounds; someone in marketing discovered that this was America.[17] One can question the desirability of these forms of consumer culture. If legality can be coldly abstract and divisive, consumerism tends to emphasize material values over all others, to divide by class and to fuel insatiable desires for commodities that deplete other resources for building meaning and a sense of community. Paradoxically, advertisers who sell subgroup images in global economic markets may play into the seeming danger of fragmentation and exoticism precisely while homogenizing culture worldwide.

As a result there is some danger that both civic culture and consumer culture ultimately may seem too thin and abstract to provide social cohesion. To define *American* in terms of civic culture is to assert that "[t]here is no American people, merely an American Idea."[18] To define *American* in terms of consumer culture is to assert merely the marketing of America. Cultural glue needs more. Especially in the face of heated disagreements, solidarity and respect may require something more textured than abstract commitments.

The third source of solidarity, the crosscutting ties that link Americans, offers precisely this virtue of concreteness. One may see such linkages not simply as an alternative to civic and consumer culture but as their enriching complement. Americans are linked through concrete social relations, not by a single unity but through overlapping communities, the way a family may extend across marriages, divorces, and other intimate relations.[19] A community of communities can evoke sufficient allegiance to the ground rules that let the subcommunities thrive,[20] and the abstract quality of ground rules is humanized and enlivened by the actual network of connections shared by members.

This kind of sharing further qualifies any emphasis on identity as a source of solidarity. Certainly one way to become American has long been to affirm a particular religious or ethnic identity.[21] Americans also ironically claim commonality as a nation of strangers.[22] Claiming outsider status is a familiar American practice.[23] The "one" American is yoked to "the many." Especially American may be the unsettling of even these identities through the tradition of undermining tradition.[24]

In this view unity is less important than solidarity. Unity implies coherence, which may be elusive. By contrast solidarity does not require unity, identity, or similarity; rather, it puts differences aside in the name of affection, self-interest, or short- or long-term purposes. Rather than emerge from commonality, solidarity grows through interactions. Rather than a community of common identity or interests, repeated interactions among heterogeneous peoples can provide social glue.

Anthropologists, sociologists, and historians have long heralded the virtues of crosscutting ties. Complementarity, interacting across lines of difference, integration through swaps across groups with different strengths and resources—these processes have been identified in pluralistic cultures that function well. Moreover, students of culture increasingly question the presentation of any culture as homogeneous.[25] In a famous examination of solidarity Clifford Geertz studied villages marked by a communal sharing of food within neighboring households, despite diverse belief systems; those ties were disrupted when people moved to larger towns, and similarity-based identities seemed to matter more.[26] This implies not only the futility of a search for the common culture of a diverse society but even danger in the creation of myths about national identity.[27] Such myths serve to justify channeling people into singular identities or eliminating any person who does not conform.

Recent scholarship has exposed the notion of the "melting pot" as a mythical construct that served historically to distract from the divisive features in American life.[28] Before the Revolution English officials tried unsuccessfully to impose uniformity on the untidy variety in colonial life, laws, and politics. Traditions of governance and cultural renewal that emphasized the local and resisted central authority made uniform laws, customs, and even coinage often unavailable prior to the war. The preservation of state sovereignty alongside federal supremacy marked an ingenious compromise in the founding of the nation. Myths of the melting pot emerged with the new nation but perhaps applied only to American Negroes, who did indeed overcome regional, linguistic, and tribal differences during and after slavery.[29] Protected by the rule of law, as well as a complex constitutional structure, the nation preserved and promoted a plural society despite fears of potential instability. "Americans continue to celebrate pluralism in the past but are reluctant to honor it in the present."[30]

This messiness might be pursued to an even more radical conclusion: ambivalence about our pluralism is itself an American tradition. As Michael Kammen suggests, "conservatism *and* liberalism, individualism *and* corporatism, hierarchy *and* egalitarianism, emotionalism *and* rationalism, autonomy *and* co-operation are all integral to the mutuality of pluralism."[31]

The diversity that characterizes even seemingly homogeneous cultures further challenges the assumption that unity is necessary for stability. Associations and subgroups function as democratic bulwarks against centralized power. Ties of cooperation and respect and the work of self-governance through democratic politics are enhanced by overlapping but disconnected ties among different groups of people. The very multiplication of people's felt alliances enlarges the grounds for solidarities.

Constitutional scholar Kenneth Karst has argued that the proliferation of an individual's connections to groups defined by race, religion, family, occupation, and hobby create new kinds of commonality that serve to unify a national society that might succumb to cultural divisions. He gives the example of the "bloody" battles between Catholics and Protestants who battled in mid-nineteenth-century Philadelphia. Had they continued to live cheek by jowl in their own separate communities, the battles

> might have been bloodier still. But market individualism went about its usual work of multiplying ways of life with the result that both homogeneity and separateness were destroyed. Each of the groups became stratified by class and otherwise differentiated within itself, making new integrations possible for succeeding generations. Opportunity called individuals and families, both Catholic and Protestant, to join the move West; in their new surroundings they formed communities in which the old divisions just didn't matter so much. Their grandchildren intermarried and produced children of their own. As daily life in Hawaii makes beautifully clear, nothing else integrates quite so effectively as a baby.[32]

The solidarities created by crisscrossing connections may never appear as strong as those tied to an overarching value like nationalism or feelings of tribal unanimity. Yet these solidarities may be strong enough to foster mutual aid against fractionalizing violence. The connections of intermarriage and overlapping group membership offer something at once more fragile and more reliable than unity. The recognition that a stranger belongs to the soccer team that plays in the same league as your uncle's team generates a bond founded in concrete encounters rather than idealized histories or shared mythic heroes.

Aviam Soifer, an insightful scholar of groups in American history, observes that illusions of unity cannot sustain tolerance when communal differences surface, as they inevitably must. "Tolerance, ironically, must be bound to group struggle. It requires recognition of the guilt and fear we all encounter, rooted in uncertainties about our own identities. We strive for independence, yet any meaningful freedom is deeply dependent upon our social networks. To be real, tolerance requires recognition that we all use groups to define ourselves and others, inescapably and differently."[33]

For a democratic society, then, unity is neither the precondition nor the crucial means. Instead, engagement in a communal debate about the future affords the ties of shared struggle. A national identity, no less than a religious or racial one, implies a preexisting, stable frame that suppresses differences. Preoccupation with what it means to be an American is no less constraining than preoccupation with being Chicano or a woman. Each preoccupation tries to summon a solidarity prior to action; each skips the hard work of crafting connection in the very processes of deliberation and action. Solidarity, Hannah Arendt reminded us, does not arise from understandings prior to politics but from the process of politics that permits its construction.

The links of a common fate join those who share this nation. That fate, as David Hollinger has written, "can be common without its will being uniform, and the nation can constitute a common project without effacing all of the various projects that its citizens pursue through their voluntary affiliations."[34] After September 11, 2001, more Americans expressed commitment to the common project even as they reclaimed their connections with different religions, ethnicities, occupations, regions, and generations. Some observant Jewish males donned yarmulkes with stars and stripes. Some Sikhs wore T-shirts reading "Proud to Be American" along with their turbans. People sent canned goods and stuffed animals, tissue and blood, boots and jelly to survivors of the disaster and to the police, firefighters, and cleanup crews in New York. Some declared, "We're all New Yorkers," whereas others proclaimed themselves Texans or second-graders, offering support. Some saw dangers of a new American separatism, whereas others felt sudden solidarity with victims of terrorism in other parts of the globe. Group identities, then, are hardly the condition of solidarity, nor are they corrosive to it. They are one ingredient of our complex sense of self as we each go about creating a collective future.

NOTES

1. Arthur M. Schlesinger Jr., *The Disuniting of America* (New York: Norton, 1992), 113.

2. Eric Foner, "What Is an American?" in *Who Owns History? Rethinking the Past in a Changing World* (New York: Hill and Wang, 2002), 149–66.

3. See Gerald Stern, "It's Not Right," in *Outside the Law: Narratives on Justice in America,* ed. Susan Richards Shreve and Porter Shreve (Boston: Beacon Press, 1997). Thus, the issue is not just slavery but new forms of exclusion developed during Reconstruction and since. See generally George Lipsitz, "The Pos-

sessive Investment in Whiteness: Racialized Social Democracy and the 'White' Problem in American Studies," *American Quarterly* 47 (1995): 369–427.

4. See Michael Kinsley, "The Spoils of Victimhood," *New Yorker,* March 27, 1995, 62.

5. See, e.g., Deborah Barfield, "Minority Legislators Fight State Budget Cuts," *Newsday,* March 13, 1996, A36; Sharon Cotliar, "Towns Make English Official," *Chicago Sun-Times,* Aug. 25, 1996, 15; Robert D. Hershey Jr., "Bias Hits Hispanic Workers," *New York Times,* April 27, 1995, D1; Irene Middleman Thomas, "Survival of the Fittest," *Hispanic* 9 (June 1996): 32.

6. Peter Irons, *Justice at War* (New York: Oxford University Press, 1983); Page Smith, *Democracy on Trial* (New York: Simon and Schuster, 1995); John Tateishi, *And Justice for All: An Oral History of the Japanese American Detention Camps* (New York: Random House, 1984).

7. Robert Williams, *The American Indian in Western Legal Thought* (New York: Oxford University Press, 1990); Vine DeLoria, *Custer Died for Your Sins* (New York: Macmillan, 1969); Vine DeLoria, *American Indian Policy in the Twentieth Century* (Norman: University of Oklahoma Press, 1985).

8. See *United States v. Virginia,* 518 U.S. 515 (1996); *Taylor v. Louisiana,* U.S. 419 (1975): 522; Deborah Rhode, "Association and Assimilation," *Northwestern University Law Review* 106 (1986): 81; Judith Resnik, "Asking about Gender in Courts," *Signs* 21 (1996): 952; Reva B. Siegal, " 'The Rule of Love': Wife Beating as Prerogative and Privacy," *Yale Law Journal* 105 (1996): 2117.

9. Adeno Addis, "Role Models and the Politics of Recognition," *University of Pennsylvania Law Review* 144 (1996): 1377, 1441.

10. Foner, "What Is an American?" xii, 149.

11. Philip Gleason, "American Identity and Americanization," in *Concepts of Ethnicity,* ed. William Petersen, Michael Novak, Philip Gleason (Cambridge, Mass.: Harvard University Press, 1980), 62.

12. See Kenneth Karst, *Belonging to America* (New Haven, Conn.: Yale University Press, 1989). A more critical attack argues that American civil identity has always involved multiple, competing traditions, including nativist and inegalitarian, as well as liberal republican strands. See Rogers M. Smith, "Beyond Tocqueville, Myrdal, and Hartz: The Multiple Traditions in America," *American Political Science Review* 87 (Sep. 1993): 549; and Jacqueline Stevens, "Beyond Tocqueville, Please!" *American Political Science Review* 89 (Dec. 1995): 987.

13. Stanley Hoffman, "Thoughts on the French Nation Today," *Daedalus* 122 (1993): 63, 64.

14. Sanford Levinson, "The Constitution in American Civil Religion," *Supreme Court Review* (1979): 125.

15. Mary Anne Glendon, *Rights Talk: The Impoverishment of Political Discourse* (New York: Free Press, 1991).

16. Todd Gitlin, *The Twilight of Common Dreams: Why America Is Wracked by Culture Wars* (New York: Metropolitan Books, 1995).

17. See Joan Beck, "Get the Facts Straight and Start Dealing with Racial Realities in the Once-a-Decade Head Count," *Chicago Tribune,* July 11, 1996, 23.

18. Michael Lind, "Are We a Nation?" *Dissent* (summer 1995): 355, 356.

19. See Judith Stacey, *In the Name of the Family: Rethinking Family Values in the Postmodern Age* (Boston: Beacon Press, 1996). The classic statement of this view is Georg Simmel, *Soziologie* (Berlin: Doneker and Humblot, 1968).

20. See Horace Kallen, *Cultural Pluralism and the American Idea* (Philadelphia: University of Pennsylvania Press, 1959); Randolph Bourne, "Trans-National America," in *War and the Intellectuals: Essays by Randolph S. Bourne, 1915–1919*, ed. Carl Resek (New York: Harper and Row, 1964); Michael Walzer, "Multiculturalism and Individualism," *Dissent* 41 (spring 1994).

21. See David A. Hollinger, *Postethnic America: Beyond Multiculturalism* (New York: Basic Books, 1995).

22. Jodi Dean describes a way to pursue solidarity in a pluralist society: citizens should not try to see the stranger as the other of a citizen; but citizens should try to recognize themselves as strange. Jodi Dean, *Solidarity of Strangers: Feminism after Identity Politics* (Berkeley: University of California Press, 1996), 42. For an insightful rejoinder to Kristeva see Bonnie Honig, "Ruth, the Model Emigree," in *No Place Like Home: Democracy and Foreigners* (Princeton, N.J.: Princeton University Press, 2001).

23. R. Laurence Moore, *Religious Outsiders and the Making of Americans* (New York: Oxford University Press, 1986).

24. Joseph A. Maxwell, "Diversity, Solidarity, and Community" (paper presented at the annual meeting of the American Educational Research Association, New York, April 1996).

25. See James Clifford, *The Predicament of Culture* (Cambridge, Mass.: Harvard University Press, 1988); Elizabeth Mertz, "Legal Loci and Places in the Heart: Community and Identity," *Law and Society Review* 28 (1994): 971; Regina Austin, "The Black Community: Its Lawbreakers, and a Politics of Identification," *Southern California Law Review* 65 (1992): 1769; Roy Wagner, *The Invention of Culture*, rev. ed. (Chicago: University of Chicago Press, 1981).

26. Clifford Geertz, *The Religion of Java* (Glencoe: Free Press, 1960).

27. "Generally speaking, nationalist ideology suffers from pervasive false consciousness. Its myths invert reality. . . . It preaches and defends continuity, but owes everything to a decisive and utterly profound break in human history" (Ernest Gellner, *Nations and Nationalism* [Ithaca, N.Y.: Cornell University Press, 1983], 124–25). See also Michael Walzer, *What It Means to Be an American: Essays on the American Experience* (New York: Marsilio, 1992).

28. See Michael Kammen, *People of Paradox: An Inquiry into the Origins of American Civilization* (Ithaca, N.Y.: Cornell University Press, 1980).

29. Ibid., 82–85.

30. Ibid., 85.

31. Ibid., 92. Partisan groups operating in the swirl of these multiple trends often take on the coloration of opponents, and the paradoxes expand to include new groups and individuals.

32. Karst, *Belonging to America*, 176.

33. Aviam Soifer, *Law and the Company We Keep* (Cambridge, Mass.: Harvard University Press, 1995), 69.

34. Hollinger, *Postethnic America*, 157.

CHAPTER 4

The Myth of Culture War

The Disparity between Private Opinion and Public Politics

Paul DiMaggio

In June 1999, speaking before Congress in opposition to gun control, Representative Tom Delay attributed school violence to such apparently disparate features of modern life as daycare, abortion, evolution, the entertainment industry, individualism, moral relativism, and contraception. *New York Times* correspondent Francis Clines described the speech as "Joshua's trumpet to a full-scale cultural war."[1]

For almost a decade now journalists and political pundits have told us that a culture war is raging. Bitter disputes over matters that most Americans once regarded as inappropriate for government intervention—abortion, sexuality, artistic expression, parenting—have divided communities and reshaped the contours of national politics. Signs of struggle have been evident in incivility on the airways, violence on the far right, partisan ill temper in congressional debate, and electoral volatility, all of which have appeared to be on the rise.

Social scientists have also warned of political polarization. James Hunter, an expert on conservative Christianity and author of the book *Culture Wars,* has written, "Every day presents us with disheartening signs that America is fragmenting" and has argued that "tensions over social issues . . . are undermining the cohesion of our union."[2] Another sociologist, Os Guinness, wrote of "the cultural chasm that has opened up in American society since the sixties."[3]

According to Hunter and Guinness the United States has been in the midst of a "culture war" in which supporters of traditional morality vie with secular relativists for control of American institutions. Over this war's course, they assert, Americans have become polarized around contrasting positions on social and cultural issues that reflect fundamental moral division. This underlying division is believed to structure debates on many social and cultural issues, including abortion, sex education, gender roles and sexual behavior, bilingual education, government support for the arts, multiculturalism in secondary and higher education, gun control, and affirmative action.

This view is attractive because it helps us to articulate and come to grips with anxieties about many unsettling features of contemporary public life. Moreover, it seems consistent with much of what we see on television or read in the press. But the argument also fails to fit the facts. Americans are far more united in their opinions on social and cultural issues than talk of culture wars would lead one to believe; indeed, their views on many issues were becoming *more* united at precisely the time that scholars and journalists were warning of growing polarization. Rather than representing an accurate diagnosis of the American political condition, the culture wars account has served as an interpretive frame with an intrinsically conservative bias, attributing to the general populace a strident antagonism thus far visible mainly among political elites and well-financed social-movement organizations.

THE PRESS AND THE "CULTURE WAR"

Although controversial in academic circles, the "culture wars" perspective has had enormous influence on American political discourse. Journalists, always eager to provide drama and thematic consistency for the frequently humdrum and disconnected events they must report, have found the metaphor of culture war attractive. Between 1990 and 1994 the culture wars figure gradually came to structure the media's understanding and interpretation of many political conflicts.

The term first appears in the Nexis database in 1987, when sociologist Todd Gitlin and historian Ruth Rosen employed it in a *New York Times* article entitled "Give the 60's Generation a Break." This was an unusual instance, however, both because it preceded the next appearance by many months and because the authors were sympathetic to the left. By the term's next sighting it had become a byword of political conservatives, many of whom hailed the purported conflict. For example, in 1990 Congressman Henry Hyde described his proposed constitutional amendment to ban flag burning as "one front in a larger culture war."[4]

Although the publication of James Hunter's scholarly *Culture Wars* introduced the notion to academics in 1991, it was Patrick Buchanan's call to arms at the 1992 Republican presidential nominating convention that made the phrase a household expression.

Despite its embrace by the political right, the term proved irresistible to mainstream journalists, no doubt because it served as such a handy and dramatic frame for dealing with so many issues. Indeed, trend spotters in the media and advertising industry who had been writing about social division since the early 1980s were particularly attuned to talk of polarization from Washington and the universities.[5] Some pundits hailed President Clinton's 1992 election as marking a "truce" in the culture war, and references fell off immediately thereafter.[6] But they revived again when the Christian Coalition organized a conference called "Winning the Culture War" for conservative political operatives in spring of 1993.[7]

By mid-1994, journalistic attention to the putative culture war reached a new peak. More important, for the first time, *culture war* had become a generally accepted shorthand for a wide range of social conflicts. Instead of referring to the hot debate of the day—whether it was about school prayer, the National Endowment for the Arts, or abortion—the term came to describe many issues at once, to characterize a chronic syndrome rather than acute outbreaks of social division. It also came to be employed in an offhanded fashion in articles only marginally concerned with cultural conflicts, one of those lazy phrases that substitute for thought among journalists pressured by deadlines. One reporter even referred to a rock festival as "Generation X's first clear victory in the culture wars."[8] Finally, with the religious right's extraordinary success in the 1994 off-year elections, references to culture war reached a crescendo in the first months of 1995.

To be sure, not every journalist joined the swelling chorus. E. J. Dionne Jr. of the *Washington Post* wrote of a "false polarization" in which public controversy obscured mass "consensus on where the country should move."[9] He was in the minority, however.

HAS AMERICA BECOME MORE POLARIZED?

It is tempting to infer the presence of polarization (either within the population as a whole or between specific groups), in circular fashion, from the very political conflict and volatility that such polarization is presumed to cause. For example, in 1995 former senator Warren Rudman, trying to explain the partisan and extreme tone of congressional debate, told a

National Public Radio reporter, "We may be seeing in Congress a microcosm of what's happening out in the country. . . . [W]hat we are seeing is a polarization out there in the country, and what is happening in Congress is a reflection of that."[10]

To see the surface as the tip of a deeper, larger iceberg is a natural way to look at things. But is it an accurate one? To find out, Bethany Bryson, John Evans, and I reviewed twenty years of data on Americans' opinions on a wide range of social and cultural issues—gender roles, race, school prayer, abortion, crime, family values, sexuality, and feelings toward African Americans, liberals, conservatives, and the poor.[11] We drew our evidence from answers to forty-four questions asked at repeated intervals from the early 1970s to the early 1990s by the General Social Survey and the National Election Study. These are the surveys that social scientists use most often to explore recent social trends. They are based on high-quality national samples, and the researchers who prepare them ask questions in the same way each year and avoid changes in survey procedure that might make comparison misleading.

To test the accuracy of the perception that Americans have become more polarized, we first had to specify what polarization *is*. This is more difficult than it sounds, for journalists or politicians use the word *polarization* to refer to two different things. In the first instance it refers to a shift in opinions of the whole population from moderate centrist views toward more extreme positions, leaving a yawning gap in the middle of the ideological spectrum. In the second usage *polarization* refers to disagreement between specific kinds of people thought to be at odds with one another, such as men and women, blacks and whites, or Republicans and Democrats. Each type of polarization may lead to political turbulence, but they are analytically distinct, as either kind may increase (or decline) without a parallel change in the other. We looked at both kinds.

TRENDS IN THE DISTRIBUTION OF ATTITUDES

First, we asked: *Has there been a trend among all respondents away from moderate opinions and toward more extreme responses? To what extent has the public separated into two distinct camps?*

Have Americans' opinions on social issues become more extreme and less centrist? No, with one celebrated exception, the abortion issue. Respondents to the General Social Survey were asked if abortion should be legally available under each of seven different circumstances, and their responses were combined to create a scale ranging in value from "0" (opposition to abortion for any reason) to "7" (support for abortion on demand). Tracked over time, this scale reveals polarization: between 1972 and 1993 declining numbers of people espoused centrist views, and more took extreme positions. But Americans *were already* deeply divided in their attitudes toward abortion by the early 1970s, so this polarization, although statistically significant, may not have been politically consequential.

Far from being the archetypal issue of an era of social division, however, the abortion debate was uniquely polarizing.[12] On virtually every other issue polarization either remained constant or actually declined. The public actually has become *more unified* in its attitudes toward race, gender, and crime since the 1970s. For race and gender this reflects a liberal trend: almost all respondents now reject crudely racist positions and support women's right to work and be active in public affairs. For crime the decline in polarization reflects a conservative trend, with the public favoring tougher sentencing policies, the death penalty, and gun control.

Given all the talk about polarization, we were surprised to find so little of it. Perhaps, we reasoned, we missed the main story by looking at the population as a whole. Maybe the culture wars are waged only by people who follow the controversies of the day: voters, the politically active, and college graduates. We repeated our analyses for each of these groups, and we also looked separately at men and women under thirty, in case growing division was a generational phenomenon. Still, our search for polarization was in vain.

TRENDS IN DIFFERENCES BETWEEN GROUPS

Next we compared groups that might be expected to differ in their views on social issues and asked: *Have differences in opinion between these groups become larger over the past two decades?* Even if the distributions of social attitudes among the general population had not polarized during the 1970s and 1980s, it is certainly possible that growing gulfs between the attitudes of African Americans and Euro-Americans or between evangelical Christians and people with liberal religious views might be responsible for widespread perception of social fragmentation.

Once again, our efforts to find polarization were disappointed. The generation gap that loomed so large in the 1960s and early 1970s had clearly waned by the 1990s. Of eighteen opinions on social issues that we examined, differences between people older than forty-five and those

younger than thirty-five had diminished significantly for twelve and remained the same for the rest. Related to this, the education gap—the difference in attitudes between the college educated and people with only
high school degrees or less—also declined for issues as diverse as race
and sex education.

We have heard so much about the gender gap in voting over the past
decade that we expected differences between the social attitudes of men
and women to have increased as well. Surprisingly, this is not the case.
Between the 1970s and the 1990s women's and men's opinions on crime
and sex education converged, and on no issues did they become more
distinct.

As we analyzed our data, press accounts of reactions to O. J. Simpson's acquittal rendered tensions between black and white America especially apparent. But although blacks' and whites' attitudes on many
social and political issues are far apart, such differences have actually
diminished over the past twenty years. This convergence of opinion
reflects two trends. First, white Americans have rejected crude forms of
racism, so racial attitudes (as the surveys have measured them) have
grown more similar. Second, with the emergence of a sizable black middle class, African-American opinion on many issues has grown more
heterogeneous.

On many of the issues that the media has placed under the heading
of "the culture war"—abortion, flag desecration, family values, the National Endowment for the Arts, and so on—conservative leadership has
come from the Christian right. The 1970s and 1980s were periods of expansion for evangelical Christianity, providing a base for religious figures
eager to influence public policy. Given the rise of the religious right, and
opposition to the religious right from within mainline Protestant denominations, we expected to find a growing opinion gap between members of theologically conservative religious groups who attend church regularly, on the one hand, and members of liberal denominations and
agnostics, on the other.

Remarkably, the opposite was the case: the religiously conservative
and religiously liberal have become *more similar* in their attitudes toward abortion, gender roles, sexual morality, race, sex education, and
divorce. Differences persist, but the religiously conservative are less
monolithic than many believe, and on many issues large differences have
diminished significantly. The reason is simple: whereas religiously conservative denominations used to draw disproportionately from south-
easterners with modest levels of formal education, by the 1980s evan-

gelical Protestantism had spread throughout the United States, and its adherents were becoming similar in their educational attainment to other Americans.[13]

We found only one major exception to the trend toward stable or declining polarization among groups: people who told pollsters they were "strong" Republicans and Democrats drew apart on many issues between the early 1970s and 1995. Differences increased in attitudes toward abortion, divorce law, crime, race, government assistance to minorities, and the poor. These developments appear to reflect a shift in the basis of party identification from economic issues and foreign policy in the early 1970s to social issues, especially race, in the 1990s.[14]

Taken as a whole, our results could not be more inconsistent with conventional wisdom. On every salient between-group dimension except party identification Americans have become either a little or a lot more unified. Men and women, blacks and whites, members of conservative faith communities and religious liberals—in each case social attitudes have either stayed the same or converged. Even on the wedge issues (race, abortion, school prayer, sex education) between-group differences have remained stable or have grown smaller.

What should we make of this? We have seen that journalists seem to believe that America has become more divided. Attacks on abortion clinics and government buildings and confrontations between federal agents and armed rightist groups provide vivid indications of the terrible toll that moral conflict can exact. And other evidence demonstrates that partisanship in Congress grew ever more strident and divisive over the period we reviewed.[15]

The question, then, is this: *How is it that our public politics have become more polarized while our private attitudes and opinions have become more united?*

WHY DO AMERICANS THINK THEY ARE MORE DISUNITED THAN THEY ARE? TWO CHRONIC FALLACIES

There are three general ways of explaining the dramatic disparity between trends in public opinion and the perception of culture war that our research revealed. First, this disparity may reflect chronic habits of mind that render us ill equipped to assess the strength of the social fabric. Second, it may be that there really *are* significant divisions in the American polity, but they are divisions in something other than public opinion. Third, something about the political environment of the 1990s may have changed so that similar or lower levels of disagreement now generate more political turbulence.[16] There is some truth in each of these suggestions.

To argue that Americans have not become more divided in their political views is not to deny that our political debates are raucous, passionately joined, and often disagreeable. Unfortunately, it is all too easy to assume that public disputes or even the violent acts of a few extremists betoken deep and growing underlying division among the citizenry as a whole. Such an assumption reflects two common fallacies in our political reasoning: the fallacy of *change;* and the fallacy of *proportionate sampling.*

By the "fallacy of change" I mean many observers' tendency to pronounce every notable political event as betokening momentous transformation and to view political developments as results of directional trends rather than as cyclic fluctuations. There are, of course, many more blips than trends in almost every realm of life. But in a culture (and a profession, journalism) preoccupied with the present, it is sometimes difficult to tell the difference.

It is natural, therefore, for pundits observing a surge in debates over social issues to assume that Americans are becoming *more* divided. Such an assumption, however, reflects a confusion of political climate and political weather, of the condition of American politics with meaningful change in that condition. The fact that polarization has remained stable or declined a bit over the past two decades does *not* mean that Americans are united in their social perspectives. *It only means that they are no more divided than usual.*

The United States has always been a contentious polity. Consider the cultural conflicts of the 1960s, not to mention the antiwar movement and the struggle for African-American civil rights. Or recall the political divisions of the Great Depression, when Communists and Socialists received unprecedented political support at the same time that right-wing demagogues like Father Coughlin excited the enthusiasms of huge national followings. At the turn of the last century, violence associated with labor unrest claimed more lives in the United States than anywhere else except Russia.[17] And the Civil War was no picnic. Only a chronic case of collective amnesia leads us to view the disagreements of the 1980s and 1990s as historically notable.

The second fallacy is the "fallacy of proportionate sampling," by which I mean the assumption that public conflicts mirror private divisions in fixed proportion—that every terrorist act represents some proportionate number of peaceful extremists, that every explosion of anger is proportionate to some larger armory of yet undetonated rancor, or that every public expression of a view reflects a proportionate number of men and women who share it. This assumption tends to legitimate political extremism by assuming that violent acts or extreme speech represent in exaggerated form a broader movement of which they are visible signs. Thus legitimated, generals of spectral armies can claim media attention and exert political influence far out of proportion with the size of the public for whom they speak.

A moment's reflection reveals that the fallacy of proportionate sampling is just that. With a few dollars and a bit of technical know-how anyone can create her or his own Web site, mailing list, letterhead, or, regrettably, terrorist incident. Even at the mass level political scientists have demonstrated that members of the public are more willing to articulate some of their opinions than others. People differ, they have learned, not just in what they believe but in their readiness to express their views. Positions held by passionate minorities can come to overshadow and even appear more widely held than the opinions of reticent majorities.[18] Thus one can never assume that a rise in the frequency of visible public conflicts reflects a commensurate growth in dissensus.

HAS SOMETHING *OTHER* THAN SOCIAL ATTITUDES CHANGED?

We often think of politics as being about "issues" on which citizens have attitudes or "preferences" that they seek to institutionalize in public policies. But politics can also engage passions, identities, beliefs, and values, none of which are necessarily closely linked to people's attitudes on specific issues.

One possibility is that Americans have become more passionate about the beliefs that divide them, not more divided in the beliefs themselves. Polarized opinions only sometimes yield passionate public debates. For example, public opinion about abortion is polarized, *and* abortion is a topic of fierce controversy. Public attitudes toward legalized prostitution are also highly polarized, but debate on this topic is neither widespread nor emotionally intense.[19]

The General Social Survey has tapped emotions by using "feeling thermometers" to elicit respondents' affect toward various groups (African Americans, conservatives, the poor, Russians or Japanese, liberals, and so on). We found no evidence of polarization in any of these measures of emotional fever, either within the population as a whole or between different groups. A similarly cool emotional state is suggested, as well, by polls that show that few Americans mention specific "culture wars" issues when asked about the most important challenges facing our society.[20]

It is possible, of course, that other forms of political affect—for example faith in democratic institutions or willingness to participate in the political system—*have* intensified or polarized. Surely a division of the citizenry into distinct groups of activists and alienated political dropouts would have corrosive effects on public life. But plausible as this may be, the data do not reflect it.[21]

Perhaps Americans are agreeing less about facts, even as they are agreeing more about values. The convergence of social attitudes between black and white Americans might tempt one to think that racial divisions in the United States are healing. Yet when one looks *not* at what black and white Americans believe to be *just and appropriate* but at what they believe to be *factually true* about such things as the origins of the AIDS epidemic, the prevalence of racism, or government involvement in the drug trade, one sees alarming divisions.[22] Perhaps we would find growing cleavages over facts (despite narrowing differences in attitudes) if we were to compare the beliefs of secular liberals and conservative evangelicals on such matters as abortion, sexual practices, and the behavior of federal government officials.

It is also possible that Americans have become more divided in their deepest values, even as their attitudes on most issues have converged. A centerpiece of James Hunter's argument is that the values of "orthodox" traditionalists (who derive morally binding norms from their religious beliefs and Scripture) are at odds with the values of "progressivist" relativists (who believe in the moral equivalence of different value systems and in reason as the ultimate source of moral authority) on a wide range of issues. Sociologist Wayne Baker has found that Americans' values have indeed become more polarized between absolutism and relativism in recent years.[23] Significantly, however, Baker reports that this divergence has *not* led to polarization in the social attitudes that these values are often presumed to shape.[24]

Rhys H. Williams identifies two reasons such worldviews have relatively little effect on specific attitudes. First, people's judgments are more complex than our theories tell us they are. Rather than deduce our social and political attitudes from first principles, most us approach each issue inductively, applying different rules to issues in different domains. Second, people's attitudes are bound as directly to their social relations as to their values.[25] Most of us think deeply only about the issues we care about, and few of us care deeply about many issues. Outside the narrow zone of urgent concern, what we tell pollsters may have as much to do with what we think our friends believe than with any deductive process of moral reasoning.

In this sense attitudes help to assert our social identities. They tell each of us (and others) who we are and what we stand for and against. Most of us have many "social identities" based on our genders, our racial or ethnic backgrounds, our jobs, our neighborhoods, even our hobbies. Each of these identities may have different implications for our views on particular issues. For example, Catholic physicians who work among the underprivileged may oppose abortion as Catholics, support family planning as advocates for poor women, and oppose antiabortion legislation as a threat to medical authority.[26]

Three important implications flow from these observations. First, because most people have more than one important identity, their perspectives on social issues are more complex, and their ability to see many sides of an issue greater, than they might otherwise be.

Second, because different social identities entail different perspectives, most people possess *alternative* understandings of social issues, different ways of thinking about them that lead to contrasting attitudes or preferences that may ebb and flow as particular social identities become more or less salient.[27] Sociologist Christian Smith argues that most conservative Christians simultaneously adhere to the "legacy of Christendom"—the belief that the faithful should use government to establish the Kingdom of God on earth—*and* endorse the pluralism and individualism characteristic of America's civic culture. "Most of the people we interviewed," he writes, "tried to resolve this dissonance by compartmentalizing both beliefs, strongly affirming them as separate commitments, and preventing each from having to face the full implications of the other. When we began to press people to . . . choose one above the other, they fought long and hard to keep them in their separate compartments."[28]

Third, it follows from the first two points, that social movement groups and political organizers gain converts not only by changing people's attitudes but also by changing the political salience of people's various social identities—for example, by persuading blue-collar Hispanic Catholics to think of themselves as Christians rather than union members or Latinos. I will argue below that much culture war rhetoric can be understood as an effort by political conservatives to do just this.[29] But first we need to consider change in the political environment in which these efforts at persuasion take place.

WHY AMERICANS THINK THEY ARE
MORE POLITICALLY DIVIDED THAN THEY ARE

Actual politics, of course, is connected only indirectly to what we usually think of as "public opinion." As Susan Herbst has argued, the temptation to think of public opinion as the aggregate of what individuals tell pollsters in the (compromised) privacy of their homes is a peculiarly modern perspective. Until relatively recently, "public opinion" was understood to be the opinions formed and expressed by people speaking together in specific institutional settings like salons, pubs, or community meetings.[30]

In practice, all opinion that matters is organized. Public conflict emerges not simply, or even primarily, as a function of the opinions that people hold but as a result of the way in which groups and institutions organize those opinions. For example, polarized attitudes toward legalized abortion generate more social conflict than polarized attitudes toward legalized prostitution because many institutions mobilize people to influence abortion policy, but few work to put prostitution on the political agenda. As John Evans and Bethany Bryson have shown, institutional factors have shaped the extent to which denominations in different religious traditions (Catholic, evangelical, mainstream Protestant, and liberal Protestant) have polarized over abortion. Within-tradition divisions grew most significantly where church leaderships permitted members with different positions on abortion to form special-purpose caucuses to advance their views. They did *not* increase where dissenting special-purpose groups were prohibited. In other words attitudes matter most when they become the basis for organizing people into contentious groups.[31]

The 1970s and 1980s witnessed two significant changes in the way institutions organized and disseminated opinions on cultural matters. The first involved changes in media practice. Between 1980 and 1990, social and cultural views expressed in public became more diverse in ideological content and less restrained in style of expression (although to no greater degree than in the 1930s or 1960s). Above all, more conservative views were included in public debate, and the range of permissible right-wing opinion widened during the 1980s with the emergence of conservative policy institutes, talk shows, and religious media.[32] The fallacy of proportionate sampling makes it natural to presume that mass opinion became more divided as well, even though this was not the case.

Communications scholar Joseph Turow has argued that changes in the communications marketplace may eventually exacerbate social divisions. Technological developments make it easier and easier for marketers to target specific groups. Because advertisers are much better at getting people to act on interests and inclinations they already possess than at cultivating new interests or changing people's minds, the media increasingly create separate programs or messages for people of different views, reinforcing the opinions and preferences characteristic of the groups to which they belong.[33] Fortunately, against such balkanizing tendencies stands the fact that most of us belong to many different social groups with crosscutting perspectives and orientations that counterbalance the forces of fragmentation.

A second institutional change that was crucial for both the organization and appearance of culture war reflected developments in the political parties. Recall that the only publics that became more divided in their views (relative to one another) over the past decades were Republicans and Democrats. In conventional political theory political parties are supposed to take the rough edges off conflicts in civil society by vying for the allegiance of the "median voter" (political scientists' term for the centrist majority). By contrast, through 1994 at least, the parties had themselves become sources of cleavage, sowing divisions only dimly reflected in public attitudes. As political scientist Ted G. Jelen has documented, moral politics increasingly shaped the party identification of both white evangelical and mainline Protestants during the 1980s. Before then, views on cultural and social issues were largely unrelated to party identification; afterward, moral conservatives—white evangelicals in the first half of the decade, other white Protestants during the late 1980s—shifted to the Republican Party.[34]

This shift responded to a well-orchestrated campaign by elements of the Republican Party to boost the primacy of cultural issues in its appeal. Cultural conservatives like William Bennett and Patrick Buchanan attempted to define the major axis of conflict as one separating supporters of "traditional values" from cultural elitists endowed with many imputed, if shadowy, negative identities. This strategy was sensible insofar as the party's views on other issues were less appealing to voters than its moral stances. It paid off in a large increase in the proportion of evangelical Christians who identified themselves as "conservatives" during the first two years of the Clinton presidency. This group played an important role in the Republican sweep of the 1994 elections.[35]

Much of the traditional Republican leadership opposed this strategy, however, for fear that a too passionate embrace of moral conservatism could jeopardize the centrists whom Ronald Reagan had attracted to the Republican coalition. The success of the moral conservatives throughout much of the 1990s reflected a number of institutional changes that reduced party organizations' ability to exert discipline over divisive candidates, officeholders, and special interest groups. Such developments may or may not polarize public opinion in the long run, but they certainly contribute to the *perception* that opinion has been polarized.

"CULTURE WARS" AND THE POLITICS OF FRAMING

As the millennium approached, evangelical columnist Charles Colson asked his fellow moral conservatives, "Will we lose the Culture War?" Christian conservatives, he lamented, were losing ground on several fronts, with the public indifferent or even unsympathetic to many of their causes. Yet Colson took heart in the fact that 84 percent of conservative and 33 percent of liberal respondents to a national survey endorsed the view that it is "important for society" to "promote respect for traditional values." The strategic lesson Colson drew was that moral conservatives should avoid skirmishes and stick with the war. "Our culture is embroiled in nothing less than a clash of worldviews," he wrote. "Christians must stop focusing on social issues one at a time. Instead we must delve beneath the surface and identify the underlying principles. . . . Otherwise we may win a few battles, but still lose the war."[36]

Colson's remarks exemplify the logic of the culture war as a rhetorical project. When moral conservatives have tried to persuade Americans to accept their views on social issues one by one, their success has been limited. When they have welded the issues together into a compelling narrative frame, they have had more success.

By *frame* I mean a package that contains a repertoire of identities, a set of beliefs, and an integrative story that knits those beliefs into a coherent whole.[37] The "culture war" is best understood as a frame of this kind. Its rhetoric invites religious conservatives to make their faith (rather than their gender, age, race, occupation, or neighborhood) their primary identity and to define this identity as germane to many political positions (rather than treating their moral views as irrelevant to Caesar's realm). Class and race play little explicit role in the culture war narrative. Instead, the culture wars frame melds such disparate topics as sex education, family leave, abortion, government subsidies for the arts, and gun control into a coherent and navigable political terrain (while leaving uncharted, and therefore less politically salient, such matters as economic inequality, racial discrimination, or campaign finance reform).

Ironically, proponents of the culture war used precisely the same deconstructive techniques to call attention to disrespectful treatment of religious conservatives that feminists and people of color had employed in their struggles for equality. James Hunter has made arresting use of Antonio Gramsci's notion of cultural hegemony—once a staple of neo-Marxist cultural studies—to explain the political resentments of moral traditionalists.[38] Once the term migrated from the academy to the political arena, the declaration of culture war became a conservative effort to hoist liberalism by its own petard: to use the techniques of identity politics to raise the consciousness of the theologically and morally conservative.

A further irony is that the capacity of political leaders to mobilize conservative Christians around religious identity depended in no small part on the latter's increasing integration into the social mainstream. The Christian right emerged as theologically conservative Christianity expanded from its southeastern (and working- and lower-middle-class) base to recruit well-educated, upper-middle-class adherents throughout the United States.[39] Thus it happened that some Christian conservatives recognized and resisted the marginality imposed on them only as they became less marginal.

Like most identity groups that find common ground in resistance to elite-imposed status offenses, members of conservative faith communities possess many other identities that influence their political opinions. Using the combined criteria of self-identification, conservative political views, and intention to vote, James Hunter and Carl Bowman estimate that only about one in five evangelical Christians is part of the "Christian right."[40] Nancy Ammerman, who used field methods to study fundamentalist congregations, and Christian Smith and his colleagues, who interviewed evangelicals, likewise discovered much diversity in conservative Christians' political views.[41] Most religious traditionalists, we may presume, continued to base their issue preferences on other available identities or on reasoned consideration of alternative positions.

CONCLUSION

If by *culture war* we mean polarization of attitudes, then the culture war is a myth. But if we understand it as a campaign to construct new forms of political identity and define the terms of political engagement, then it warrants our close attention.

In fact, the culture war is both of these things, an effective myth that has shaped the public's understanding of the issues that divide it, making some identities more salient and others less accessible, and connecting the former to a galvanizing trope. Its rhetoric fits the interests and perspectives of political conservatives more comfortably than it does those of liberals or the left. Insofar as Americans understand their politics in terms of the culture wars story—as opposed to, for example, alternative narratives built around economic inequality, globalization, institutional racism, or communitarian democracy—we will attend to different problems and elect representatives who make different choices than would otherwise be the case.

NOTES

1. Francis X. Clines, "In a Bitter Cultural War, an Ardent Call to Arms," *New York Times,* June 17, 1999, 21.

2. James Hunter and Carl Bowman, *The State of Disunion: 1996 Survey of American Political Culture* (Ivy, Va.: In Medias Res Educational Foundation, 1996), 4.

3. Os Guinness, *The American Hour: A Time of Reckoning and the Once and Future Role of Faith* (New York: Free Press, 1993), 167.

4. Elaine S. Povich, "House Panel Won't Touch Flag Issue," *Chicago Tribune,* June 20, 1990, 5.

5. Joseph Turow, *Breaking Up America: Advertisers and the New Media World* (Chicago: University of Chicago Press, 1997).

6. Michael Barone, "The New Political Order," *U.S. News and World Report,* Nov. 16, 1992, 113.

7. Ralph Hallow, "Cultural Warriors Fault Movies, TV, Schools, Press," *Washington Times,* May 14, 1993, A4.

8. Scott Aiges, "A Whole Lotta Lolla," *New Orleans Times-Picayune,* July 30, 1993, L20.

9. E. J. Dionne Jr., *Why Americans Hate Politics* (New York: Simon and Schuster, 1992).

10. Interview with former senator Warren Rudman on *Weekend Edition,* National Public Radio, Saturday, Aug. 12, 1995.

11. For a more detailed account see Paul DiMaggio, John Evans, and Bethany Bryson, "Have Americans' Social Attitudes Become More Polarized?" *American Journal of Sociology* 102 (1996): 690–755.

12. There were signs of growing division in the public's attitudes toward "poor people," but these changes were not statistically significant. Although change in average attitudes was negligible, people migrated to more extreme views on either side of the stable mean during the 1970s and 1980s. There is also some evidence that attitudes toward government assistance for members of minority groups, which had been converging until the mid-1980s, may have begun to repolarize thereafter.

13. James Hunter, *Evangelicalism: The Coming Generation* (Chicago: University of Chicago Press, 1987); Robert Wuthnow, *The Restructuring of American Religion* (Princeton, N.J.: Princeton University Press, 1988).

14. There was only one other minor exception: people who describe themselves as "liberal" and "conservative" became more different in their views on abortion. This occurred because attitudes toward abortion became more central to the way that people characterize themselves ideologically. See Michael Hout, "Abortion Politics in the United States, 1972–1994: From Single Issue to Ideology," working paper, University of California, Berkeley, Survey Research Center, 1995.

15. Keith T. Poole and Howard Rosenthal, *Congress: A Political-Economic History of Roll Call Voting* (New York: Oxford University Press, 1997).

16. A fourth possibility, which I believe can be dismissed quickly, is that our empirical work was flawed, either because the data were poor or because we looked at the wrong questions. The General Social Survey and the National Election Study are the two leading sources of social science data on opinion trends, each conducted by a leading research organization and subject to regular, exacting review by experts whom the National Science Foundation recruits to review proposals for research support. If we can be confident that any surveys collect reliable data on Americans' attitudes (and I believe we can), then these are the ones. We took more seriously the question of whether the set of attitudes available for trend analysis may have biased our results but concluded that they did not for the following reasons. To be sure, new questions appear when particular issues heat up, and to the extent that polarization is greater on "new" issues that have only recently entered public discourse than on "old" ones, trend studies (which rely on many years of data) may underestimate polarization. But such bias is balanced by the fact that surveys make room for questions about issues that have become controversial by eliminating questions on issues about which most people have come to agree, potentially leading trend studies to overestimate polarization. Moreover, although we lacked trend data on some hot-button issues (immigration, National Endowment for the Arts funding, bilingual education), we did have information on many others (e.g., sex education, gun control, and race); and, as we have seen, except for abortion, these evinced no more polarization than less contentious matters.

17. Charles Lindblom and John A. Hall, "Is the United States Falling Apart?" *Daedalus* 126 (1997): 183–208.

18. Robert Huckfeldt and John Sprague, "Choice, Social Structure, and Political Information: The Informational Coercion of Minorities," *American Journal of Political Science* 32 (1988): 467–83; Elizabeth Noelle-Neumann, *The Spiral of Silence—Our Social Skin*, 2d ed. (Chicago: University of Chicago Press,

1993); Timor Kuran, *Private Truths, Public Lies: The Social Consequences of Preference Falsification* (Cambridge, Mass.: Harvard University Press, 1995).

19. Data on attitudes toward prostitution are from the 1996 General Social Survey.

20. Christian Smith, with Michael Emerson, Sally Gallagher, Paul Kennedy, and David Sikkink, "The Myth of Culture Wars: The Case of American Protestantism," in *Cultural Wars in American Politics: Critical Reviews of a Popular Myth*, ed. Rhys. H. Williams (New York: Aldine de Gruyter, 1997), 175–95.

21. John Evans, Bethany Bryson, and I used data from the General Social Survey and National Election Study to see if participation in voluntary associations, voting, and other forms of political participation had become more unequally distributed between the early 1970s and early 1990s or if such political activists and political dropouts had become more divided in their social views over that period. Neither was the case.

22. Jennifer Hochschild, *Facing Up to the American Dream* (Princeton, N.J.: Princeton University Press, 1995).

23. Wayne Baker, "Americans Are Polarized: Cross-Cultural and Longitudinal Comparisons of Beliefs about Moral Authority," manuscript, University of Michigan, 1997.

24. John Evans and Bethany Bryson, "Locating Actual Cultural Conflict: Polarization over Abortion in Protestant Denominations, 1972–1995," manuscript, Princeton University, 1997.

25. Rhys H. Williams, "Afterword," in *Cultural Wars in American Politics: Critical Reviews of a Popular Myth*, ed. Rhys. H. Williams (New York: Aldine de Gruyter, 1997), 283–95.

26. Multiple social identities have nothing to do with the "multiple personalities" that play such prominent roles in psychological thrillers and treatises on psychopathology. Think of them as sets of feelings and self-images—what psychologists call "self-schemata"—that go along with the various social roles that people play in their everyday lives.

27. Paul DiMaggio, "Culture and Cognition," *Annual Review of Sociology* 23 (1997): 263–87; John Zaller, *The Nature and Origins of Mass Opinion* (New York: Cambridge University Press, 1992).

28. Smith et al., "Myth of Culture Wars," 191.

29. For a thorough and relevant discussion of the relationship between social identities and movement strategies see Mary Bernstein, "Celebration and Suppression: The Strategic Uses of Identity by the Lesbian and Gay Movement," *American Journal of Sociology* 103 (1997): 531–65.

30. Susan Herbst, *Numbered Voices: How Opinion Polling Has Shaped American Politics* (Chicago: University of Chicago Press, 1993).

31. Evans and Bryson, "Locating Actual Cultural Conflict."

32. Ellen Messer-Davidow, "Dollars for Scholars: The Real Politics of Humanities Scholarship and Programs," in *The Politics of Research*, ed. E. Ann Kaplan and George Levine (New Brunswick, N.J.: Rutgers University Press, 1997), 193–234.

33. Turow, *Breaking Up America*.

34. Ted G. Jelen, "Culture Wars and the Party System: Religion and Re-

alignment, 1972–1993," in *Cultural Wars in American Politics: Critical Reviews of a Popular Myth,* ed. Rhys H. Williams (New York: Aldine de Gruyter, 1997), 145–57.

35. Stanley B. Greenberg, "After the Republican Surge," *American Prospect* 23 (1995): 66–76.

36. Charles Colson, "Will We Lose the Culture War? An Effective Battle Strategy," *Breakpoint* (Sep. 8, 1999): radio-program transcript originally available at the now-defunct www.breakpoint.com.

37. William Gamson, *Talking Politics* (New York: Cambridge University Press, 1992).

38. James Hunter, *Culture Wars: The Struggle to Define America* (New York: Basic Books, 1991).

39. Wuthnow, *Restructuring of American Religion.*

40. Hunter and Bowman, *State of Disunion.*

41. See Nancy T. Ammerman, *Bible Believers: Fundamentalists in the Modern World* (New Brunswick, N.J.: Rutgers University Press, 1987); and Smith et al., "Myth of Culture Wars," 175–95.

CHAPTER 5

America's Jews

Highly Fragmented, Insufficiently Disputatious

Jack Wertheimer

During the 1997–98 academic year five Orthodox Jews filed a lawsuit against Yale University, claiming Yale's policy requiring all freshman and sophomores to live in a mixed-sex dormitory was discriminatory because it forced them into an environment whose mores were sharply at odds with their strict religious and ethical sensibilities. The students requested either to be exempted from the requirement or to be housed in a single-sex residence "where rules against visitation by members of the opposite sex and against cohabitation are enforced."[1]

The response of the secular organized Jewish community to the lawsuit was telling. The community relations sector, the organizations whose primary responsibility is to improve relations between Jews and their neighbors, reacted with virtual silence. Jews engaged in the realm of public policy curtly rejected the lawsuit as baseless. Meanwhile, some non-Orthodox Jewish religious leaders condemned the undergraduates for seeking to establish a "ghetto Judaism" at Yale.

This little vignette dramatizes the current state of disputation within the organized Jewish community of the United States. The culture wars of the late twentieth century surely divided the Jewish community, as they did other groups in American life. After all, in suing Yale the Orthodox students were doing more than simply questioning the morality of campus housing arrangements. They were also challenging the reflexive universalism and liberalism of the larger Jewish community, which regards such arrangements as a nonissue. Much of the organized Jewish community, in turn, rebuffed the students, with the most stinging criticism coming from Jewish religious leaders of a different outlook.

To some observers, this disagreement may seem quite unremarkable. Don't Jews have a long history of disputation? If anything, divisiveness has been the hallmark of Jewish life historically. Indeed, one could enumerate a long list of schisms that have punctuated Jewish communal life stretching back to sectarian strife in first-century Palestine. Still, what is striking about the recent fragmentation is the virtual absence of serious *debate:* even as social barriers among Jews are rising ever higher and shrill invective has become all too common, there are fewer opportunities for a genuine *clash of ideas.* Jewish life in the United States in recent decades has come to resemble a startling sociological anomaly: fragmentation virtually unaccompanied by serious moral disputation.

Once again, the case of the Yale students illustrates the larger pattern: whereas the issue they raised—sexual morality on the campus—ought to have provoked some reflection in a community that sends a disproportionately high percentage of its youth to colleges and universities, Jewish communal leaders either dismissed the matter entirely or castigated the Yale students as parochial. Much like the talking heads who dominate cable television, Jewish communal leaders concerned themselves with the technical issues: did the students have a legal case? The larger moral and cultural issues elicited no sustained debate. Driven by a desire to be inclusive and universal, the organized Jewish community avoids debates over potentially divisive issues and marginalizes those who take exception.

This is not to suggest that Jews do not participate in the serious debates of our time. Individual Jews, to be sure, do engage in feisty argumentation on both sides of the cultural divide. But only rarely do these individuals speak as Jews. Thus, when a person of Jewish background publishes an op-ed article in a major newspaper on abortion or affirmative action or gun control, that writer does not speak for or specifically to the Jewish community. Similarly, when Jews in Hollywood produce films, they are not driven by a Jewish agenda any more than is a critic of Hollywood violence and pornography who criticizes those same movies in the name of Jewish values.

As for the institutions of the Jewish community—the subject of this essay—organizations that speak for Jews rarely engage in serious debate with one another.[2] To some extent this absence of sustained debate is inertial: during the middle decades of the twentieth century the Jewish community had achieved such wide agreement on key issues that it con-

tinues to act as if the earlier consensus is still strong. But on a deeper
level many communal leaders fear debate, and they strive instead to paper over differences rather than bring genuine disagreement into the open.
At a time of multicultural ferment, when gays, blacks, Latinos, women,
fundamentalist Christians, and just about everybody else ebulliently pro-
motes their own identities and interests in public, Jews are loathe to give
credence to positions based on the particularistic traditions of Judaism.
Much of the public policy agenda of the organized Jewish community is
still rooted in a post–World War II conception of American civil religion
that soft-pedals particularism. Because American society has changed in
recent decades and many minority groups now unabashedly put forward
their own demands, this approach warrants rethinking. It also warrants
rethinking because—dare one say it?—it may not be all that "good for
the Jews."

THE FRAGMENTED WORLD OF AMERICAN JUDAISM

For much of the twentieth century Jewish institutional life was marked
by a division of labor between "church" and state: institutions in the former category addressed religious issues, whereas the so-called secular organizations addressed a range of public-policy matters.[3] In sway to the
model of American Protestantism, the religious sector of American Jewry
has fragmented into several "denominations," each presenting its own
somewhat different version of Judaism.

In the closing decades of the century these denominations clashed
sharply with one another. They no longer shared a common set of assumptions about the most basic questions of religious belief, as the once-
taken-for-granted questions of "Who is a Jew?" and "Who decides?"
dramatically illustrate. Jewish religious movements today act unilater-
ally and with no consultation.

Traditionally, Jewish identity consisted of a mixture of tribal and religious elements. As defined by the rabbis of the Talmudic period, a Jew
was one who either had been born to a Jewish mother or had converted
to the Jewish faith. (The latter was expected both to adopt Jewish religious norms *and* to identify with the historical experience of the Jewish
people.) Until recently, Jews of different denominations, whatever their
theological disagreements, could agree on who was a member of the Jewish community. Not only was the ancient rabbinic standard universally
accepted, but the barriers to intermarriage created by internal Jewish

taboos, as well as by Gentile hostility, saw to it that the standard was fairly easily maintained. But with today's massive increase in exogamy the traditional definitions have come under attack.

The most obvious target has been the doctrine of matrilineal descent. Why, some ask, should a child with only one Jewish parent be treated differently by the official religious community if that parent happens to be the child's father rather than its mother? Should not community and synagogue alike embrace such children and thereby help "interfaith" families identify as Jews? Is it not self-destructive to risk the loss of hundreds of thousands of children solely to maintain a principle that, whatever may be said for it historically, no longer suits our circumstances?

In 1983 the Reform movement, the denomination with which the plurality of American Jews identify, formally adopted a resolution accepting any child of intermarriage as a Jew. No longer was descent from a Jewish mother a necessary condition. Nor, for that matter, was formal conversion to Judaism. Rather, the child's Jewish identity was redefined as an act of personal choice, the only proviso being that the "presumption" of Jewish status was "to be established through appropriate and timely public and formal acts of identification with the Jewish faith and people. The performance of these *mitzvot* [commandments] serves to commit those who participate in them, both parent and child, to Jewish life."[4]

The Reform resolution equally introduced a different conception of Jewish identity. No longer is Jewish descent sufficient; no longer is conversion necessary for a person not born to a Jewish mother. Rather, public acts of Jewish affirmation are necessary to substantiate the presumption of Jewish identity. In this way Jewish identity was transmuted from a matter of fate into one of faith; it is an act of personal choice rather than an obligation conferred through birth. Indeed, as the debate over this resolution unfolded, some even defended patrilineality as a means of *toughening* the requirements, given that under its stipulations the child of an interfaith family who was born to a Jewish mother would not be accepted as a Jew if that child never publicly demonstrated a commitment to the Jewish religion and people.

This ruling has been rejected by the Conservative and Orthodox movements of American Judaism, both of which maintain the traditional rabbinic position on Jewish identity.[5] They contend that the reasoning behind the original rabbinic definition remains unchanged: children are still most powerfully influenced by their mothers. And these movements re-

gard it as damaging to the morale of the Jewish community when boundaries are continually redefined to accommodate members who have broken a fundamental taboo by intermarrying.

Unlike other disagreements over matters of theology and religious
practice, this question of personal status—and Jewish disagreement over
it—has important social repercussions. The Internet forum of Reform rabbis has been buzzing with stories of Conservative rabbis who will not allow the teenagers in their synagogues to fraternize with their peers from
local Reform temples on the grounds that this could lead to their dating
young people not considered Jewish according to traditional criteria. Or
consider the dilemma of a Conservative rabbi asked by a female con-
gregant to officiate at her marriage to a young man who is Jewish only
according to Reform's patrilineal dispensation. A rabbi who acquiesces
will be committing an act punishable by expulsion from the organization of Conservative rabbis; a rabbi who declines will end up alienating
at least two families on account of "intolerance." We are rapidly approaching the time, moreover, when there will be rabbis who are themselves offspring of interfaith families and who will not be recognized by
their colleagues *as Jews.*

Conversion to Judaism, the recourse long available to those not born
Jewish who want to join the Jewish group, now also divides American
Jews of different denominations. The conversion process traditionally unfolds in a series of steps: a term of study leading to a commitment to Jewish religious observance and an identification with the Jewish people; the
convening of a rabbinic court *(beit din),* which supervises the conversion; the actual conversion ceremony, in which the convert is immersed
in the waters of a ritual bath *(mikveh)* and, if male, undergoes an actual
or symbolic circumcision.

Each of the religious movements treats these phases differently. Many
Orthodox rabbis in the United States do not accept conversions performed by their more liberal counterparts because such conversions do
not bind the individual to Orthodox observance. Following the ruling
of a leading decisor of the past generation, Rabbi Moshe Feinstein, many
Orthodox rabbis contend that non-Orthodox rabbis are by definition not
qualified to constitute a religious court, so no conversion performed by
non-Orthodox rabbis can ever be acceptable. Reform rabbis, by contrast,
operate as they see fit: they offer educational programs of varying
lengths, often perform conversions without a *beit din,* and do not necessarily require either circumcision or immersion. Caught in the middle
are Conservative rabbis, who adhere to all three steps outlined above but

whose conversions are often not recognized by Orthodox rabbis, whereas they themselves are hard-pressed to accept conversions performed under Reform auspices. Reviewing recent Reform response on conversion, a Conservative rabbi concluded that "innocent children and their parents should be advised that without proper *halakhic* procedures [Jewish legal requirements, such as circumcision and immersion] . . . they may have problems later being accepted as a Jew by non-Reform movements. The child would grow up thinking he or she is Jewish and be surprised to find out it is only accepted by the Reform [movement]." It is an open secret that most Conservative rabbis recognize Reform conversions only on a case-by-case basis.

Despite the pluralism of American Jewry, then, its religious movements tend neither to accept each other's definitions of who is a Jew nor to accept each other's converts. At best, each operates independently, with little regard to the others' positions or values. At worst, each movement acts as if convinced that it alone will survive and so does not hesitate to take unilateral actions that have deleterious consequences for other Jews. In short, American Judaism is characterized by deep social and religious chasms but lacks the vocabulary and institutions—and perhaps the will— to bridge them.

THE CIVIL RELIGION OF ORGANIZED JEWISH LIFE

At first glance the external or "state" sphere of organized Jewish life operates differently and appears to be far more cohesive than the religious one. The organizations setting Jewish public policy work in tandem and annually issue "a joint program" (or, as it has been called more recently, "an agenda for public affairs"), a plan for concerted action. For several decades, however, this regime has come under fire from critics who have challenged the basic assumptions of the public policies of the organized Jewish community. Frustrated by the indifference of the policy establishment to their dissatisfaction, a growing number of organizations have opened offices in Washington, D.C., to lobby as they see fit. (Several Orthodox groups have set up shop, and both the Conservative and Reform movements support such offices in Washington.) With increasing frequency these Jewish lobbyists are taking positions diametrically opposed to the proclaimed positions of the organized Jewish community. Thus, despite its surface unity the public policy arm of the Jewish community is also fragmenting—with Jewish groups actively lobbying government leaders even as they ignore each other. To appreciate the seriousness of

the new divisions over public policy, we need to appreciate the historical context that shaped both the emergence and collapse of communal
consensus.

That consensus was forged only gradually in the post–World War II
years, after a half century of bitter internecine conflict on a wide range
of ideological and social issues. In the first half of the twentieth century
American Jewry divided as Uptown natives and Downtown "greenhorns"
clashed over who should speak for American Jews and whether Jewish
leaders should defend their people's interests through dignified, behind-
the-scenes negotiations or by mobilizing the masses to take to the streets.
They quarreled perhaps most bitterly over the question of a Jewish homeland: was Zionism a threat to Jewish security in the United States? Underlying these conflicts were profound class and cultural differences
between native and immigrant Jews and between political radicals and
conservatives.

Under such circumstances it was virtually impossible to forge a consensus on communal priorities—even during the crisis years of the Holocaust. In the postwar era, by contrast, the community knitted together
socially when second-generation East European Jews rapidly achieved
social mobility and the influence of German Jewish leaders waned. As
the postwar era unfolded, the Uptown/Downtown interethnic divisions
gradually disappeared.

This new social cohesion facilitated the construction of a "functional
consensus" regarding American Jewry's communal agenda. In his insightful analysis of the postwar era the historian Arthur Goren identifies
the dual components of the new agenda—"assuring Israel's security and
striving for a liberal America."[6] Both were linked to America's self-cho-
sen role as the international guardian of democratic ideals and fair play:
the American Jewish community insisted that the United States owed Israel strong support because the Jewish state was an embattled bastion
of democracy surrounded by autocratic states. Which nation was more
deserving of support from America, the defender of democracy around
the world? On the domestic front American Jewish organizations after
World War II busied themselves with civic affairs to insure that no group
in America suffered unfair treatment; the defense of Jews was now understood as part of a larger campaign of social action rather than solely
as a parochial cause. Jewish needs both at home and abroad were therefore explained in universal terms. Israel deserved support because it embodied what was best in America rather than because it was a separate
country with special needs; anti-Semitism was fought not as an attack

on Jews but as a symptom of other prejudices that were a blight on America. Couched in these terms, the defense of Jewish interests facilitated *integration* into America rather than highlighted Jewish particularism. Thus, the Jewish agenda consisted of a campaign to encourage the United States to live up to its noblest ideals in its pursuit of democracy abroad and justice at home. An America that lived up to such ideals, it was believed, would offer the best protection to its Jews.

These twin goals energized Jewish organizations and committed them to a new activism in both foreign affairs and domestic policy. Each of the major religious denominations of American Judaism, for example, formed social action commissions in the early postwar years. Throughout the 1950s rabbinic organizations issued resolutions supporting union workers—despite the fact that most Jews were no longer in working-class occupations. Organizations of the Reform movement routinely called for government-funded housing and medical care for the poor; Conservative rabbis rejoiced when the Supreme Court handed down its school desegregation decision in 1954, and the Rabbinical Council of America, the largest organization of Orthodox rabbis, approved resolutions at its 1951 convention supporting price and rent controls.

The defense agencies of American Jewry also reoriented themselves. Whereas formerly they had concentrated on fighting anti-Semitism, they broadened their agenda to encompass all forms of social action. They supported legislation to end racial discrimination and to strengthen unions; they urged the government in Washington to embrace an internationalist policy that included foreign aid to democratic nations (such as Israel); and they favored social welfare programs. In 1945 the American Jewish Congress created a Commission on Law and Social Action dedicated to the twin tasks of "focus[ing] attention . . . on [social] abuses which must be ended, and promot[ing] . . . public policies which will make discrimination illegal and assure democratic rights for all racial and religious minorities."[7] A year later the American Jewish Committee's executive committee, noting "the closest relation between the protection of the civil rights" of all citizens and the members of particular groups, resolved to broaden its agency's mandate beyond the battle against anti-Semitism to "join with other groups in the protection of the civil rights of the members of all groups irrespective of race, religion, color or national origin."[8]

By 1953 the *Joint Program Plan* of the National Community Relations Advisory Council (NACRAC, later renamed NJCRAC when the word Jewish was added in 1971), the coordinator of most Jewish community relations agencies in the country, set forth a similar rationale for its involvement in social policy matters: "The overall objectives of Jewish community relations are to protect and promote equal rights and opportunities and to create conditions that contribute to the vitality of Jewish living. . . . These opportunities can be realized in a society in which all persons are secure, whatever their religion, race or origin."[9] Based on this latter premise, the NJCRAC (recently renamed the Jewish Council for Public Affairs) would develop liberal policy positions on a wide range of social questions that had little direct bearing on relations between Jews and their neighbors.

CRACKS IN THE CONSENSUS

During the late 1960s and early 1970s this consensus in organized Jewish life came under attack by small fringe groups. In keeping with the general mood of disenchantment with "establishments," groups on the left and the right challenged the Jewish establishment. To an extent these critics borrowed arguments and tactics from the civil rights movement and feminists on one side of the ideological spectrum and from the emerging Christian right on the other. Groups on the Jewish left, for example, challenged Jewish organizations for offering unqualified support to Israeli government policies after the Six Day War—and especially after the Yom Kippur War of 1973. It was the view of the generally young critics who joined these left-wing groups that the established leadership had demonstrated its moral bankruptcy and inability to lead by failing to criticize the Israeli government.

Almost simultaneously, small groups on the right of the spectrum mounted their own attacks on the consensus positions of the Jewish community. First came the Jewish Defense League and Soviet Jewry activists who twitted the established leaders for their timidity in the face of anti-Semitic thugs at home and abroad. Moreover, conservative critics broke ranks with the community over the ever more liberal agenda on social issues.

By the late 1960s Jewish neoconservatives associated with *Commentary* magazine challenged other assumptions of the postwar consensus. In a far-reaching manifesto for change Murray Friedman urged "a new direction for American Jews." First on his list of priorities was a strong American national defense because it was the guarantor of Israel's security. He also called for reversing the Jewish "ideological bias [which] systematically favors governmental over private-sector solutions, and systematically discounts what people can do to solve their problems by dint of their own struggle." Friedman singled out the annual *Joint Program Plan* of the NJCRAC as the prime expression of the "old and now largely discredited liberal agenda." In the same spirit he called for a break "with the formulas of the past"—including support for Great Society programs and "excessive reliance of agencies on government grants."[10]

Most globally, the coalition of right-wing forces urged the Jewish community to reassess the wisdom of its political alliances. In 1971 Norman Podhoretz, then editor of *Commentary,* announced the shift in thinking that led to his journal's turn to neoconservatism: "whatever the case may have been yesterday, and whatever the case may be tomorrow, the case today is that the most active enemies of the Jews are located not in the precincts of the ideological Right, but in the ideological precincts of the radical Left. . . . Jews should recognize the ideology of the radical Left for what it is: an enemy of liberal values and a threat to the Jewish position."[11]

Around the same time, Orthodox Jews who associated with the religiously right-wing Agudath Israel movement also broke ranks with the liberal consensus of the Jewish community. Beginning in the mid-1960s, this group targeted the most sacrosanct of American Jewish principles— the separationist doctrine. From the very beginning of the republic, historian Naomi W. Cohen has demonstrated, "Jewish spokesmen set themselves up as guardians of the 'authentic' American tradition, often urging conformity with the 'spirit' of the national, religion-blind Constitution."[12] In the years after World War II Jewish organizations worked unceasingly to shore up the wall separating church and state, believing that anything short of strict separation endangered Jewish security and opened the floodgates to the forces bent on Christianizing America.

Early in the 1960s the consensus position was challenged by Orthodox Jews who came out in favor of state aid to parochial schools. Marvin Schick, a leading partisan of the Orthodox campaign, observed that for countless Protestants and Catholics, from public-school officials to teachers to politicians, the issue of state aid was a practical matter about which "reasonable men might differ." By contrast, "the bulk of the organized and articulate Jewish community, robot-like invoked the holiness and oneness of the First Amendment and proclaimed their opposition to any 'breach in the wall separating church and state.' This idol worship, however, did not paralyze the thought processes of Orthodox leaders who were . . . [starting to think] it might be a good thing for the state to do something which might help the Hebrew Day School."[13]

By the 1970s and 1980s, religiously Orthodox and politically conservative Jews had moved the discussion beyond aid to parochial schools. They now were wondering whether America might be a better country if prayer had a place in the public school and religious symbols were displayed in the public square. Rather than promote the "no establishment" clause of the First Amendment, this coalition emphasized the "free exercise" of religion so that religiously observant Americans, including Jews, could practice their religion unencumbered. "To their thinking," writes the historian Jonathan Sarna, "the threat posed by rampant secularism was far more imminent and serious than any residual threat from forces of militant Christianity."[14]

THE CURRENT CIVIL RELIGIOUS REGIME

Judging from the annual pronouncements of Jewish community relations specialists, these criticisms have had scant impact. True, the *Joint Program Plan* and its successors, the *Agendas for Public Affairs,* include statements of demurral by member organizations on specific policy recommendations. But on balance the Jewish community continues to embrace its historic liberalism. In recent years the *Joint Program Plan* has endorsed public-school education, coupled with unwavering opposition to any aid to parochial schools; complete opposition to capital punishment; a statement on AIDS that instructs the Department of Health and Human Services to remove "the HIV virus from the list of 'dangerous and contagious diseases' for which aliens are excluded from this country"; and a strong endorsement of environmental programs, including a call for the "elevation of the Environmental Protection Agency to Cabinet status."

Surely one might debate whether these policy positions offer the best solution to contemporary problems in the United States. But on what basis have they been enunciated in the name of the American Jewish community? And why should that community invest its moral and political capital in support of policies that do not affect Jews as a group and about which American Jews as individual citizens undoubtedly hold a variety of opinions?

Over the years a number of explanations have been offered to justify these forays into the public policy arena. Perhaps the major one is that the Jewish tradition itself *commands* political activism. In the words of one *Joint Program Plan:* "American Jewish activism reflects the essence of the Judaic concept of '*mitzvot*,' to act upon commandments."

This, however, only begs the question of how particular commandments within the tradition translate into *specific policies*. It is precisely over the application of general principles of justice and compassion that decent people disagree. Is the death penalty clearly an act of social evil? The Torah commands capital punishment. If we call for strict gun control, are we protecting the innocent or depriving them of the means to defend themselves against criminals? Once again, the Torah calls for such self-defense. Is the American welfare system supported by the Jewish policy establishment congruent with Jewish teachings of *tzedakah* (justice, charity)? Traditionally the preferred form of Jewish giving has been one that safeguards the dignity of the recipient. The *Joint Program Plan*'s response—enveloping all of its stances in the mantle of some amorphous "Jewish tradition"—is evasive. Such a romance of "tradition" does more than trivialize that tradition, stretching it elastically beyond recognition. By obscuring the real grounds of its positions, the "agenda for public affairs" itself is inimical to the tradition of honest democratic debate.

A second rationale—namely that most American Jews do, in fact, concur with the public policy positions taken by their "spokesmen"—is not implausible on the face of it. Jewish leaders, it is argued, reflect the will of American Jews. There is some truth to this claim. But if Jews are generally to the left of Protestants and Catholics, all things being equal, it is also true, as survey research indicates, that activists are considerably further to the left than the communities they claim to represent. Moreover, the very process by which individuals rise to leadership in the community-relations agencies strongly favors those who hold liberal views: such lay and professional leaders are not randomly selected but gravitate to the field because they are social activists. Individuals who dissent from the party line are marginalized. Finally, organizations tend to pick their battles carefully, and Jewish ones are no different; on matters that do not concern them directly many Jewish organizations defer to coordinating bodies. (Indeed, a perusal of the actual policy positions of national agencies represented in the Jewish Council for Public Affairs demonstrates that organizations as diverse as the American Jewish Committee and the Women's League for Conservative Judaism actually take positions far more nuanced than those put forth in their name by the "agenda for public affairs.") It is therefore questionable whether the will of the people is fairly represented by the public policy arm of the Jewish community.

A third justification for Jewish activism is that it serves the group interests of Jews to encourage those forces in society that are tolerant and socially "conscious." Certainly, this was a major lesson that Jewish policy organizations derived from the horrors of the Holocaust. The destruction of European Jewry convinced many that the fate of Jews was directly linked to the welfare of society at large and necessitated a more cosmopolitan concern for the weak and needy. And throughout the nineteenth century many European Jews saw Jewish survival as linked to the Enlightenment tradition and the universalism of the democratic revolution. In recent decades, however, this concern has progressively extended its reach to absurd lengths. It is not hard to glimpse the connection between ending discrimination and the fate of Jews. But precisely how *tikkun olam,* the repair of the world, requires *specific policies* of environmental regulation, say, is less obvious.

In the end the most plausible justification for the positions espoused by the community is a frankly political version of the above logic of group interest. As a small minority, the argument goes, the Jewish community must forge links with coalition partners in the hope that these partners will speak for Jewish interests. Here, at last, is a rationale that lends itself to hard-nosed evaluation. Specifically, we can ask if the Jewish community's coalition partners have "delivered" in return for Jewish support of *their* agendas. For example, has Jewish cooperation with other minority groups on racial or urban matters been rewarded with support for Israel or a strong effort by these groups to root out anti-Semitism in their own ranks? Have efforts to form coalitions with one set of partners foreclosed the possibility of joint action with other groups? And has the strong tilt of the Jewish community toward the social program long advocated by the left wing of the Democratic Party impeded coalition building with those in the center and those on the right of the political spectrum? Unfortunately, these important questions are rarely debated by organizations most directly engaged in setting the public-policy agenda for the Jewish community.

TOWARD PARTICULARISM:
WHAT ARE JEWISH INTERESTS AND VALUES?

Perhaps the divided world of American Jewry cannot be made whole. But as we look to the future, we may reasonably ask whether it might not prove quite salutary to expose the divisions in American Jewish life so that a healthy public debate might ensue.

Circumstances have changed radically since the terms of discussion in the Jewish community were set in the immediate postwar period. Simply put, American Jews have achieved virtually everything that the postwar generation dreamed of: unfettered socioeconomic mobility, entrée into all sectors of society, and respectability for Judaism and things Jewish. Although Jews must remain ever vigilant, levels of anti-Semitism remain relatively low by historical standards. Overt discrimination and physical violence are the exceptions, but when they do occur, government leaders have responded forcefully and unequivocally to protect Jews. For some Jews these measures of security and success confirm the sagacity of the communal agenda. Accordingly, they urge the community to stay the course and advocate for more of the same.

But this myopic nonchalance neglects the critical feature of today's circumstances. Only the character—and not the condition—of threat facing Jews has changed. Today internal Jewish weakness is a far greater present danger than anti-Semitism. The community is losing large numbers of members to the twin processes of assimilation and intermarriage. The very Jewish population that is succeeding so well in integrating into American society is simultaneously almost devoid of a strong sense of distinctiveness. And the organized Jewish community lacks the sharp boundaries that would confidently clarify to its members who is a Jew or what is Judaism. In sum, the current Jewish communal "agenda for public affairs" is preoccupied with fighting the last war and is disregarding the present crisis.

Conditions in contemporary culture are only intensifying this dilemma. These include the growing inability of most American families to transmit their religion and culture intact to the next generation; "religious switching" is endemic in American society, and ethnicity is rapidly melting away. More generally, families are hard-pressed to serve as vehicles for the transmission of a strong identity as they are buffeted by massive dislocation and social change. Extended families tend to scatter widely. And even the nuclear family is under great strain because of high divorce rates, the multiple pressures faced by families with two wage earners, and a popular culture that is hostile to traditional family life and to the concept of religious obligation. The result is a growing "culture of disbelief" subversive to Judaism no less than to other religions.

As a result the public policies favored by the Jewish community may actually contribute to subverting Jewish survival. Certainly, it is no longer clear that the particularistic values of Judaism and the long-term interests of the Jewish community neatly coincide with liberal universalism. All this increases the urgency for a rethinking process in the Jewish community and a reassessment of the terms of discussion of the postwar public-policy consensus.

Fortunately, the mood in the Jewish community has been shifting, and there is now a new openness in a number of quarters to such reconsideration. As we go forward, several policy areas will warrant further scrutiny: First, Jews need to reexamine their embrace of American individualism, which in our time is increasingly untempered by countervailing values of altruism and voluntarism. A Jewish community preoccupied with individual self-advancement will look favorably on individualism, but that ethos is hostile to the maintenance of Jewish identity. American individualism, for example, frowns on young people who accept their parents' values uncritically and favors the collapse of ethnic and religious boundaries. Similarly, religious syncretism, unbounded choices, and constant self-invention render the task of teaching basic Jewish techniques for group survival far more difficult.

Second, the Jewish community must reconsider its reflexive fear of any potential breach in the wall of separation between church and state. Communal leaders have justified such an approach by citing, often incorrectly, historical precedent and by arguing that only an impenetrable wall of separation will guarantee Jewish rights and interests. But here too, much depends on one's definition of Jewish interests. It is not "good for the Jews" to keep religion out of the public square when religion—including Judaism—has something important to teach about morality and civilized behavior. It is not a Jewish interest to deprive parochial schools of government funding or to fight voucher programs when Jewish day schools, a critical vehicle for strengthening Jewish life, are starved of funds.

Third, the Jewish community must reassess its historical fear of asserting Jewish perspectives and interests in an unembarrassed fashion. The old habit of homogenizing Jewish teachings to blend smoothly with prevailing mores needs to be reconsidered. Under the bland banner of *tikkun olam,* the repair of the world, the Jewish community has taken positions in favor of a host of policies that cannot be squared with a fair reading of traditional Jewish texts. A more rigorous reading of those texts would force the community to reexamine its policy positions on what truly constitutes social justice, philanthropy, proper family structures, and sexual morality.

Such a reassessment of fundamental issues will not reknit the Jewish community into a unified body. Strong differences in outlook undoubtedly will remain on how to read, let alone apply, specific texts. At the least, however, the shibboleths that have so long dominated communal discourse will come under scrutiny—and the underlying disagreements will be exposed. At best, Jews may become far better informed about the particularity of their tradition and clarify for themselves where boundaries need to be established between Judaism and other religions, between Jews and Gentiles, between the Jewish community and other ethnic groups. The Jewish community then may also contribute a more nuanced set of positions on the great issues that divide all Americans today. In the process, it may even make new friends.

NOTES

Sections of this essay have appeared in different forms in *Commentary* and the *American Jewish Yearbook*. My thanks to the editors of those publications for their help.

1. For a detailed discussion of the Yale Five and their case see Samuel G. Freedman, *Jew vs. Jew: The Struggle for the Soul of American Jewry* (New York: Simon and Schuster, 2000), chap. 5.

2. The major exception to this generalization is the periodic eruption of communal debate over the policies of the state of Israel. Going back to the early 1970s, with the emergence of the dovish "Breira" organization, American Jews have fiercely contended with one another over what Israelis ought to be doing. One could speculate as to the psychological roots of this displacement: do American Jews need their Israeli brothers and sisters to play some kind of surrogate role, or are American Jews acting out their sibling rivalry? However we regard the decades-long engagement of American Jews in telling Israelis how to manage their Arab neighbors, it is nonetheless striking how little American Jewish groups debate each other over how their own members ought to live in the United States.

3. Most denominational organizations, in fact, take positions on a range of public-policy questions, but this is not their primary work.

4. Walter Jacob, ed., *American Reform Responsa: Collected Responsa of the Central Conference of American Rabbis, 1889–1983* (New York: CCAR, 1983), 550.

5. The Reconstructionist movement, with which approximately 1 percent of American Jews identify, adopted a version of this position already in 1968.

6. Arthur A. Goren, "A 'Golden Decade' for American Jews: 1945–1955," *Studies in Contemporary Jewry* 8 (1992): 4–8.

7. Commission on Law and Social Action of the American Jewish Congress to Jewish community leaders and workers, memorandum, n.d., Blaustein Library of the American Jewish Committee.

8. Naomi W. Cohen, *Not Free to Desist: A History of the American Jewish Committee, 1906–1966* (Philadelphia, Pa.: Jewish Publication Society of America, 1972), 383–85.

9. Quoted in Peter Y. Meddin, "Segmented Ethnicity and the New York Jewish Politics," *Studies in Contemporary Jewry* 3 (1987): 32–33.

10. Murray Friedman, "A New Direction for American Jews," *Commentary* (Dec. 1981): 37–44, esp. 41.

11. Norman Podhoretz, "A Certain Anxiety," *Commentary* (Aug. 1971): 10.

12. Naomi W. Cohen, *Jews in Christian America: The Pursuit of Religious Equality* (New York: Oxford University Press, 1992), 5–6.

13. From Marvin Schick, ed., *Government Aid to Parochial Schools—How Far?*, excerpted in Naomi W. Cohen, "Schools, Religions, and Government— Recent American Jewish Opinions," *Michael* 3 (1975): 377.

14. Jonathan D. Sarna, "Christian America or Secular America? The Church-State Dilemma of American Jews," in *Jews in Unsecular America,* ed. Richard John Neuhaus (Grand Rapids, Mich.: William B. Eerdmans, 1987), 18.

PART II

Refiguring the Boundaries of Citizenship

Race, Immigration, and National Belonging

CHAPTER 6

Once Again, Strangers on Our Shores

Mary C. Waters

Americans have a fundamental ambivalence about immigration. We are a nation of immigrants, yet racism and xenophobia are constitutive parts of our national psyche. Although we voice warm feelings about our immigrant ancestors, we see the present crop of immigrants as unworthy or even as demonic others, and the United States has a long history of trying to restrict immigration.

The current debate on immigration perfectly embodies this ambivalence. In the nearly four decades since the Hart-Celler immigration reforms opened the doors to non-European immigration, the largest flow in the nation's history has profoundly transformed U.S. society. For some the new immigrants, like the ones that preceded them, are a noble testimony to the success of the American experiment and the character of the immigrants who have fashioned it. Immigrants are seen as strengthening the best in American traditions, revitalizing decaying neighborhoods and stagnant industries and adding new talents and energies to the U.S. civic culture.

For others, however, this influx is nothing short of a disaster that displaces native workers, swells the minority "underclass," and exacerbates racial and ethnic conflict. Many Americans find particular cause for concern in the "nonwhite" character of the recent immigrants who have increasingly come from Asia, Latin America, and the Caribbean. In 2000, 51 percent of the foreign born were from Latin America and the Caribbean, 25.5 percent were from Asia, 15.3 percent were from Europe, and 8.1 percent from other countries.

Few people argue, at least out loud, that past immigration was bad for America. Instead the current debate hinges on the question of how today's immigrants differ from earlier ones. Restrictionists usually make two distinctions between the post-1965 immigrants and the earlier waves of European immigrants. First, arriving after the rise of the welfare state, today's immigrants are not encouraged to work as hard as previous immigrants, who did not enjoy such government help. Second, the immigrants themselves are different because we are now admitting racially different groups into a society that no longer advocates assimilation.

But evidence suggests that both these claims are exaggerated. When political refugees are taken out of the equation, working-age immigrants are no more likely to use welfare than working-age natives. A study by the Carnegie Endowment for International Peace and the Urban Institute concluded, "There is no reputable evidence that prospective immigrants are drawn to the United States because of its public assistance programs." In any event recent welfare reform legislation restricts access to welfare among legal immigrants.[1]

Meanwhile, the argument that nonwhite immigrants are less likely to assimilate than European immigrants simply ignores the intensity of turn-of-the-century beliefs that southern and central European "races" were genetically inferior to the northern and western European groups who came to the United States in earlier times and composed the "core American culture." In a full-page ad in the Sunday *New York Times* on June 22, 1913, William Ripley, a Harvard economics professor, deemed "the hordes of new immigrants" to be "a menace to our Anglo Saxon civilization"; these hordes were producing a "swarthy and black eyed primitive type population."[2]

The weakness of the restrictionists' comparisons does not mean we should abandon that methodological instinct. Indeed, the experience of European immigrants and their descendants was irrevocably shaped by two conditions that no longer apply for current immigrants: the hiatus in immigration between the depression and 1965 and the economic growth and social mobility that characterized the American economy between World War II and the 1970s.[3] These changes speak powerfully to the question of whether today's immigrants will be absorbed in the same way that earlier waves of immigrants were.

The immigrants from Europe who arrived between 1880 and 1920 are an assimilation success story. As their children and grandchildren rose from poverty to affluence, earlier pronounced differences in education, income, and occupational prestige between people of northern and western European ancestry on the one hand and southern and central European ancestry on the other virtually disappeared by 1980.[4] The "ethnic miracle" of the Jews, Italians, Greeks, Poles, and Slavs who were once despised and are now so accepted by American society is cause for optimism about the newer wave of post-1965 immigrants and their children and grandchildren.

Yet these immigrants achieved their progress in an era in which further immigration from Europe was cut off abruptly and in which in the years after World War II America saw rising income equality and sustained economic growth that benefited the middle and working classes. Today's immigrants arrive in a different milieu. There is no sign that the constant new supply of immigrants will be suddenly cut off. And since the mid-1970s the United States has seen rising income inequality and declining or stagnant real wages—especially for the working and lower-middle classes.

THE DEMOGRAPHICS OF IMMIGRATION

The so-called Great Pause in immigration in the 1920s and the restrictions that effected it halted the flow of European immigrants for three generations. That sharp break cut off the supply of raw materials for ethnicity—so that what it came to mean to be Jewish or Italian or Polish in the United States principally reflects what happened in the United States subsequently.[5] In the absence of appreciable numbers of new arrivals successive generations of acculturated Americans, not unassimilated greenhorns, became the majority among the new ethnics. Today most Italian Americans or Polish Americans are second, third, and fourth generation. They did not cease being Italian or Polish and become just plain "Americans." But their ethnicity became less intense and increasingly intermittent, voluntary, even recreational. If some still enjoyed ethnic holidays or special foods, their ethnicity rarely determined their occupation or residence. As more and more of the later generations of white ethnics intermarried, their ethnic identity became even more attenuated, and individuals felt increasingly free to choose whether to identify with their mother's or father's or grandmother's or grandfather's ethnic origins.[6] As a result the vast majority of Italian Americans live in neighborhoods that are not predominantly Italian American. As fewer new immigrants from Italy arrived, the nation's Little Italys gradually shrank and evolved into places visited by suburbanites in search of restaurants or other ethnic stores.

New immigrants from Mexico, Latin America, the Caribbean, and Asia face different circumstances. Given the continual stream of immigration, the members of these various immigrant communities will vary greatly in their level of assimilation, and the meaning of being Korean American, Mexican American, or Dominican will not diminish in quite the linear fashion experienced by earlier European immigrants.[7] Although some will undergo marked assimilation, they will be replaced by new individuals who will keep the ethnic group "fresh." Ethnic neighborhoods will not shrink and become quaint shrines to an earlier way of life but will remain vibrant new neighborhoods, even when the same people do not stay in them. The third-generation Chinese American who intermarries, moves to the suburbs, achieves social mobility, and develops a merely "symbolic" identity as Chinese American will be replaced by a first-generation Chinese American who lives in Chinatown, speaks little English, and lives a visibly rich ethnic Chinese lifestyle.

This replenishment powerfully shapes not just the immigrants' quest to define their identity but also the way immigrants present their collective self to outsiders and, thus, public opinion about immigration. Simply put, the visible aspects of the ethnic group—speaking a language other than English, occupational specialization, residential concentration—will not be diluted, and it will strike the average American that the new immigrants are not assimilating as the European immigrants did in earlier times, even though a great deal of assimilation is taking place among second- and third-generation Asians, West Indians, and Latinos.

Language provides a good example of this mismatch between perception and reality. Complaints about immigrants who refuse to learn "our" language, resentful anecdotes about voting signs in Spanish, and efforts to certify English as the hallowed language have all been a staple of talk radio and politicking. Meanwhile, the rushing stream of new immigrants ensures that many people in Los Angeles and Miami speak only Spanish. And this will happen despite irrefutable evidence that the new immigrants are rapidly acquiring English—sometimes in the course of a single generation. In a recent study of Miami and San Diego, Portes and Schauffler found only 1 percent of the second-generation youth they studied knew little or no English; 73 percent reported they are able to speak, understand, read, and write English "very well" and another 26 percent "well." In effect, even in Miami, the city in the United States where it is easiest to live one's whole life speaking only Spanish, there is a virtually universal switch to English in one generation.[8]

This ethnic replenishment has another effect that obscures underlying assimilation: it gives rise to population projections that heighten fears about the changing racial composition of the United States and generate well-known predictions that whites will soon become a minority throughout the country. But all these forecasts assume no intermarriage and no change in ethnic identity. They assume that Mexicans, for example, will always marry other Mexicans and that all of *their* descendants will identify as Mexican.

If people at the turn of the century had made similar estimates of the future numbers of Jews, Italians, and Slavs, they would have missed the actual trajectory of those immigrants' progeny. And indeed fears about unassimilable immigrants and soaring population were directed at the Italian, Jewish, and Polish parents and grandparents of those who now worry about "their" unassimilable immigrants. In the last century the Irish were seen as a "race" apart from other European groups, and cartoons portrayed them as apes. If blacks were called "smoked Irish," the Irish in turn were dubbed "niggers turned inside out."[9] They were also stereotyped as ignorant criminals and fecund child bearers who lacked discipline and good family values. Surely it would have been difficult to predict how popular, how quintessentially American, such a denigrated group would become in the next century.

Actually, the growth of the Irish from 4.5 million immigrants to 40 million Irish Americans by the 1980 census happened not because the allegedly fecund Irish were too different culturally to assimilate but precisely because they *were* able to assimilate.[10] The Irish had high rates of intermarriage with other white groups, and the offspring of those marriages tended to favor "Irish" as their preferred identity. And if turn-of-the-century projections had radically underestimated the Irish, similar forecasts would have failed to predict the decline in the boundaries separating white ethnic groups or that differences between southern and central European immigrants and northern and western European immigrants would gradually become a moot point. In all these cases groups such as Italians and Poles and Greeks, once seen as racially distinct, now intermarry to such a great extent with other white European groups that they are virtually indistinguishable. As Richard D. Alba reports, "In 1990 census data, more than half (56 percent) of whites have spouses whose ethnic backgrounds do not overlap with their own at all. . . . Only one-

fifth have spouses with identical backgrounds."[11] All of this makes ethnicity a matter of choice for Italian, Irish, and Scottish ancestry, who now
have the option to "choose" to identify with one or more of their ethnic ancestries and discard or "forget" others.

Even though the demography of current Caribbean, Latin American,
and Asian immigrants will be more complex than the earlier generation's,
significant intermarriage and identity changes are already occurring
among the descendants of these immigrants. Rates of intermarriage have
been growing since 1960 for all groups, even for those defined as "racial"
groups.[12] Although it is still the case that only a small proportion of marriages by whites are with nonwhites and Hispanics (2 percent), the rate
of increase in recent decades has been dramatic; "in 1960 there were
about 150,000 interracial couples in the United States. This number grew
rapidly to more than one million in 1990. When marriages with Hispanics
are added the intergroup marriages totalled about 1.6 million in 1990."[13]
Although greater than 93 percent of whites and of blacks marry within
their own groups, only 70 percent of Asians and of Hispanics do so.
Black-white intermarriages are still the least prevalent, but among
younger people there is evidence of dramatic change. Alba reports that
"10 percent of 25 to 34 year old black men have intermarried, most with
white women."[14]

Because immigration is ongoing, there may be two stories to tell about
the new immigrants—one a story of new arrivals and the replenishment
of ethnic culture, the other a story of quiet assimilation into a blended
culture. But if the second story is obscured by the first, there could be
growing public support for restricting immigration.

One might counter that the fluidity of white ethnic categories contrasts
with the seemingly impermeable boundaries of race that Mexican, Korean, and Jamaican immigrants encounter in the United States. But those
who believe that current immigrants from Asia, Latin America, and the
Caribbean are less "assimilable" than those from European countries may
be committing two important errors. First, as complaints about the Hebraic and Celtic "races" remind us, the legal and social systems of racial
classifications in the United States are fluid, the product of a complex
and contingent process, and subject to change over the coming decades.
At the least, as intermarriage blurs the boundaries between groups, our
ideas of what constitutes a "race" will change accordingly, just as they
did with the Irish and Jews.

Those who fear the new immigrants will not assimilate commit a second error: they mistakenly assume the cultures of non-European groups

will continue to be very different from the "core American culture." Yet in the past that core American culture has absorbed a number of different groups who were viewed as racially different, and there is every reason that American culture will continue to do so. Indeed, Muller argues, "The continuing addition of new ethnic groups helps to broaden and enrich the national culture. . . . A nationwide Gallup survey taken in 1984 found that 61 percent of the public agreed that immigrants improve our culture."[15] In effect, both sides of the assimilation equation are moving targets. Groups that seem "racially" different now may not always seem so, and the core American culture that groups are assimilating into is itself constantly changing and evolving as it absorbs new influences.

CHANGES IN THE ECONOMY
AND SECOND-GENERATION DECLINE

The second major difference between contemporary and previous immigrants is economic. The children and grandchildren of the European immigrants who arrived in the peak years of immigration around 1900 benefited from the spectacular expansion of the U.S. economy between 1940 and 1970. As Barry Bluestone has summarized, "In the U.S. real average weekly earnings grew by 60 percent between 1947 and 1973. Median family income literally doubled. . . . And over the same period personal wages and family incomes became tangibly more equal. . . . Along with growth and greater equality, poverty declined across the nation."[16]

The existence of manufacturing jobs offering security and good pay meant that blue-collar workers with a high school degree or less could attain a stable middle-class lifestyle, as a rising tide really did lift all boats. By the 1980s the descendants of southern and eastern European immigrants and northern and western European immigrants had achieved economic parity.

This level of economic growth and widening opportunities was not sustained after the early 1970s. During the final decades of the twentieth century the restructuring of the U.S. economy from manufacturing to services was accompanied by rising inequality between rich and poor, especially in the nation's urban centers. The result has been described as an hourglass economy, with many jobs for highly skilled workers in professional services and information processing and many unskilled low-level jobs. The unionized blue-collar manufacturing jobs that supported middle-class lifestyles have become scarce. One result has been to increase the value of formal education in the labor market: "In 1963, the mean annual earnings of those with four years of college or more stood at just over twice (2.11) times the mean annual earnings of those who had not completed high school. . . . By 1987, the education to earnings ratio had skyrocketed to nearly three to one."[17]

These disparities intensified in the 1980s, when the average real wages of male high school dropouts fell by 18 percent, and male high school graduates suffered a nearly 13 percent loss in real earnings. Only men with a master's degree or more registered an increase in inflation-adjusted earnings, and college graduates' earnings stayed about the same. This happened partly because all the employment growth in the economy during the 1980s came in the services sector, where wages polarized between high school dropouts and college graduates four times faster than in goods-producing industries.[18]

This new economy poses tough challenges for the children of unskilled immigrants no less than for native-born Americans who lack college degrees. Both face a generational erosion of real family income relative to their parents. Simply achieving their parents' low level of education will yield diminishing returns in earnings. As a result, to achieve a middle-class lifestyle the second generation must vault from their parents' lower-level service jobs and education to a completed college education. The unforgiving economy of today means that current second generations must accomplish in one generation what it took the Irish, Italians, and Poles several to accomplish. In the absence of well-paying blue-collar jobs for those without a high school diploma, the current second generation is climbing a ladder on which the middle rungs are missing, as historian Joel Perlmann has put it.[19]

These circumstances have played havoc with the ethnic bargain enjoyed by white ethnic immigrants. Their experience suggested each succeeding generation would become more similar to native-born Americans. Whatever the psychic costs of shedding identity for the third and fourth generation descendants, assimilation offered the substantial economic rewards of upward mobility.

Today's second-generation immigrants are no longer assured of this payoff, as Herbert Gans warned in the early 1990s. He outlined several possible outcomes for the second generation, including an ironic version of "Americanization": the children of immigrants—especially of parents who have not escaped poverty—refuse the low level, poorly paid jobs of their parents and, in their economic slide, begin to look increasingly like those poor young whites, blacks, and Hispanics who reject low-wage jobs.

It makes sense, then, that "becoming American" can be every immigrant parent's worst nightmare for their children.[20]

Another possibility is an equally ironic form of refusing to assimilate. Instead of "becoming American" by adopting negative attitudes toward school, opportunity, and hard work, the children of immigrants embrace their parents' ethnic community and values and end up doing better. The people who have secured an economically viable ethnic niche acculturate less than did the European second and third generation, and those without such a niche escape dead-end immigrant and other jobs mainly by becoming persistently jobless Americans.

Race further complicates the relationship between the ethnic bargain and economic decline for immigrants of color. In their study of second-generation children in Miami and San Diego, Alejandro Portes and Rubén Rumbaut identified a pattern in which those groups who come with strong ethnic ties, access to capital, and fewer ties to U.S. minorities— Koreans and Chinese—experience "linear" ethnicity. The orbit of ethnic networks helps transmit parental authority, traditional values, and access to job opportunities. As a result resistance to acculturation ends up providing better opportunities for their second generation.[21]

In another pattern second-generation youth whose parents lack the ability to provide jobs develop an "adversarial stance" toward white society similar to that of many American minorities and may even come to identify with them. Immigrants may thus lose their ethnic distinctiveness only to become indistinguishable from native blacks or Latinos. For them assimilation may mean joining the street culture of the urban ghetto.

In striking contrast to Chinese and Korean children, Haitians feel pressured by black American peers to adopt "black culture" in school and to identify as blacks rather than as Haitians or West Indians. The peer culture imparts a skeptical view of upward mobility and school success. Portes and Zhou discern a similarly sad fate for members of the second generation who cast their lot with America's minority groups: "Children of nonwhite immigrants may not even have the opportunity of gaining access to the white mainstream, no matter how acculturated they become. Joining those native circles to which they do have access may prove a ticket to permanent subordination and disadvantage."[22]

Portes and Zhou's findings have been replicated for other ethnic immigrants. Suarez-Orozco found that successful Central American immigrant children maintained a dual frame of reference.[23] They contrasted their experiences in the United States with their experiences at home and developed an immigrant attitude toward school that helped them to do well. According to Gibson, whereas native minority youth equated school achievement with yielding their specific cultural attributes, second-generation Punjabi Sikhs in California embodied "accommodation without assimilation."[24] Viewing school as a way to bring honor to their families rather than as an avenue of individual mobility, they acquired the cultural skills and language they needed to succeed in school yet retained their Sikh identities and culture. Matute-Bianchi discovered that among California high school students immigrant and American-born children who identified as Mexican did better in school than those who identified as Chicanos or "Cholos," an oppositional identity based in the American race and ethnic classification system.[25]

I found something similar among second-generation West Indian youth in New York City. Students from middle-class backgrounds were likely to maintain ties to their parents' ethnic identities and to resist identifying as black Americans. Poor and working-class youth in segregated neighborhoods were far more likely than their middle-class counterparts to reject their parents' stress on West Indian heritage and to strongly identify as black Americans. These identities were closely related to perceptions of racism in American society. Those who believed that discrimination blocked their way developed more oppositional theories of how to "make it" and tended to identify with American black youth. The type of identification was highly correlated with levels of educational success and thus future prospects.[26]

One final twist of the racial dynamic complicates the story. Intensifying the payoff to "ethnic" rather than "minority" identification, membership in cohesive ethnic enclaves has a positive impact not just on the aspirations of job seekers but on the perceptions of the employers who consider hiring them. After all, employees also use the identity of "not-native minority," which functions to reassure employers about the work habits of immigrants. As the employers articulate it, the newcomers are much more willing to accept lesser jobs, for their frame of reference is the situation they left back home, not the American context used by American minorities for comparison.

Several recent studies have attempted to measure this odd form of "racial" discrimination that works in favor of immigrants of color, in which white employers take their immigrant status to be more important than their nonwhite status. In a survey of hiring practices among Chicago area employers, Kirschenman and Neckerman found that employers strongly preferred immigrants over inner-city blacks.[27] Kasinitz and Rosenberg found the same preference among employers in the Red

Hook section of New York City.[28] In a review of the effects of immigrants on American cities, Muller concludes that immigrants do not reduce the overall earnings of native minorities but that there may be a substitution effect on unskilled black workers.[29]

But will the children of immigrants continue to enjoy these advantages? Will the second generation still be able to tap into the social networks that provide access to jobs and reassure employers? Will they resist the same disdain toward low-level service jobs that native minorities feel? Will potential employers see them as racial minorities and pass them over for employment in favor of even newer immigrants, perhaps from their parents' country of origin? Will they be more successful than native minorities in staying in school through college? For now, the answers to all these questions are pending.

Becoming an American includes learning about American racial attitudes and prejudices. Although Latin American and Caribbean first-generation immigrants may not see themselves in terms of U.S. racial categories, the second generation probably will, at least in part. Many Dominicans in New York are dark-skinned and would be classified as black by most Americans. These immigrants often label themselves white because in the Dominican Republic to be partly white means to be non-black.[30] Will the children of these immigrants adopt the American view and identify as black? What impact will the way others see them have on the way the children of the immigrants see themselves? Some researchers argue that whether immigrants see themselves as "ethnics" or "minorities" will influence political and social outcomes for the group.[31] It is quite possible that as the second generation experiences racial discrimination, it may embrace a black identity and adopt an oppositional identity.

At present the evidence on outcomes for the second generation, based as it is on ethnographic case studies and small-scale surveys, is sketchy. The question of how much second-generation decline there is awaits more systematic survey research. Yet the question of decline directs our attention to the intersection of two major problems in current American society—rising income inequality combined with constricting opportunities for the least educated and continuing racial discrimination and racial exclusion.

However uncertain the prospects of our newest Americans, the fluidity of racial and ethnic identities, as well as their entanglement in broader forces of economic opportunity and labor-market access, make this much clear: if the culture of current immigrants and their children does matter to the ongoing debate about immigration policy and diversity in the United States, it is not because the "culture" of people with African, Asian, or Hispanic roots will prevent them from becoming "true Americans." Rather, the race of newcomers matters if a declining economy and ongoing discrimination means that we cannot deliver the American dream of upward mobility the immigrants seek for their children and grandchildren.

Ironically, recent attempts to restrict the access of immigrants to the social welfare safety net may produce the very conflicts restrictionists claim to want to prevent. The most radical proposals deny schooling, and even citizenship, to the children of illegal immigrants. By creating separation and exclusion—thereby ensuring a lack of assimilation and second-generation decline—such policies pose a serious threat to social cohesion in the United States.

NOTES

1. Poor immigrants are actually much less likely than poor natives to use welfare; about 16 percent of poor immigrants receive cash assistance, compared to 25 percent of poor natives. See Carnegie Endowment for International Peace and the Urban Institute, "Immigrants and Welfare," *Research Perspectives on Migration* (Sep./Oct. 1996): 3.

2. Cited in Thomas Muller, *Immigrants and the American City* (New York: New York University Press, 1993), 40.

3. Douglas Massey was the first to choose these two factors as the most important historical differences between the experiences of European immigrants who arrived at the turn of the century and more recent immigrants. See his "The New Immigration and Ethnicity in the United States," in *American Diversity: A Demographic Challenge for the Twenty-First Century,* ed. Nancy Denton and Stewart Toldnay (Albany: State University Press of New York, 2002), 75–98. Although Massey explores the impact of these changes on the meaning of ethnicity, I concentrate here on the possible impacts of these changes on support for immigration restrictionism and on the future outcomes of the second generation.

4. Stanley Lieberson and Mary C. Waters, *From Many Strands: Ethnic and Racial Groups in Contemporary America* (New York: Russell Sage Foundation, 1988).

5. See Massey, "New Immigration."

6. Mary C. Waters, *Ethnic Options: Choosing Identities in America* (Berkeley: University of California Press, 1990); Richard D. Alba, *Italian Americans: Into the Twilight of Ethnicity* (Englewood Cliffs, N.J.: Prentice-Hall, 1985).

7. Massey, "New Immigration," 18.

8. Alejandro Portes and Richard Schauffler, "Language Acquisition and Loss among Children of Immigrants," in *Origins and Destinies: Immigration, Race,*

and Ethnicity in America, ed. Silvia Pedraza and Rubén G. Rumbaut (Belmont, Calif.: Wadsworth, 1996), 437.

9. Noel Ignatiev, *How the Irish Became White* (New York: Routledge, 1995), 41.

10. See Michael Hout and Joshua Goldstein, "How 4.5 Million Irish Immigrants Became 40 Million Irish Americans: Demographic and Subjective Aspects of the Ethnic Composition of White Americans," *American Sociological Review* 59 (Feb. 1994): 64–82.

11. Richard D. Alba, "Assimilation's Quiet Tide," *Public Interest* (spring 1995): 13.

12. Gary Sandefur and Trudy Mckinnell, "American Indian Intermarriage," *Social Science Research* (1986): 347–71; Akemi Kikumura and Harry L. Kitano, "Interracial Marriage: A Picture of the Japanese Americans," *Journal of Social Issues* 29 (1973); Harry L. Kitano, L. K. Chai, and H. Hatanaka, "Asian American Interracial Marriage," *Journal of Marriage and the Family* 46 (1984): 179–90; Stanley Lieberson, *A Piece of the Pie: Blacks and White Immigrants since 1880* (Berkeley: University of California Press, 1980); Belinda M. Tucker and Claudia Mitchell-Kernan, "New Trends in Black American Interracial Marriage: The Social Structural Context," *Journal of Marriage and the Family* 52 (Feb. 1990): 209–18; Claudette Bennett and J. Gregory Robinson, "Racial Classification Issues Concerning Children in Mixed Race Households" (paper presented at the annual meeting of the American Statistical Association, Fort Lauderdale, Fla., 1993).

13. Roderick Harrison and Claudette Bennett, "Racial and Ethnic Diversity," in *State of the Union: America in the 1990s,* vol. 2, *Social Trends,* ed. Reynolds Farley (New York: Russell Sage Foundation, 1995), 165.

14. Alba, "Assimilation's Quiet Tide," 17.

15. Muller, *Immigrants and the American City,* 245.

16. Barry Bluestone, "The Inequality Express," *American Prospect* 20 (winter 1995): 82–83.

17. Ibid., 83.

18. Ibid.

19. Remarks at the Jerome Levy Institute of Bard College Conference on the Second Generation, Bard College, New York, Oct. 25, 1997.

20. See Herbert J. Gans, "Second-Generation Decline: Scenarios for the Economic and Ethnic Futures of the Post-1965 American Immigrants," *Ethnic and Racial Studies* 15, no. 2 (1992): 173–93.

21. Alejandro Portes and Rubén G. Rumbaut, *Legacies: The Story of the Immigrant Second Generation* (Berkeley: University of California Press, 2001). See also Alejandro Portes and Min Zhou, "The New Second Generation: Segmented Assimilation and Its Variants," *Annals of the American Academy of Political and Social Science* 530 (1993): 74–97.

22. Portes and Zhou, "New Second Generation."

23. Marcelo M. Suarez-Orozco, " 'Becoming Somebody': Central American Immigrants in U.S. Inner-City Schools," *Anthropology and Education Quarterly* 18 (1987): 287–99.

24. Margaret Gibson, *Accommodation without Assimilation: Sikh Immigrants in an American High School* (Ithaca, N.Y.: Cornell University Press, 1989).

25. Eugenia Matute-Bianchi, "Situational Ethnicity and Patterns of School Performance among Immigrants and Nonimmigrant Mexican Descent Students," in *Minority Status and Schooling: A Comparative Study of Immigrant and Involuntary Minorities,* ed. Margaret Gibson and John Ogbu (New York: Garland, 1991).

26. Mary C. Waters, *Black Identities: West Indian Immigrant Dreams and American Realities* (Cambridge, Mass.: Harvard University Press, 1999).

27. Joleen Kirschenman and Kathryn Neckerman, "We'd Love to Hire Them, but—The Meaning of Race for Employers," in *The Urban Underclass,* ed. Christopher Jencks and Paul Petersen (Washington, D.C.: Brookings Institution, 1991), 203–34.

28. Philip Kasinitz and Jan Rosenberg, "Missing the Connection? Social Isolation and Employment on the Brooklyn Waterfront," working paper of the Michael Harrington Institute, Queens College, Queens, New York, 1994.

29. Muller, *Immigrants and the American City.*

30. Sherri Grasmuck and Patricia Pessar, "First and Second Generation Settlement of Dominicans in the United States: 1960–1990," in *Origins and Destinies: Immigration, Race, and Ethnicity in America,* ed. Silvia Pedraza and Rubén Rumbaut (Belmont, Calif.: Wadsworth, 1996).

31. Peter Skerry, *Mexican Americans: The Ambivalent Minority* (New York: Free Press, 1994); Robert C. Smith, "Doubly Bounded Solidarity: Race and Social Location in the Incorporation of Mexicans into New York City" (paper presented at the Social Science Research Council, Conference of Fellows, Program of Research on the Urban Underclass, June 1993).

CHAPTER 7

Expelling Newcomers

The Eclipse of Constitutional Community

Cecilia Muñoz

For a nation of immigrants the United States has long been ambivalent about immigration. On the one hand, we have a rich tradition of treating immigrants generously. The attitude of welcoming strangers, embodied informally in the symbolism of the Statue of Liberty and the integration of each generation of new immigrants into the fabric of American life, has nurtured a formal tradition that codified generosity in legal forms: the relative ease and universalist criteria that encouraged becoming an American citizen; a doctrine of birthright citizenship, quite different from most European societies, that automatically conferred citizenship on children born in the United States; and a reluctance to grant citizens and noncitizens different rights and benefits, save the right to run for president and to vote.

On the other hand, there is a less welcoming tradition, embodied in the fear and resentment of immigrants, that has subverted rather than grounded the tradition of democratic pluralism. Long ago Ben Franklin worried about the Germans streaming into Pennsylvania. Their culture, he feared, would render them incapable of becoming Americans. Their language, he complained, might overtake English as the common language in culture and commerce. Worse still, nativist emotion has given rise to a chronic disregard for the rights of people even perceived as immigrants. As recently as the 1950s Mexican Americans were the targets of roundups known as "Operation Wetback," in which thousands of persons, including legal U.S. residents and citizens, were "repatriated" to Mexico without due process of law.

We are a far cry from the nativist crusades of the 1920s, and in general the United States is successfully absorbing millions of new Latino, Asian, West Indian, and other immigrants. Yet a growing fear of immigrants in the 1990s, both of their economic threat and their cultural and racial differences, bred an emotional climate of restrictionism evident in English-only referenda, in Pat Buchanan's bids for the Republican nomination for president, and in California's Proposition 187. A few years ago, in an eerie parallel to Operation Wetback, the city council of Chandler, Arizona, enlisted the police to "clean up" a neighborhood scheduled for redevelopment. With the help of Border Patrol officials Chandler police spent several days accosting anyone who appeared Mexican, requesting that they demonstrate their right to be in the United States. Many native-born U.S. citizens were questioned multiple times as they drove to work, did their shopping, and took their children to school. Unfortunately, such practices are becoming more common as the presence of immigrants increases across the country.

To an extent barely recognized in public debate, a series of recent laws and policies has radically challenged the old immigration regime. American society has been quietly refiguring the boundaries of national community and sacred notions of citizenship. The erosion of constitutional community began with the California governor's race in 1994, spilled over into national legislation with provisions of the welfare and immigration bills of 1996, found expression in a 1998 proposal in Congress to revoke the concept of birthright citizenship, and continues with the increased use of racial and ethnic profiling in the enforcement of immigration and other laws.

Efforts to restrict immigrants and to give them a secondhand form of citizenship endanger not just the dignity of immigrants or traditional American values but the very practice of democracy in everyday life. They have undermined the civil rights enjoyed by citizens of specific ethnic groups. They have made suspicious appearances—and thus biological criteria—a ground for withholding fundamental liberties. They have created new divisions within the national community, not just between immigrants and citizens but between citizens from dominant ethnic and racial groups and citizens who look "different" or have Asian- and Latino-sounding names and between undocumented immigrants and their U.S.-citizen children. They have subjected large numbers of U.S. citizens and legal immigrants to the infringements and invasions of arbitrary state power. If immigration poses any threat to our nation, as restrictionists like to claim, the danger comes mainly from their own efforts to convince the rest of America that some of their neighbors are too "different" to become true Americans and from the policies that would go to almost any lengths to get rid of them.

THE RECENT IMMIGRATION DEBATE

The erosion of civil rights and constitutional community emerged in a distinctive political environment. Perhaps the defining moment in the immigration debate of the 1990s came in the summer of 1993, when California governor Pete Wilson, in an open letter to President Clinton, called for changes in immigration control policy. Wilson claimed undocumented immigrants were responsible for California's economic crisis because of their illegitimate use of public services.

Wilson had been languishing at a low point in popularity. Almost immediately after his call for restrictions on immigrants he experienced a twenty-point surge in popularity. After funneling major financial and political support to what was then a little-known ballot proposition drafted by extremist restrictionists, the "Save Our State" initiative, or Proposition 187, Wilson rode this particular issue back to popularity and reelection as governor in 1994. The authors of this initiative were the late former commissioner of the Immigration and Naturalization Service (INS) Alan Nelson and former INS western regional director Harold Ezell. The latter was known for his inflammatory anti-immigrant statements in the 1980s, and the former was working as a consultant for the Federation for American Immigration Reform at the time he drafted the initiative.

Proposition 187, which passed by a 59 percent to 41 percent margin, established the principle that dominated the rest of the decade: almost no policy is too extreme if it is designed to control immigration. One of its provisions required all children enrolling in public school to identify their own immigration status and that of their parents. If the purpose of this seemingly innocuous procedure was noxious indeed—to deny children an education and provide a vehicle for deporting their parents—its consequence was even more radical. In targeting not only undocumented children but U.S.-citizen children whose parents did not have immigration status, it guaranteed children of foreign appearance would have increasing encounters with arbitrary state power. In addition, it required state and local officials, including health care providers, teachers, and law enforcement officers, to report anyone they suspected of being in the United States illegally. As the furor over the proposition grew, anyone with a Hispanic or Asian appearance or surname was automatically suspect in many people's minds.

In the end the draconian consequences of Proposition 187 were suspended by litigation that has effectively stopped its implementation. But an important symbolic victory had been won. Governor Wilson was easily reelected, and an important political message had been sent: even extreme anti-immigration measures made great politics.

Subsequent congressional campaigns in California and the presidential campaign of 1996 underscored this perception. Republican congressional candidates in California campaigned on proposals that they sought to enact in Congress, such as the Gallegly Amendment, which would have allowed states to deny a public education to undocumented students. In addition, Republican presidential nominee Bob Dole and vice presidential nominee Jack Kemp both reversed longstanding proimmigration positions during their campaigns in what was widely viewed as an attempt to woo California voters by following Governor Wilson's model for success. Although their resounding defeat among Latino voters in California has begun to reshape politics, so far the change has been more in the area of style than substance. For example, in his 2000 election campaign George W. Bush wooed Latinos with highly effective bilingual ads, at the same time avoiding entirely the difficult questions of immigration policy.

Although Governor Wilson was careful to limit his rhetoric to illegal immigrants, in short order federal legislation was enacted attacking legal immigrants and naturalized citizens. These proposals, enacted into law in 1996, contained elements extreme enough to rival Proposition 187, and America is still living with their consequences.

The events set in motion in California in the early 1990s culminated in the enactment of major welfare and immigration reform bills in 1996. These laws, which codified many of the ugly proposals first floated in the California debate, have seriously eroded the rights of immigrants and naturalized citizens and created a double standard for Americans of immigrant origin. They have worsened existing discrimination against Americans who are perceived as or mistaken for immigrants. All this has betrayed America's historic commitment to equality and the pluralistic notion that anyone can become a full American regardless of his or her origin.

The first of these proposals enacted into law was the Welfare Reform

Act of 1996. Before then, the American government granted to immigrants the same access to social services enjoyed by citizens. But the 1996 reform bill reversed the legal position immigrants enjoyed as the equals of Americans in most respects. In the process the implementation of the act provided the states with significant opportunities to erode the rights of citizens because they or their family members are immigrants.

Welfare reform divided the U.S. population into three groups, each with different eligibility for receiving government-funded social services. The first, U.S. citizens who can document their citizenship, continues to be eligible for all government-funded programs, provided they meet income and other eligibility requirements. The second, "qualified noncitizens" (generally meaning legal immigrants), are ineligible for the four major safety-net programs (Temporary Assistance to Needy Families [TANF], Supplemental Security Income, Food Stamps, and Medicaid) until they can demonstrate that they have worked for ten years. The states also have the authority to decide their eligibility for such programs at the state level. The third group, nonqualified immigrants (generally meaning those without immigration status), continue to be ineligible for welfare programs, even though this category includes hundreds of thousands of immigrants who are lawfully present in the United States. The states have the authority to determine whether or not they will be eligible for a variety of other social services that are provided at the state level, such as nutrition programs, prenatal care, and other basic services.

Welfare reform overturned a long tradition that held that immigrants legally in the country had the same responsibilities and the same access to social services as citizens. Although it cut off access and disposed of the benefits, Congress left intact the responsibilities immigrants are expected to uphold, including paying taxes to support safety-net services they may no longer receive, serving in the military, and other aspects of good citizenship. At one point in the debate the Senate even approved language that would have allowed the government to deny services to naturalized U.S. citizens if they had not fulfilled the requirement that they work for ten years, but this language was dropped from final legislation. Although a substantial portion of the benefits that were eliminated for legal immigrants has been restored, at this writing few restorations apply to immigrants who have arrived since 1996, leaving this population of taxpaying new Americans without a safety net.

While welfare reform was busy circumscribing eligibility, it was also expanding the state's power to monitor immigrants and reduce their presumptive right to privacy. The reporting provisions of the bill expanded the verification procedures through which states determine who qualifies for publicly funded services. Government service providers must now determine if applicants are qualified immigrants, when the applicants arrived in the United States, the financial circumstances of the immigrants' sponsor, and other factors in determining eligibility.

This is more than a mere administrative formality; it is a threat to substantive democracy. In the more than fifteen years since employers were required to verify their employees, it has become clear that the requirement to determine immigration status invites discrimination against people who are mistaken for immigrants. Nearly a dozen studies, including a 1990 report by the General Accounting Office, *Immigration Reform: Employer Sanctions and the Question of Discrimination,* have documented the widespread pattern of discrimination that resulted from the 1986 Immigration Reform and Control Act's requirement that employers verify the work authorization of their new employees. Applicants with Hispanic surnames are frequently assumed to be noncitizens and thus can be denied services until they produce immigration papers—even if the applicant is a native-born U.S. citizen. In addition, citizenship documents such as birth certificates are likely to be scrutinized more closely when they belong to someone with a "foreign-sounding" name.

Even more forbidding, welfare reform enables states to submit quarterly reports to the attorney general with the names and addresses of persons who are known to be illegally in the United States. This provision, which directly echoes Proposition 187, provides a mechanism some states employ to frighten U.S.-citizen children away from services for which they are eligible because receiving them is tantamount to turning their parents in to the INS. In 1998 the San Diego County Board of Supervisors instructed county officials to send a letter to recipients of the food stamp and CalWORKS (TANF) programs informing them that their family members will be reported to the INS. Although the letter was ultimately not sent, San Diego County's intention has echoed in the delivery of social services in that county, as well as elsewhere in the state.

The threats that welfare reform has posed to American values, due process, and civil rights have been compounded by the impact of the 1996 Immigration Reform Act. The worker verification mandated by the 1986 Immigration Reform and Control Act (IRCA), which required employers to check their newly hired employees' immigration status, had already intensified discrimination in employment, creating a Kafkaesque world of arbitrary justice, of presumed guilt, and of punishment without crime. Employers selectively check the documents of "suspect" employees or insist that Latino or Asian workers present a greater number or specifically selected documents to be able to work. It is true, as studies show, that much of the discrimination triggered by the law results from confusion or ignorance on the part of employers who do not understand the intricacies of immigration or citizenship law. Nonetheless, the deprivations of rights and of the expectation of routine fairness are no less real.

The case of Rosita Martinez underscores dramatically the impact of such provisions. The Marcel Watch company insisted that Martinez, an employee of Puerto Rican birth—and therefore a U.S. citizen—could not work until she showed her green card. When Ms. Martinez's case was heard before a judge, the employer insisted that she was a "foreigner" and that the law required him to see her green card.

As unsavory as some of these practices are, the 1986 law at least offered some protection against arbitrary infringements. By contrast, the 1996 immigration reform law did not even maintain this level of procedural recourse. On the contrary, it radically limited the force of antidiscrimination protections. For starters the 1996 law added an intent standard; that is, any victim of discrimination must now prove that her or his employer *intended* to discriminate. This would seem to discount discrimination that results from employer ignorance, the most common employment practice under this law. The result is a policy regime that targets immigrants and those perceived to be immigrants and subjects them to an entirely different set of workplace eligibility criteria than those who are perceived to be natives of this country. It also, in essence, legally sanctions stereotyping and bigotry. And it continues the process of constricting the boundaries of our national community.

The third realm in which the 1996 law erodes citizenship and civil rights, the provisions on judicial review, may be the most constitutionally ominous. Unlike technical eligibility requirements or employer conduct, it involves immigrants in encounters with the state itself and thereby affects their perceptions of its legitimacy.

The 1996 immigration law permits arbitrary actions by the INS and eliminates judicial review of INS decisions, with potentially horrific consequences. Among the most egregious assaults on traditional notions of individual rights and protections in Anglo-American law, noncitizens can be arbitrarily deported from the United States if they cannot establish residence under standards of proof that are not articulated under the law. Persons seeking political asylum can be turned away at the airport by low-level INS officers as they seek entry and summarily returned to the countries from which they fled—to possible imprisonment, torture, or death—without opportunity for a hearing or the ability to obtain legal assistance. In addition, in a blatant act of court stripping, INS decisions on individual cases of removal and adjustment of status cannot be reviewed by the courts, which makes the INS, in effect, the final judge of its own actions. And it permits such self-scrutiny despite ample evidence that the agency regularly abuses its discretion.

Similarly, the law mandates the expedited removal of persons convicted of certain crimes, expands the definition of such crimes to include relatively trivial offenses, and applies these provisions retroactively. The consequences of such mandates, even if unintended, were utterly foreseeable: the creation of an informal system of two-tiered citizenship, with some citizens getting more ample helpings of rights and due process than others. Since the law was enacted, long-term U.S. residents who have been in the United States since they were children are being detained and deported for relatively minor offenses that were committed sometimes decades ago, despite the fact that they have lived exemplary lives since these incidents occurred. The law provides no discretion for a judge to provide relief in these cases.

One poignant example of the implications of these changes in the law is the case of Olufolake Olaleye, who in 1993 attempted to return baby outfits worth $14.99 to an Atlanta store. She was accused of shoplifting the clothing because she did not have a receipt; thinking this was a simple misunderstanding, she appeared in court without a lawyer. To end the ordeal, she pled guilty to shoplifting, was fined $360, and was sentenced to a twelve-month suspended sentence and twelve months of probation. When she paid her fine, the probation was terminated.

When these events occurred, Ms. Olaleye was approved but not yet sworn in for citizenship. Because the 1996 law functions retroactively, her shoplifting offense became an "aggravated felony" under immigration law. The fact that it is not considered an aggravated felony under criminal law is irrelevant; she was denied her citizenship and placed in deportation proceedings. Without a change in the law Ms. Olaleye will be banished from the United States without the possibility of return, all for failing to produce a receipt when returning $14.99 worth of baby clothes for her two children, who are native-born U.S. citizens.

One notable case that received widespread media attention is the case of Jesus Collado, who came to the United States from the Dominican Republic as a child. When he was a teen, he was arrested and charged after his girlfriend's mother filed a complaint against him for allegedly engaging in sexual relations with her daughter, who was underage. In 1996, seventeen years later, he was detained by the INS solely on the basis of this incident. He was released from detention after several months of separation from his wife and children but still faces a deportation hearing before a judge who is not provided discretion under the law to allow him to remain in the United States.

The final assault of the 1996 immigration bill, a departure of frighteningly resonant symbolism, can only be described as "racing toward Big Brother": The law updated the employer sanctions regime by adding a computerized verification system that allows employers to verify the work authorization of new hires by accessing INS data. These "pilot" projects, mandated by statute in the five most populous states, are currently being used to verify real workers, despite evidence of problems with the INS database. An extensive recent study, based on previous experiments by the INS and the Social Security Administration (SSA), demonstrates that as often as 28 percent of the time, the system is not able to correctly verify the workers whose information is submitted.

Still worse, the statute provides no protection for workers who are the victims of errors in the system. Under the law, if the computer system is unable to verify an employee after the first or second try, neither the government nor the employer is responsible for determining the nature of the problem preventing verification. That obligation is tossed back to the employee, who must discover what information is in the computer records and correct any errors. In a final absurdity, nearly twenty years after 1984 there is no procedure in place that allows an individual access to information in the computer about his or her work eligibility.

The INS has gone still further in the use of verification and identification information as an immigration enforcement mechanism through the creation of Operation Vanguard, through which it examined the employment records of an entire industry. Operation Vanguard, which was implemented in Nebraska and Iowa in 1998 and 1999, involved demanding the employment files of the entire meatpacking industry in those states and comparing that information to INS and SSA records. The records of more than twenty-four thousand workers were examined, and nearly five thousand came back as "suspect." But of the one hundred to show up for interviews with the INS—no one knows exactly what happened to the thousands who never came forward—only thirty-four turned out to be undocumented workers. These results suggest serious problems with the quality of the data and enormous inconvenience for the thousands of workers affected, many of whom may have lost their jobs without cause. The INS views the operation as a resounding success and plans to deploy it in other industries.

It is true that the United States has a long, if imperfect, tradition of extending rights to the vulnerable. But it is also true that the current regime of immigration enforcement undermines the rights of Hispanic Americans and others often perceived as immigrants.

It is important that we dwell on the implications of the contradiction between confident expectations of the enjoyment of civil rights and the ethos of suspicious appearances derived from biological notions of race and ethnicity. The environment that has developed in the wake of the September 11 terrorist attacks makes this even more apparent. Close observers of the government's response to these events have noted a series of disturbing policy changes—interrogations of thousands of American Muslims and Arab Americans selected solely because of their ethnicity, indefinite and secret detentions, heightened surveillance, secret trials, monitoring of attorney-client communications, special visa requirements for Arabs and Muslims, military tribunals, and restrictions on student visas, among others.

Comparatively less attention has been paid to the crisis facing immigrants, their citizen family members, and their communities in the aftermath of September 11. A number of extraordinary policy shifts have taken place within the government in the period since the attacks, most of them the result of administrative actions made relatively quietly within the Justice Department or other federal agencies. Some of these changes have breathtaking implications that could affect generations of immigrants and those perceived to be of immigrant heritage.

For example, in the spring of 2002 the Justice Department reversed decades of legal precedent by declaring that state and local law enforcement agencies have "inherent" authority to enforce civil violations of immigration laws. Although many local police departments have announced that they will not engage in immigration enforcement for fear of alienating communities they seek to serve, this policy shift has created enormous fear within immigrant communities and has fostered a general reluctance to call police and fire authorities to respond to emergencies. Some immigrant advocate groups at the local level describe the environment as akin to siege.

Similarly, the Justice Department has announced that it will now enforce an obscure provision of immigration law in a way that will make it a criminal—and hence deportable—offence to fail to report a change of address to the INS within ten days of moving. The first high-profile use of this new policy was against a legal resident with several U.S.-born children who was pulled over for driving slightly over the speed limit; this incident led to the initiation of deportation proceedings for his failure, years before, to file a form with the INS that he had never heard of. If this policy shift continues to be enforced retroactively, literally millions of immigrants would be vulnerable to criminal and deportation proceedings.

Finally, in creating the new Homeland Security Agency, Congress essentially abolished the Immigration and Naturalization Service altogether, integrating its functions into the multiple pieces of the new agency. Significantly, the version of the bill that created the new agency excluded even the administration's proposals to restructure the INS and lacks targets or deadlines for the processing of visas and naturalization petitions, as well as protections for civil and human rights. Observers of this area of policy uniformly predict that handling times and backlogs will grow, perhaps dramatically, and immigration enforcement, inspections, and admissions decisions are likely to be made from a security perspective, an extraordinary development in a nation built by immigrants, whose policies have emphasized the reunification of families and resettlement of refugees.

Debate about America's immigration policy has always been something of a referendum on our immigrant past, something of a referendum on the direction in which current immigration is taking the country. In a country whose destiny has been shaped by immigration it is only fitting that the debate be vigorous and thoughtful. The current debate has a good deal more vigor than thought, however; denying the link between today's immigrants and those of the past, it has become a smoke screen behind which policies that jeopardize the rights of all Americans are enacted. At some level immigration enforcement has historically been conducted at the expense of American civil and constitutional rights, particularly those of Hispanic Americans. But more than thirty years after the enactment of this century's most significant civil rights laws, and at a moment in which the influence of Hispanic Americans on U.S. society is growing, it is long past time to insist that the immigration debate be conducted in a way that respects the contributions of all Americans and, more important, respects their rights.

Over the last decade, immigration policy, rather than helping to forge a national community, has threatened to create separate societies, subject to vastly different standards when it comes to fundamental rights—the right to work, to receive services, even to walk down the street without having one's status as an American questioned. U.S. Latinos are increasingly subject to procedures that in theory are applied to all Americans but in practice are not. The larger society has accepted these policies because the political environment fosters the notion that immigration control requires such abridgments. In no other realm do policies engender discrimination and then establish modest civil rights protections designed to undo the harm created by them.

At issue is the country's willingness to continue a tradition of being enriched by those who seek to come to America and to link their destinies with ours. It is a unique American tradition that both the immigrants and the larger society emerge from that process transformed and better for it. It is also uniquely American that this evolution has been greeted with fear and skepticism that periodically reach a fever pitch and produce policies of which we are later ashamed. Tragically, the United States has taken several steps down the path, perhaps more precisely a slippery slope, of weakening core democratic principles. The challenge for the nation is to reverse this trend and forge a dialogue on immigration policy that threatens neither our national values nor the rights of American residents and citizens.

CHAPTER 8

The United States in the World Community

The Limits of National Sovereignty

Douglas S. Massey

The large immigration of recent years has stimulated popular debate and popular unhappiness over the impact of immigration on American life. As recently as the 1950s only 2.5 million immigrants arrived in the United States, with 60 percent coming from Europe or Canada, 25 percent from Latin America or the Caribbean, and only 6 percent from Asia. Given the relatively small numbers, mostly of European origin, no one paid much attention. By the 1980s, however, immigration to the United States had nearly tripled to 7.3 million persons, only 12 percent of whom came from Europe or Canada, with 47 percent originating in Latin America and another 37 percent in Asia. During the 1990s an additional 10 million immigrants entered the country, exceeding the record pace set in the prior decade by 37.7 percent. As before, the vast majority of these new arrivals were Asian or Latin American. Not surprisingly, immigration has become a hot political issue.

In seeking to account for this tidal shift, most Americans envision a world of desperately poor people driven from their homes by privation and political repression, people who come to the United States seeking freedom and fortune. Of course, the United States has been freer and richer than most of the world for many years, but surely the United States was no less freer and richer before the 1970s.

In truth, that master image, informing as it does both popular resentment and policy debate, has been flawed in at least two ways. First, Americans tend to look at immigrants as if they were making truly personal choices. Second, our policy elites and political leadership class mistakenly act as if immigration was something to be understood and remedied within the confines of our national borders. In fact, both of these tendencies are symptoms of the same provincialism, which fails to see how much both the self and the nation are shaped by powerful structural forces in the global arena.

Why, then, are there so many immigrants? What happened between the 1950s and the 1980s to transform American immigration so radically? Many observers point to the 1965 Amendments to the Immigration and Nationality Act, which scrapped a discriminatory national origins quota system enacted in the 1920s and repealed a ban on Asian immigration dating to the 1880s. In place of these biased policies it substituted an impartial system that distributed visas on the basis of family ties to legal U.S. residents and, to a lesser extent, according to U.S. labor-market needs. It allocated a maximum of twenty thousand visas per year to each country but exempted immediate relatives of U.S. citizens from this limitation.

The new rules were phased in and implemented fully by 1968. During the 1970s immigration rose by 35 percent over the prior decade. For the first time in American history a majority of immigrants to the United States (more than three quarters) were not of European origin. In the minds of scholars and citizens this remarkable transformation followed from the provisions of the 1965 act itself, which eliminated Western Europe's privileged access to immigrant visas. Soon voters were clamoring for new legislation to restore the lost "control" over immigration that had been forfeited by the 1965 amendments. If legislation had caused the problem, the thinking went, then new legislation would solve it.

Actually, the transformation of American immigration had little to do with the 1965 amendments, and successive legislative acts did not—and could not—restore the conditions of the 1950s. The dramatic decline of immigration from Europe stemmed from changes there, not from anything that happened in the United States. After World War II Western Europe underwent a profound transformation that converted it from a region of emigration to one of immigration. By the mid-1960s labor shortages had grown so acute in northern and western Europe that governments there established formal programs to recruit immigrant workers. By the 1970s even the nations of southern Europe—Italy, Spain, Portugal, and Greece—had begun to attract immigrants. Europeans stopped coming to the United States because of structural shifts in European society itself, not because of changes in U.S. immigration policy.

The 1965 amendments also had nothing to do with the expansion of Latin American immigration. On the contrary, they functioned to restrict entry from this region. Prior to 1965 immigrants from the Western Hemisphere were exempted from national origins quotas and could enter without numerical restriction. The 1965 amendments imposed the first-ever ceiling on immigration from the Western Hemisphere (120,000 persons), and a quota of twenty thousand visas per country was applied in 1976. Contrary to popular belief, the upsurge in immigration from Latin America and the Caribbean occurred in spite of, not because of, the 1965 amendments to the Immigration and Nationality Act. Were these amendments never to have passed, immigration from the region would have been substantially greater that it actually was.

The one change that can be traced directly to the 1965 amendments was opening the door to Asian immigration that had been slammed shut at the end of the nineteenth century. But immigration from Asia would have expanded anyway, even without the amendments. In the wake of South Vietnam's collapse the United States was reluctantly compelled to accept hundreds of thousands of "boat people" as refugees. Most of them were "paroled" into the United States by the attorney general for political and humanitarian reasons, outside of the numerical limits and entry criteria established under the 1965 amendments.

Whereas only 335 Vietnamese entered the United States during the 1950s and 4,300 arrived during the 1960s, 172,000 were admitted during the 1970s; 281,000 arrived during the 1980s; and 125,000 entered during the first half of the 1990s. The U.S. misadventure in Indochina also led to the entry of thousands of Cambodian, Laotian, and Hmong refugees, who collectively totaled 300,000 by 1990. All told, about a third of Asian immigration after 1970 stemmed from the U.S. intervention in Indochina.

Thus, none of the drop in European immigration, none of the expansion of Latin American immigration, and only a portion of the increase in Asian immigration can be traced to the 1965 amendments to the Immigration and Nationality Act. Whether or not this legislation had ever passed, immigration to the United States would have been transformed. But if a change in U.S. law did not bring this about, what did?

The forces driving immigration to the United States are the same as those bringing immigrants to every other developed country in the world today. Migration is no longer restricted to a few settler societies, such as the United States or Canada. During the 1980s, immigration became a worldwide phenomenon focused on five core receiving areas: North

America (Canada and the United States), Europe (the countries of the EEC plus Switzerland, Scandinavia, and Austria), the Persian Gulf (Saudi Arabia, Kuwait, Bahrain, and the United Arab Emirates), the Western Pacific (Australia and Japan, along with Korea, Hong Kong, Taiwan, Singapore, and Malaysia), and the southern cone of South America (Argentina).

In 1998 my colleagues and I completed a systematic study of the causes of international migration within these five regions.[1] I completed my own detailed statistical analysis of the forces driving Mexican migration to the United States.[2] Both exercises yielded the same conclusions: immigration is initiated by structural changes in developed and developing nations that occur as a result of their incorporation into the global market economy, and, once begun, immigrant flows are perpetuated through self-sustaining social processes—the relay systems built out of networks of kith and kin—intrinsic to immigration itself.

The spread of markets into nonmarket or premarket societies contributes to immigration in a variety of ways. Since World War II, capitalism has steadily expanded into ever further reaches of the globe. The emergence of developing nations from their precapitalist pasts, and the shift of former socialist countries from command to market economies, creates profound upheavals in those societies. The coming of markets and capital-intensive methods of production disrupts traditional social arrangements and displaces people from customary livelihoods. The result is an increasingly mobile population of workers who actively search for new ways to support themselves. That is why most international migrants come not from poor, isolated places that are disconnected from world markets but from regions and nations that are undergoing rapid development as a result of their insertion into global trade, information, and production networks. Development—not the lack of development, as is commonly assumed—is the engine of the movement of peoples.

As developed nations participate in the global economy, they suffer new competitive pressures that segment domestic labor markets, creating strong demand for workers at the low and high ends of the skill continuum but weak demand in the middle. This splitting is most acute in certain global cities that play a key role in financing and coordinating the expanding global economy. The concentration of managerial, administrative, and technical expertise in these places concentrates wealth and increases the demand for low-wage services so that global cities attract a disproportionate share of the world's immigrants. In the United States, for example, roughly half of all immigrants go to just six urban areas that play central roles in the world economy (New York, Los Angeles, Chicago, San Francisco, Houston, and Miami).

Immigrants are channeled to these places because the same processes of market expansion that create mobile populations in developing regions also create the links of transportation, communication, and culture that make migration possible, even likely. In addition, the foreign policies and military actions that wealthy nations undertake to maintain international security, protect foreign investments, and guarantee access to raw materials further create entanglements and obligations that encourage the movement of refugees, asylees, and military dependents. The largest flows in Asia come from nations that have housed significant U.S. troop concentrations since 1945, namely Japan, Korea, the Philippines, and, of course, Indochina, which together account for 42 percent of Asian immigration.

Once begun, migration tends to perpetuate itself, in part through processes that affect the individual, in part through the social networks in which individuals are embedded. At the individual level international migrants tend to begin as "target earners," seeking to earn money quickly, attain a predetermined income goal, and return home. Yet a migrant who comes home may not be satisfied with a return to the status quo. Working in a more advanced industrial economy can lead to irreversible changes in a person's motivation. Once again, that makes additional migration more likely. So in a spiral of rising desire, satisfying the needs that originally led to migration creates new needs, just as access to high wages and the goods they buy creates new standards of material well-being and ambitions for upward mobility. Migrants grow accustomed to higher incomes. They alter their consumption patterns and adopt new lifestyles that cannot easily be maintained through local labor, making additional trips necessary.

But it's not just motivations that shift. Migrants acquire new forms of human capital—personal attributes and abilities that make them more productive and desirable in foreign labor markets. In the course of traveling and working abroad they come to learn the host country's language, employment practices, job routines, and ways of life. They make important contacts with employers, learn how to enter the country legally or illegally and discover how to manage daily life in a foreign setting. There is, then, a technology as well as a psychology of immigration, which only diminishes the costs and risks of foreign travel, while the potential benefits of foreign labor increase.

In sum, once tried, migration tends to be repeated. The more some-one migrates, the more he or she is likely to continue migrating, yield-ing a self-sustaining process of human capital accumulation that produces more trips of longer duration.

Migration has powerful effects on migrants' social capital, as well as on their human capital. Social capital refers to value that accrues from people's relationships with others. Thus, for someone considering a trip to the United States, whatever the emotional value of a tie to a current or former U.S. migrant, such bonds have a certain practical value. It's worth more than sentimentality. One can draw on it to gain access to a high-paying foreign job or to learn of cheap housing or to find out where to go if one is seriously ill. Such ties to migrants already in the host coun-try thereby lower the costs and risks—and raise the benefits—of mov-ing across national borders. In another spiral of value creation each ex-perience of migration spreads value to the migrants' friends and relatives and changes their calculus of risk and reward. To put it differently, the expansion of networks of people linked to migrants expands the social capital flowing through the entire community, which expands the col-lective inducements to migrate for everybody.

It is precisely these causal dynamics that successive adjustments to the Immigration and Nationality Act since 1965 have ignored. And it is these same dynamics that explain why such amendments have failed to restore the conditions of low, ethnically homogenous immigration characteris-tic of the 1950s. Despite encouragement by recent immigration legisla-tion, Europeans have not rejoined the flow of immigrants. Meanwhile, immigration from Asia and Latin America has continued to increase. Cur-rent U.S. policies simply do not come to terms with the fundamental forces responsible for immigration. Indeed, U.S. policy is at war with itself, si-multaneously seeking to discourage immigration with repressive sanc-tions but encouraging it through other means.

The case of Mexico most clearly reveals the inherent contradictions of these policies. From 1942 to 1964 the U.S. government actively re-cruited some 4.5 million Mexicans into the United States as temporary workers, creating the very conditions that allowed immigration to flour-ish. After 1965 the United States reversed itself and sought to discour-age the flow it had created. New restrictive policies were implemented, including lower ceilings for legal immigration, sanctions against em-ployers for hiring illegal migrants, a ban on the receipt of federal benefits by immigrants, and the allocation of more resources to the U.S. Border Patrol.

These repressive measures were spectacularly unsuccessful. By 1965 the processes of social and human capital formation had become self-sustaining. Even more ironically, even as the United States worked to strengthen its enforcement apparatus and increase barriers to the legal and illegal entry it had provoked, it pursued other policies that further increased the flow of immigration.

Under U.S. law each legal entry generates entitlements for subsequent entry for close relatives such as wives, children, parents, and siblings. The allocation of immigrant visas according to the principle of family reunification thus increases the efficiency of migrant networks and enhances the formation of social capital in sending regions. This process notably intensified in 1986 with the passage of the Immigration Reform and Control Act (IRCA), which sought to discourage undocumented migration by applying employer sanctions and increasing the budget of the Border Patrol; but it also authorized a massive amnesty program for undocumented migrants that legalized 2.3 million Mexicans between 1987 and 1990.

The paradoxical effect of legitimizing their status in the United States and solidifying their ties north of the border was to make it easier for migrants to sponsor the subsequent immigration—illegal and legal—of friends and relatives at home. Coming from a family containing someone who was legalized under IRCA became the strongest single predictor of new undocumented migration, raising the odds of illegal entry by a factor of nine, to around 35 percent in any given year.[3] Legalization also created new entitlements for admission under U.S. law, and by 1994 some 30 percent of all Mexican residence visas went to relatives of persons who had been legalized under IRCA. Thus, whereas U.S. policy grew more restrictive in some ways, in others it acted strongly to promote immigration.

The United States also encouraged Mexican immigration through its sponsorship of the North American Free Trade Agreement (NAFTA). Under this agreement powerful market forces were guaranteed to penetrate more deeply within Mexico, setting off structural transformations that inevitably displace people from livelihoods and promote migration. Since the mid-1980s Mexico has moved rapidly to eliminate tariff barriers and state subsidies that protected its industries from competition. Government-owned industries were sold off, and a state-sponsored system of communal agriculture was privatized. As a result of these changes the Mexican economy grew increasingly volatile, with periodic devaluations, recurrent bouts of inflation, falling wages, rising joblessness, and oscillations in interest rates. As other nations have discovered, the creation of a competitive market economy can be a wrenching, transformative experience.

Mexican families turned to international migration as a means of adapting to this new economic environment. By allocating workers to different labor markets (local, urban, and international) households diversify risks to family income, and by sending one or more members abroad for work they gain access to capital in the form of migrant savings. The new economy provided new means to achieve these goals, for with market integration comes new transportation links to make travel to the United States cheaper and easier, and new means of communication to transmit information rapidly throughout the continent. The expansion of travel for business, education, and pleasure in North America also creates cross-border ties and obligations.

Perhaps the most important factor fueling Mexican migration, however, is the huge stock of human and social capital available in Mexico to support international movement. After fifty-five years of continuous movement back and forth, social connections and personal experience with the United States run deep. Representative surveys reveal that half of all adult Mexicans are related to someone living north of the border and that a third have been to the United States at some point in their lives.[4] Tabulations from the 1992 Survey of Mexican Population Dynamics suggest that about a fifth of all adult Mexicans have worked in the United States.[5]

Given ongoing integration in the North American market and the huge quantity of human and social capital available to support Mexican immigration, there is probably little that the United States can do to reduce it. The most we can reasonably hope to accomplish is to direct ongoing flows in directions that are consistent with our interests. Efforts to prevent these flows, which arise as a natural consequence of social and economic forces well established on the continent, will be counterproductive, yielding the worst of all possible worlds: continued immigration on terms that are unfavorable to the country and disastrous for immigrants themselves.

The internal contradictions of U.S. immigration policy contribute directly to social and economic fragmentation in the United States. But the greatest danger does not lie in the most often cited division of our society along ethnic lines, the kinds of visible and often flamboyant tensions evident in virulent fights between blacks and Latinos, whites and Vietnamese fishermen in the Gulf of Mexico, or Anglos and Cubans in

Florida. Rather, the most virulent danger lies along the fault lines of class. Although current policies have not succeeded in reducing the volume of immigration or in redirecting it away from Third World sources, they have exacerbated class polarization and income inequality. Efforts to suppress population flows that stem from the consolidation of the North American market and are otherwise encouraged by U.S. policy have put downward pressure on wages and working conditions, giving rise to an underground economy that benefits neither immigrants nor natives.[6]

The turning point came with IRCA's passage in 1986, when the United States enacted employer sanctions, strengthened the Border Patrol, militarized the border, and generally embarked on a more repressive, punitive approach to immigration enforcement. Before this time legal and illegal migrants earned the same wages, worked the same hours, and generally experienced the same working conditions. Afterward, the labor market position of undocumented migrants deteriorated markedly. Compared to legal migrants they earned systematically lower wages, worked fewer hours, were more likely to earn below the statutory minimum wage, and were more likely to experience irregular terms of employment. Moreover, whereas analyses based on the 1980 census suggested that immigration had few significant influences on the employment or wages of natives, studies done using data from the 1990 census uncovered significant negative effects. U.S. attempts to suppress immigration seem to have increased class polarization, undermined the economic status of native workers, and marginalized immigrants in American society.

To the extent that punitive policies influence the behavior of migrants at all, they have the perverse effect of transforming circular flows into more permanent, settled communities. If the greatest risks are encountered at the border, once inside the country migrants rationally choose to stay put. Thus, when European governments suspended labor recruitment in 1973 and barred the reentry of guest workers, migrants who normally would have returned home stayed on and sent for family members. As a result Europe's foreign population grew, and its composition shifted decisively away from employed sojourners to dependent settlers. In the United States, implementation of repressive border policies in the late 1980s reduced the odds of return migration among Mexican immigrants and generated longer stays and more settlement north of the border.[7]

If repressive measures cannot stop immigration and also produce side effects that are against U.S. interests, what are the alternatives? A more successful, and realistic, approach to immigration policy might be to accept immigration as a natural outgrowth of incorporation within the global market economy and to work at encouraging its desirable features while trying to mitigate its negative consequences. Repressive enforcement would be reserved for immigrants from countries otherwise not connected to the United States by relations of trade, investment, or politics. Rather than trying to prevent the entry of immigrants from nations linked to the United States by well-established flows of capital, information, goods, and services, policy makers would work to achieve outcomes that serve U.S. interests: promoting short stays, limiting long-term settlement, encouraging return migration, protecting U.S. wages and labor standards, and encouraging economic growth in our trading partners and political allies. These goals could be accomplished in a variety of ways.

One way is to make temporary work visas freely available to prospective migrants so that people can reasonably expect to migrate again should their economic circumstances warrant, thus lowering the incentives to stay on in the receiving country for fear of not being able to return. A portion of immigrants' wages might be held back and paid to a foreign bank account only on the worker's return to the country of origin. Interest rates might be subsidized in foreign accounts to provide a return above the market, thus luring back migrants and their money. Finally, because migrants are often motivated by lack of access to insurance and capital markets, destination countries might enter into cooperative agreements with sending nations to establish public programs and private firms to meet these legitimate economic needs, policies that are quite feasible for Mexico within the NAFTA framework.

With state resources freed up from vain attempts to suppress immigration, receiving countries could increase internal inspections at work sites in sectors that employ large concentrations of immigrants, not to round up and deport illegal aliens but to assure employers' compliance with minimum wage laws, social insurance legislation, occupational safety and health regulations, tax codes, and mandated fair labor standards. Such an enforcement strategy has two advantages: it lowers the demand for immigrant workers by preventing employers from using them to avoid adhering to expensive labor laws, and it prevents the formation of an underground, clandestine economy.

Finally, given that international migration ultimately occurs as a result of the displacement of people from traditional livelihoods onto weak, poorly developed markets for labor, capital, and insurance, an indispensable part of any enlightened immigration policy should be the creation of binational programs to enhance market formation and economic growth in sending regions. Some of the initiatives already proposed to encourage return migration simultaneously achieve these goals: namely, the creation of social insurance programs and development banks accessible to former migrants. Funds for these enterprises might be raised through a special tax levied on migrant workers or their employers.

The globalization of capital and labor markets poses strong challenges to the nation-state and to the very idea of national sovereignty itself. It requires political leaders and citizens to move beyond nineteenth-century conceptions of territory and citizenship and expand them to embrace the transnational spaces that are being formed as a result of massive immigration. These changes are especially daunting because they must occur at a time of rising income inequality and growing fiscal pressure on the state.

Adapting to the reality of persistent international migration poses formidable challenges to the United States and its people, but these challenges will have to be met because immigration on a large scale will surely continue. Barring an international catastrophe of unprecedented proportions, international migration will most likely expand and grow, for none of the forces that energize it show any sign of moderating. The market economy is expanding to ever farther reaches of the globe, labor markets in developed countries are growing more rather than less segmented, transnational migration and trade networks are expanding, and the power of the nation-state is weakening in the face of this onslaught. The twenty-first century will be one of globalism, and international migration will figure prominently within it.

NOTES

1. Douglas S. Massey, Joaquin Arango, Ali Koucouci, Adela Pelligrino, and J. Edward Taylor, *Worlds in Motion: Understanding International Migration at Century's End* (Oxford: Oxford University Press, 1998).

2. Douglas S. Massey and Kristin E. Espinosa. "What's Driving Mexico-U.S. Migration? A Theoretical, Empirical, and Policy Analysis," *American Journal of Sociology* 102 (1997): 939–99.

3. Ibid.

4. Roderic A. Camp, *Politics in Mexico* (New York: Oxford University Press, 1993), 45.

5. Douglas S. Massey, Jorge Durand, and Nolan Malone, *Beyond Smoke and*

Mirrors: Mexican Immigration in an Era of Free Trade (New York: Russell Sage, 2002).

6. Douglas S. Massey and René Zenteno, "A Validation of the Ethnosurvey: The Case of Mexico-U.S. Migration," *International Migration Review* 34 (2000): 765–92.

7. Massey, Durand, and Malone, *Beyond Smoke and Mirrors.*

CHAPTER 9

"Who Cares Who Killed Roger Ackroyd?"

Narrowing the Enduring Divisions of Race

Jennifer Hochschild

"Who cares who killed Roger Ackroyd?" Edmund Wilson asked in a famous 1945 *New Yorker* essay, referring to Agatha Christie's *Who Killed Roger Ackroyd?* Finding such mystery novels "a waste of time," Wilson advised, "We shall do well to discourage the squandering of . . . paper that might be put to better use."[1] Wilson's warning might well be applied to arguments over the causes of racial animosity in America that have raged during the past several decades. It's not that asking who's to blame for racial hierarchy and division is entirely a waste of time. But it risks raising conflict without leading to illumination or productive results. The evidence on the causes of racial discord is as conflicting as it is voluminous, and the contenders hold equally passionate convictions about the causes of our nation's racial mess. I conclude not that there is no right answer to the causal question, but that I am unlikely to convince others that my answer is more right than theirs—and neither will they convince me.

We should turn instead to a question that we have a chance of answering and whose answer could make a real difference. We should ask not how we got into our racial fix but how we can fix it. For starters that query is likely to generate a less fractious and more productive conversation. Better yet, although there's no guarantee we will reach consensus, I hope to show that there is a surprising zone of agreement between the races that could serve as the foundation for an effort to narrow the enduring division of race.

At the outset we need to recognize the deep racial divide in perceptions of American politics, in beliefs about the problems faced by African
Americans, and in explanations for those problems. In a 1995 survey
more whites than blacks (63 to 56 percent) agreed that racial integration has been good for society. More whites also agreed that emphasizing "integration and opportunity" is the best means for "improving the
situation for blacks in America," whereas more blacks opted for the strategy of "building strong institutions within the black community." Such
results would have delighted Malcolm X, sorrowed the Reverend Martin Luther King Jr., and dumbfounded Governor George Wallace.[2]

As the black responses imply, a considerable proportion of African
Americans perceives whites to be deeply hostile to blacks, regardless of
what blacks do or how they live. In 1990 more than three-quarters of
black New Yorkers (compared with one-third of white New Yorkers)
agreed that it was "true" or "might be true" that "the Government deliberately . . . investigates black elected officials in order to discredit
them." Six in ten blacks (but fewer than two in ten whites) found it plausible that "the Government deliberately makes sure that drugs are easily
available in poor black neighborhoods in order to harm black people."
Among blacks, 33 percent (compared with only 5 percent of whites) even
thought it might be true that "the virus that causes AIDS was deliberately created in a laboratory in order to infect black people."[3] Six years
later, in a national sample, over two-thirds of blacks—compared with
one-quarter of whites—found the drug hypothesis plausible.[4]

Where blacks see improvement in America's race relations, whites see
worsening. From 1988 to 1993—the era of David Dinkins's mayoralty—
an *increasing* proportion of African-American New Yorkers, but a *de-
creasing* proportion of white New Yorkers, thought race relations in their
city were good. In 1994, after Mr. Dinkins lost the mayoralty to Rudolph
Guiliani, white New Yorkers who perceived any change in race relations
thought they were improving, but black New Yorkers who perceived
change thought race relations were worsening.[5]

African Americans and whites perceive the social and economic circumstances of race in widely different ways. Half or more of whites (compared with a third of blacks) mistakenly agree that "the average African
American" is as well off as or better off than "the average white person"
in terms of jobs, access to health care, and education. More than four in
ten whites (and about two in ten blacks) hold the same view with regard
to income.[6] The races also differ in their explanations of the causes of

disproportionate black poverty. Seldom do more than one-third of whites see serious racial discrimination; indeed, the number of whites who perceive racial discrimination is declining; and up to one-third of whites believe that compared with whites, blacks have *more* opportunities, are less vulnerable to economic upheaval, receive better health care, are treated better in the courts and the media, or are more likely to obtain good jobs and be admitted to good colleges. Thus over half of whites explain black poverty as a consequence of "lack of motivation" or "problems brought on by blacks themselves."

Conversely, three-fourths of blacks see serious racial discrimination, and the number of blacks who perceive rising racial discrimination is increasing. For example, fully 84 percent of African Americans (but only 30 percent of white Americans) agreed in 1995 that "discrimination is the major reason for the economic and social ills blacks face."[7] More generally, no more than one-third of blacks explain black poverty as resulting from "a lack of motivation" or "problems brought on by blacks themselves."[8]

The tremendous racial discrepancies that emerged in perceptions about O. J. Simpson's guilt provide one sharp example of disparities in perceptions of the power of race in American life. Fully 85 percent of blacks (but only 34 percent of whites) "agree[d] with the decision of the . . . jury" in the criminal trial. Only one in ten whites agreed that "the white establishment is always trying to bring down successful black people," although up to six in ten blacks agreed. Most important, two-thirds of whites concluded simply—and poisonously—that "blacks often use race as an excuse to justify wrongdoing."[9]

An equally sharp example of racial discrepancies in perceptions grew out of the 2000 presidential election. Even seven months after the electoral dispute in Florida was resolved, African Americans continued to disapprove much more than whites of "the way the Supreme Court is handling its job." Three times as many blacks as whites (45 percent to 15 percent) agreed that the failure to count some votes because of "problems with the ballots or voting machines" is "more likely to affect racial minorities." Most notably, fully 85 percent of blacks, compared with 45 percent of whites, perceived this failure to be "mainly a deliberate attempt to reduce the political power of minorities" rather than "mainly an accident" (which only 9 percent of blacks believed).[10]

These racial differences in sentiment and perception are not in dispute. But how to interpret them, or to explain the causes of the social, economic, and political disparities that presumably underlie them, is deeply disputed. There are almost as many candidates for interpretation as there are people who have sought one.

Some claim, simply, that racial disparities persist because whites are irremediably racist. Derrick Bell, the African-American critical race scholar, has argued that whites will never give up any position of power unless they are tricked into it, faced with an even worse threat (such as black rebellion), or able to perceive an ultimate advantage for whites from an apparent increase in racial equality.[11] Among the many historical incidents that demonstrate this claim, perhaps the quintessential case is the Compromise of 1876, which set the terms of black subjugation in the post–Civil War South for almost a century. In that political bargain the Democratic and Republican Parties mutually abandoned African Americans in the South to vicious white "Redeemers" in order to stabilize political and economic competition among white elites. Current practices are no different, argues Bell; indeed, we have entered a second Reconstruction. Latinos, white women, and the handicapped gained the most from the civil rights legislation of the 1960s, and affirmative action policies mostly benefit white women (and perhaps personnel managers and lawyers).

Stephan and Abigail Thernstrom offer a substantially different interpretation of racial disparities in perceptions and life chances. In their view overt prejudice and covert racism have declined to a degree that is historically astonishing: "Real progress has been made—more progress than those who put their lives on the line in the 1960s probably imagined. . . . The signs of progress are all around us, although we now take that progress for granted." African Americans used to suffer almost intolerable racist abuse, but those days are behind us now, and what racism remains is perpetuated mainly by continued insistence on racial disparities. "By no demographic or other measures are African Americans truly a people apart. . . . And yet if both they and whites believe they are, it may well become true."[12] Thus, the Thernstroms see people like Bell as inadvertently creating the very racial hierarchy they seek to destroy.

William J. Wilson proffers yet another interpretation of racial disparities. Since the 1960s, he argues, economic and social institutions have sorted Americans more by class than by race (or, as he claims in his recent work, by class in conjunction with racial discrimination).[13] Some African Americans were in a position to take advantage of the growing economy and of the opening up of educational, political, and residential opportunities in the 1960s. They attained a college education, moved to the suburbs, obtained and kept professional jobs, and have passed their middle-class status on to their children. Other African Americans were not in a position to take advantage of the new opportunities. They were left behind in cities where jobs disappeared because of global economic transformations. Through no fault of their own they ended up with atrocious schools, depopulated neighborhoods, and no chance to obtain steady and remunerative work. Over several decades these economically depressed communities have developed a dynamic characterized by disproportionate welfare dependency, class and racial isolation, crime, reliance on a drug economy, and other evils.

If none of these explanations for racial disparities sound appealing, still more radical ones abound. Richard Herrnstein and Charles Murray argue that blacks have, on average, a lower I.Q. than do whites, to which many of their problems can be ascribed.[14] Afrocentrists such as Molefi Asante and Asa Hilliard III argue that African Americans are harmed by the domination of European culture, with its cold rationalism, selfish individualism, and rigid and linear thinking.[15] John Ogbu and Signithia Fordham point out that African Americans' refusal to "think white"— to compete in white-dominated schools, job markets, and criminal justice systems—is a rationally self-protective response to a system that appears to promise equality of opportunity but actually is structured to ensure that blacks fail.[16] Dinesh D'Souza argues that most contemporary problems within the black community are caused by African Americans' own weakness of will or the "civilizational gap" between white and black cultures.[17] And there are still other explanations to choose from.

What are we to make of these multiple, contradictory interpretations of America's racial dilemma? If it is true that exponents of one view can almost never persuade others to change their mind, what would be the point of "squandering . . . paper" in that pointless effort? Analysts will never concur on whether white Americans are intentionally racist, whether American institutions create and maintain white racial domination regardless of anyone's intentions, whether blacks are capable of incorporation and ought to integrate into mainstream society, or whether racial disparities are as severe as ever. The politics are too entrenched and rewarding on all sides. The psychological and emotional investments are too strong and public for most people to be able to change their minds. It is even possible that the evidence is too indefinite or the real answer too complicated; explanations for racial disparities may vary for different individuals, communities, issues, or periods. Or the best explanation

may involve an interactive mix whose precise dynamics cannot be measured, controlled, or predicted.

"Who cares who killed Roger Ackroyd?" thus means "why bother trying to reach consensus, or even the right answer, on the deep underlying
causes of Americans' racial animosity and inequality?" But this is no
counsel of despair. It is a call to move away from the fruitless search for
basic causes toward the fruitful search for realistic solutions to our ills.

Robert Goodin's distinction between "causal responsibility" and
"task responsibility" is useful in this shift.[18] Causal responsibility occurs
when we try to find the agent(s) or situation(s) that created the problem,
identify thereby whom or what to blame, and begin to suggest solutions
to the problem. If white racism is responsible for the fact that African
Americans on average do less well than white Americans, then whites
are to blame, and the solution either lies in changing white beliefs and
behavior or in insulating blacks from the effects of racist attitudes and
practices. Conversely, if a "civilizational gap" is responsible for the fact
that African Americans on average do less well than white Americans,
then blacks are to blame, and the solution lies in changing black beliefs
and behavior.

Following the logic of causal responsibility is appealing for several reasons. First, blaming has emotional attractions. Angry African Americans
and white sympathizers want to shift attention away from the self-
inflicted destruction of inner cities and the possibility that some middle-
class blacks (like some middle-class whites) are victims of their own lack
of talent rather than of white racism. Conservatives want to divert attention from structural causes of individuals' inability to succeed and
from the vast upward transfer of wealth that has characterized the United
States since the 1980s. Second, blaming has real instrumental value, assuming that one can correctly identify who or what is to blame. There
is, after all, no point in alleviating recurrent symptoms when one could
instead be eliminating the underlying cause of the disorder—that dictum
holds for racial inequality as much as for a headache or fever.

But in race relations, as in medicine, one cannot always identify the
underlying cause or treat it even if it is identified. Here is where task responsibility enters the picture: it changes the question from "whose fault
is it?" to "what can we do?" Such a reorientation draws warrant from
the moral imperative to help someone who is vulnerable to you, regardless
of whether you had any role in causing the vulnerability. Even if people
have failed to take advantage of opportunities, as Goodin puts it, "others may still be able to act so as to avert [or correct] harm to them. To

suggest that those others should (or even that they *may*) stand idly by and watch people reap the bitter fruits of their own improvidence is surely absurd. . . . Those who have gotten themselves into a dangerous situation . . . are . . . enormously (perhaps uniquely) vulnerable to the actions and choices of particular others for getting them out of the mess. On my analysis, such vulnerabilities generate strong responsibilities."[19]

This argument implies that political actors should find those people and structures most available or most capable of solving a given problem and hold them responsible for its solution—regardless of whether they caused it in the first place. Political engagement here becomes a search for levers for action: Who can act? What can or must we do to get them to act? What resources do they need to ensure that their actions are effective? Who controls those resources? How can we get *them* to act? As these questions suggest, task responsibility is not necessarily any simpler or more straightforward than causal responsibility. But it has the distinct advantage of avoiding energy-wasting blaming and defensiveness and of focusing efforts on fixing problems rather than trying to understand or catalogue them.

How would task responsibility work when it comes to disparities between the races? Consider first the matter of *who* is charged with responsibility. For a child drowning in the river, task responsibility implies seeking the nearest adult who can swim. For a problem like racial inequality, the search is less simple because it engages issues of motive, as well as opportunity. Thus we must revert to the search for causes to the degree that determining the proximate cause of a problem helps us to determine people's motives for solving it.[20] Less abstractly, consider a black child in an inner-city school who cannot read both because a teacher believes that poor black boys cannot or will not learn and because the child's mother is illiterate and cannot help him with his homework. Both adults have the opportunity to help, but one has a greater incentive to do so. In this case those with task responsibility should first direct additional resources to the mother rather than the teacher because the greater motivation of the former will most likely outweigh the greater skill of the latter. This prescription obtains despite the fact that the teacher is arguably more to blame for the child's illiteracy. The theory of task responsibility would, second, require one to determine who has the leverage to remove that teacher from the classroom or to persuade her that all children can learn and deserve a real opportunity to do so.

There are two, perhaps contradictory, ways of approaching the question of *what?* from a framework of task responsibility. One strategy is to start with obvious problems that are relatively easily fixed.[21] *New York Magazine* once published a photo essay of school buildings with cardboard in windows, water running through hallways, and rooms too cold to work in because coal furnaces provided insufficient heat for the building.[22] We should not be surprised if black parents whose children attend such schools believe that the whites running the educational system are indifferent or even hostile. After all, repairing decrepit buildings is not hard—it takes only money, a little organizational skill, and the willingness to face down truculent custodial unions, corrupt contractors, and lazy school boards. It can, in short, be solved once people at a relatively low level of seniority are held responsible for its solution and are given the resources and authority they need to solve it.

Thus one might determine what tasks people are responsible for by seeing what they can do if their livelihoods depend on it. Accordingly, we should ensure that teachers teach all children, that employers treat all of their workers with dignity, that police refrain from harassment or unnecessary violence, and that social workers attend to vulnerable children in abusive or neglectful homes. If these actors are unwilling to take on the same task responsibility for black as for white clients, are themselves too vulnerable or short of resources to have any impact, or are carrying out a policy over which they have no discretion, we then turn to people and institutions to which *they* are vulnerable and who can make a difference in *their* lives: the school board or teachers' union, city budgeters, corporate headquarters, authors of welfare regulations, the police commissioner. And this process goes on until we find the link of the chain that can repair the school's windows, ensure children's safety as they walk to school, and teach them once they reach the classroom. Then, and only then, can we reasonably ask black parents not to blame white educational administrators for their children's failure.

The end of the chain of tasks in this model is collective task responsibility. In Goodin's scheme, beyond the circle of primary responsibility, people may have a "residual responsibility" to help when others abdicate. This broader community has an ongoing duty to monitor the situation in case its help is required. The limit of this less direct responsibility is "the limit of the vulnerable agent's needs and of the responsible agent's capacity to act efficaciously—no more, but certainly no less."[23] In political terms this precept requires that all citizens help to alleviate Americans' racial hostility, racial domination, and racial excuse making.

Responsibility will end when America's racial problem ends, or at least is dramatically reduced, and not sooner.

The question of *what* people should be held responsible for could follow a different logic. Instead of starting with the lowest level of actors working on the most direct tasks and moving outward from there, one might begin at the highest level of the collectivity and work on the largest tasks. That is, getting people out of destructive loops—low expectations, therefore low effort, therefore low rewards, therefore blaming others and lower expectations—may require "something more dramatic and frame-breaking" than the incremental, close-to-the-ground steps implied by subsidiarity as I have just described it.[24] In that case we should begin at the opposite end of the responsibility chain—with a large reframing of citizens' and leaders' tasks that will inspire people to move out of the blame game into the mode of collective task responsibility.

To continue with the example of inner-city schooling: what might be possible if citizens said, "Our task is to ensure that all children can read and calculate proficiently by age sixteen; how must we reallocate resources and efforts to achieve this goal?" Perhaps with such a reframing of large and urgent concerns, as recent federal legislation in fact claims to do, citizens and policy makers would be able to relinquish at least temporarily the temptation to blame and carp in order to contribute whatever they can to the immense and noble task at hand. That is the hope and goal of at least some of those endorsing high standards and frequent testing—the remaining question is whether policy makers will put enough resources and commitment into the schools so that systemic school reform really helps those who have been ignored or dismissed in the past, rather than further penalizing them.

I cannot here resolve the question of just how to put task responsibility into practice. But whether one starts small, with subsidiarity, or large, with reframing, one ends up sooner or later at collective task responsibility. How—in a political culture as individualistic as that of the United States and as full of racial mistrust as the survey data indicate—are we to persuade ourselves and others to accept a shared commitment to pursue racial equality and comity?

The answer, paradoxically, lies in what is usually perceived as the individualism and conservatism of the ideology of the American dream. For better or worse, that ideology is the most widely shared framing of what it means to be an American that is available to us. In fact, despite deep divisions between the races, most Americans of all races share a be-

lief in the American dream, almost no matter how it is defined or articulated. To put the point most paradoxically, our mutually shared values
of individualism and autonomy could bring us together in collective activity to attain our goals.

One can resolve that paradox through a clearer understanding of the
American dream and its implications for task responsibility. The dream
has four tenets. Together they explain *who* can participate in the dream,
what they participate in, *how* to succeed, and *why* the dream is worthwhile. The tenets combine into the following formula: everyone has an
equal opportunity to participate in a search for success as he or she defines
it, and everyone can reasonably anticipate some success. That success is
to be achieved through means under one's own control, such as ambi-
tion and hard work. Achievements must be associated with virtue to count
as true success.[25]

The polity—that is, Americans as a collectivity—is responsible for carrying out the tasks implied by the first two tenets. With regard to *who*,
only governmental policies can enforce strict nondiscrimination against
people of color, women, religious minorities, the poor, and other disfa-
vored groups. With regard to *what*, only governmental policies can provide all persons with the resources and institutional structure they need
to fruitfully pursue success. Those policies should include the availability of a good education through high school, enough shelter and sustenance so that one can focus on how to succeed rather than on how to
eat or stay warm, neighborhoods that are safe and decent enough so that
one can focus on how to pursue success rather than on how to make it
home alive, the availability of jobs for all who seek them, and a political process that allows all citizens to share in making decisions that affect them.

These are large duties. But they are balanced by equally large duties
that are held by citizens and encapsulated by the third and fourth tenets
of the American dream. Once the government fulfills its mandate to ensure equal opportunity and a reasonable chance to succeed, then individuals must accept responsibility for their own and their families' success
(or failure); and they have a moral obligation to pursue virtuous, not merely
material, success. Such a balance of responsibilities means, more concretely,
that there can no longer be publicly legitimate excuses for illiteracy *if*
schools are good, for unemployment *if* jobs are available, for abandoning one's children *if* social networks are in place, for abdicating engaged
citizenship *if* political channels are open to all, or for claiming victimhood
or an irresistible temptation to do evil *if* one is sane and competent.

How to get individuals to take responsibility for their own actions is the subject of even more political and personal debate than how to get the government to fulfill its duties. But the basic point is simple: *a focus on task responsibility in the context of the American dream provides essential balance between what the polity must do because individuals cannot, and what individuals must do because the polity cannot or should not.* The polity must provide the means to success for all; individuals must pursue that success as best they can, with help from those to whom they are vulnerable and with help to those vulnerable to them. When vulnerability reaches beyond individuals' ability to help, then task responsibility reverts again to the collectivity.

In the end this formulation can help us to overcome the deep and bitter racial divide. The key point is that Americans of all races generally agree on the tasks implied by the ideology of the American dream and on the proper assignment of those tasks to both government and individuals. Virtually all Americans endorse the values of political equality, equal educational opportunity, equal opportunities in general, and equal respect. At least three-fourths of all Americans agree that skill rather than need should determine wages, that America should "promote equal opportunity for all" rather than "equal outcomes," that "everyone should try to amount to more than his parents did," and that they are ambitious themselves.

These are not views held exclusively, or even mainly, by whites. Seventy percent of black, and 80 percent of white, Californians agree that "trying to get ahead" is very important in "making someone a true American." More blacks than whites—and large majorities in both races— endorse self-sufficiency as one of their primary goals. Slightly more blacks than whites agree that "there are more opportunities for Americans today than in the past." Finally, more blacks than whites (89 percent to 70 percent) deem it very important for the public schools to teach "the common heritage and values that we share as Americans."

The most socially engaged African Americans agree with ordinary citizens in endorsing the tenets of the American dream. At least 85 percent of leaders of all groups—including blacks and feminists, labor leaders and businessmen, Democrats and Republicans—endorse equality of opportunity over equality of results. At least seven of ten black leaders think earnings should depend on ability rather than being distributed equally. And black adults are passing on the values of the American dream to their children: three-quarters of white youths and even more black youths see "fair treatment for all" and "self-reliance" as extremely important values. Most recently, fully 90 percent or more of all groups agree that "our society should do what is necessary to make sure that everyone has an equal opportunity to succeed." Even at these astronomical levels of agreement, blacks are slightly more enthusiastic than whites, and young people are slightly more enthusiastic than their elders.[26]

This is a strong foundation of shared beliefs and values on which to build an ethos of task responsibility. It becomes even stronger when we consider the wide array of beliefs that blacks and whites share about the nature of political tasks facing the nation. On affirmative action, for example, most whites abhor "reverse discrimination" or "racial preferences"—and many blacks agree. Conversely, most blacks endorse programs to search out qualified minorities for college admissions or jobs, special training programs, wider distribution of information about jobs and other opportunities, the drawing of voting districts to ensure black representation in legislature—as do a majority of whites in most surveys.[27] Even on affirmative action, this most racially charged of issues, there is a core of agreement among a majority of African Americans and whites that politicians have done little to cultivate and work with.[28]

The same consensus can be discerned on crime. Throughout the 1990s white and black Americans agreed that crime is one of the most important issues facing their community. The two races are about equal in their mistrust of the criminal justice system (three in ten of both blacks and whites express "very little" confidence), and they usually agree on when it is and is not appropriate for a police officer to strike a citizen. They concur on the need to spend more to "halt the rising crime rate" and to "deal with drug addiction" (African Americans would like to increase spending on prevention of crime and drugs even more than would whites). Large majorities of both races concur that "the courts in this area do not deal harshly enough with criminals." Blacks and whites mostly concur on whether more tax dollars should be spent to solve eight major national problems (ranging from education to health care to crime and drug control).[29] Blacks are much more angry than whites over racial profiling and other biases in the criminal justice system, but that does not prevent them from wanting more and better protection.[30]

Or consider education: more than eight in ten of both blacks and whites agree that "the country needs common national standards of performance" for all schools. Even more members of both races further agree that the country needs *higher* standards of educational achievement. Solid, and sometimes huge, majorities also approve of "requir[ing] stu-

dents to meet higher academic standards in order to be promoted or grad-
uated," with summer school as a backup; support is even higher among
(largely non-Anglo) parents in large cities with many unsuccessful schools
such as Los Angeles, New York, Chicago, and Cleveland. Nonwhites support standards and accompanying tests even more than whites, although
African Americans worry more about the lack of sufficient resources for
their children's schools and excessive attention to test scores alone as a
criterion for promotion or graduation.[31]

One could repeat this exercise for a variety of policy issues, but the
point should by now be clear: there is much greater congruence between
African Americans and whites on underlying values and on perceptions
of essential public and private tasks than on causal explanations for the
racial problems our nation faces. It would be foolish to claim perfect congruence on policy issues; one could generate a list of disagreements between the races at least as long as the list of agreements. But there *is* a
list of agreements broad enough and specific enough to enable reliance
on task responsibility to be a plausible strategy for ameliorating America's racial anger and inequality and for lessening some of its deepest social problems.

NOTES

1. Edmund Wilson, "Who Cares Who Killed Roger Ackroyd?" *New Yorker,*
Jan. 20, 1945, 66.

2. *Wall Street Journal*/NBC News Poll, Oct. 27–31, 1995. By 2000, three out
of five whites and blacks agreed that the goal of achieving racial equality in the
United States was best approached through equal opportunity rather than integration or equal results (NBC News/*Wall Street Journal* News Poll, March 2–5,
2000).

3. *New York Times*/CBS News Poll, "Race Relations in New York City," June
17–20, 1990. African Americans with at least some college education found all
three charges much more plausible than did African Americans with less than a
high school education. Among whites the pattern was reversed. See Jennifer
Hochschild, *Facing Up to the American Dream* (Princeton, N.J.: Princeton University Press, 1995), 106.

4. *New York Times*/CBS News Poll, Oct. 10–13, 1996. On this survey, also,
more well-educated than poorly educated African Americans found the drug hypothesis true or plausible. My thanks to Michael Kagay of the *New York Times*
for analyzing the data on this and the previous poll for me.

5. Hochschild, *Facing Up*, 60–61.

6. *Washington Post,* Kaiser Family Foundation, Harvard University, *Racial
Attitudes Survey* http://www.washingtonpost.com/wpsrv/nation/sidebars/polls/
race_071101.htm, accessed April 22, 2001.

7. *Washington Post,* Kaiser Family Foundation, Harvard University, *The Four Americas* (Menlo Park, Calif.: Kaiser Family Foundation, 1995).

8. Evidence for this and the preceding paragraph are in Hochschild, *Facing Up,* 60–67. See also, "Conflict and Convergence: Race, Public Opinion, and Political Behavior in Massachusetts," University of Massachusetts McCormack Institute Poll (Amherst: University of Massachusetts, 1998); Gallup Organization, "Hispanics, Whites Rate Bush Positively, While Blacks Are Much More Negative," June 21, 2001 www.gallup.com/poll/releases/pr010621.asp, accessed Nov. 8, 2002; *General Social Surveys, 1972–2000: Cumulative Codebook* (Chicago: National Opinion Research Center, 2001).

9. Richard Morin, "Poll Reflects Division over Simpson Case," *Washington Post,* Oct. 8, 1995, A31, A34.

10. Supreme Court ratings are from Gallup Organization, "Hispanics, Whites Rate Bush." The views on voting are from *Washington Post* et al., *Racial Attitudes Survey.*

11. Derrick Bell, *Faces at the Bottom of the Well* (New York: Basic Books, 1992); Derrick Bell, *Gospel Choirs: Psalms of Survival in an Alien Land Called Home* (New York: HarperCollins, 1997).

12. Stephan Thernstrom and Abigail Thernstrom, *America in Black and White: One Nation, Indivisible* (New York: Simon and Schuster, 1997), 17, 492; for a similar argument see Jim Sleeper, *Liberal Racism* (New York: Viking, 1997).

13. William J. Wilson, *The Declining Significance of Race* (Chicago: University of Chicago Press, 1980); William J. Wilson, *When Work Disappears* (New York: Knopf, 1996).

14. Richard J. Herrnstein and Charles Murray, *The Bell Curve* (New York: Free Press, 1994).

15. Molefi Asante, *Kemet, Afrocentricity, and Knowledge* (Trenton, N.J.: Africa World Press, 1990); Asa Hilliard III, Lucretia Payton-Stewart, and Larry Williams, eds., *Infusion of African and African-American Content in the School Curriculum* (Chicago: Third World Press, 1990).

16. John Ogbu, *The Next Generation* (New York: Academic Press, 1974); John Ogbu, "Diversity and Equity in Public Education," in *Policies for America's Public Schools,* ed. Ron Haskins and Duncan MacRae (New York: Ablex, 1988), 127–70; Signithia Fordham, *Blacked Out* (Chicago: University of Chicago Press, 1996).

17. Dinesh D'Souza, *The End of Racism* (New York: Free Press, 1995).

18. Robert Goodin, *Protecting the Vulnerable* (Chicago: University of Chicago Press, 1985).

19. Ibid., 129.

20. Robert Goodin, personal communication, May 21, 1996.

21. This argument has affinities with the European principle of subsidiarity, as well as with Saul Alinsky's recipe for neighborhood regeneration and rebellion. Thus it does not have either a clear leftist or rightist caste. See Saul Alinsky, *Reveille for Radicals* (1946; reprint, New York: Random House, 1991).

22. Michael Tomasky, "All Fall Down," *New York Magazine,* Feb. 12, 1996, 44–49.

23. Goodin, *Protecting the Vulnerable,* 134–35.

24. Goodin, personal communication. As I wrote almost two decades ago, after reviewing the history of school desegregation policies, "incrementalism . . . does little to help either minorities or whites and does a lot to harm them. Half a loaf, in this case, may be worse than none at all" (Jennifer Hochschild, *The New American Dilemma* [New Haven, Conn.: Yale University Press, 1984], 91).

25. For further analysis of this ideology see Hochschild, *Facing Up.*

26. For citations and further evidence for the past three paragraphs see Hochschild, *Facing Up,* 55–56; *General Social Surveys, 1972–2000;* Pew Research Center Values Update Survey, Nov. 5–17, 1997.

27. Charlotte Steeh and Maria Krysan, "Trends: Affirmative Action and the Public, 1970–1995," *Public Opinion Quarterly* 60 (1996): 128–58; *Washington Post* et al., *Racial Attitude Survey.*

28. Jennifer Hochschild, "Affirmative Action as Culture War," in *The Cultural Territories of Race: Black and White Boundaries,* ed. Michele Lamont (Chicago: University of Chicago Press, 1999).

29. Bureau of Justice Statistics, *Sourcebook of Criminal Justice Statistics, 1996* (Washington, D.C.: U.S. Department of Justice), 114–15, 148–49; Bureau of Justice Statistics, *Sourcebook of Criminal Justice Statistics, 1999* (Washington, D.C.: U.S. Department of Justice), 102, 115, 126–27, 130–31; Jennifer Hochschild and Reuel Rogers, "Race Relations in a Diversifying Nation," in *New Directions: African-Americans in a Diversifying Nation,* ed. James Jackson (Washington, D.C.: National Planning Association, 2000).

30. To cite only one example: 37 percent of African Americans, compared with only 4 percent of non-Hispanic whites, claim to have been "unfairly stopped by police." "Poll: Racial Profiling," *Washington Post,* June 21, 2001 www.washingtonpost.com/wp-srv/nation/sidebars/racepoll/062101racepoll.htm, accessed Nov. 8, 2002. See also *Sourcebook of Criminal Justice Statistics, 1999:* 102, 109–11.

31. Jennifer Hochschild and Nathan Scovronick, *The American Dream and the Public Schools* (New York: Oxford University Press, 2003), chap. 4.

CHAPTER 10

The Ambivalence of Citizenship

African-American Intellectuals in Search of Community

Kevin Gaines

It has never been easy being an intellectual in America. The culture of the sound bite, the fetish of celebrity, and the eagerness of the news media to promote scandal rather than the public interest have eroded what little authority intellectuals ever had. But to be a black intellectual these days carries its own special vexations. On the one hand, African-American intellectuals have come to symbolize for many white intellectuals the separatist fragment that threatens American cultural unity. On the other hand, for many African Americans they seem distant and even disloyal figures in internal disputes over identity and the relationship of blacks to the larger American society and its legitimating myths.

In this swirl of debate that characterizes our post–cold war, post–civil rights moment, we might do well to remember Richard Wright's effort to balance a powerful affirmation of black identity without abandoning the ideal of a universal culture. Wright is particularly appropriate in this context, given his thoroughgoing engagement with the historical contradiction of Western culture: between the racist inhumanity practiced by Euro-Americans and their ideals of enlightenment, democracy, and human rights.

The hostility Wright faced as an independent critic of racism at the height of the cold war drove him to self-exile in France. Today's African-American intellectuals, by and large, find themselves in a less onerous, but still trying, condition of spiritual exile as they search for a community of their own. Spurned by many in black communities as " sellouts," African-American intellectuals are faulted for having more in common with the white world than with their communities of origin. Yet their efforts to counter this charge by serving as advocates of black interests provoke accusations among many white intellectuals, including many progressives, that they exploit an illegitimate identity politics of race at the expense of larger national or oppositional cultures.[1]

Despite their ostensible differences, these black and white detractors are cut from the same cloth. Both share considerable anxiety at the phenomenon of diversity. Both balk at identities they perceive as threats to cultural cohesion. Both assert purist notions of group identity: the dominant Anglo-American position falsely equating its group status with the national community; the minority African-American identity, in its own defensive quest for community, deeply ambivalent regarding its American citizenship and its membership in Western culture.

THE DRAMA OF RACIAL RESPONSIBILITY

A vivid manifestation of the black intellectual's quandary might be called *the drama of racial responsibility*. This occurs at those public gatherings of black intellectuals who speak in roundtable fashion on matters of concern to black communities. Inevitably, an impatient, even angry, questioner charges that the speaker's scholarly endeavors (and by implication, his or her relative success) have had negligible impact on the plight of impoverished inner-city blacks. What, after all the speeches, are they going to *do* about it?[2]

Such ritual moments expose a fault line within the black middle class, often pitting activists, social workers, ministers, small-business owners, and teachers—all overwhelmed by social crises—against black academics who are usually removed from poor black communities. It epitomizes the dilemma of black intellectuals, whose success and visibility within the academy is belied by the obscurity of their work within black communities and, more decisively, by their invisibility, with a handful of exceptions, so far as the mainstream media are concerned. Placed on the defensive by activist claims that they have abandoned their communities, many black intellectuals feel compelled to play their part in this drama. Hence there is a tendency for some black public scholars to proclaim themselves activists, asserting their organic connection to black communities. The recurrence of this spectacle suggests such claims are seldom persuasive.

Black intellectuals, then, cannot afford the luxury of being intellectuals. Like all intellectuals, black intellectuals are not exempt from the responsibilities of living in a racist society. But like it or not, they must serve someone else's agenda: they must defend or uplift the race, flatter impossibly narcissistic white liberal desires for authentic black resistance, or serve still others as legitimators of the status quo. Anything else, especially the vast and growing amount of important African-American studies scholarship, doesn't seem to count.

Such charges seem patently unfair given the relative powerlessness of all but a select few black public intellectuals. At the same time, the highly theoretical modes of inquiry favored within academic African-American studies, as well as the obscure jargon that often goes with them, fuels popular suspicions in black communities that intellectuals are indifferent to their yearning for knowledge that might raise up the race and its spirits. Such skepticism is reinforced by a preponderance of work that eschews the 1960s Black Studies movement's challenges to Eurocentric myths and scholarship through the recovery of once ignored— or denigrated—African-American histories. Instead, a recent tendency within African-American studies has been to debunk notions of black solidarity in ways that do not leave us with a clearer sense of the past struggles of black intellectuals and social movements but with a disabling sense of discontinuity, of fragmentation.

Henry Louis Gates Jr. is only the most famous symbol of this tendency. For years Gates has ably challenged Afrocentric myths and defended multiculturalism from attacks by cultural conservatives. Gates has also emphasized the realities of class polarization among blacks that undermine neonationalist illusions of racial authenticity. In his writings for the *New Yorker* through much of the 1990s, Gates consistently expressed a puckish skepticism about the very notion of black political solidarity. Similarly, the philosopher Kwame Anthony Appiah, noting that the concept of race is a fallacy, deemed scientifically unsound by scholarly consensus, contends that the political project of pan-Africanism, with race thinking at its core, is itself thus inherently flawed. And the black British critic Paul Gilroy has challenged Afrocentrism and black American notions of racial authenticity with an alternative model that situates black consciousness in a transnational, diasporic network. Gilroy's model of the "black Atlantic" describes a dynamic historical process emphasizing the migration patterns of peoples of African descent as crucial to the ongoing reinvention of black consciousness and politics.[3] In his latest book

Gilroy has argued that racial affiliations among blacks have become irrelevant in their provincialism and at worst reactionary given the many other possible identities one may claim as a basis for social activism.

Gilroy, Appiah, and Gates are correct to challenge parochial and racist expressions of black identity. But they would probably concede the persistent political cleavage along the black-white color line in the United States, most recently witnessed in the disfranchisement and intimidation of thousands of black voters in Florida in the 2000 election. With such powerful antagonists to black interests, African Americans will understandably wonder why such prominent black scholars condemn the lunatic fringe among blacks without "telling it like it is" when the rights of African Americans and the democratic legacy of the civil rights movement are under siege.

This postmodern version of African-American studies, it is tempting to argue, fails to enlighten our national culture on the legacies of race, slavery, and the civil rights movement. But perhaps it never intended to. Therein lies the key to its success, widely publicized in the case of Harvard's "Dream Team" of distinguished academics—a phrase, one suspects, that would be unthinkable to apply to nonblack intellectuals. This Barnumesque selling of African-American studies and "the black public intellectual" is of a piece with the corporate marketing of slain black leaders and their distorted legacies through the mass media or, worse, the false militancy and decadent misogyny of gangster rap. This conversion of critical black intellectuals into entertainment figures further fragments black collective memory and widens the gulf between black intellectuals and their communities of origin.

Filling the void in the 1990s were informal black scholars whose unscientific melanin theories pander to the masses[4] and, worse, cynical demagogues elevated by hypocritical news organizations whose feigned indignation did not preclude their willingness to profit from racism by extending a platform to the likes of Louis Farrakhan and Khallid Muhammad. Alienation is hardly a new condition for peoples of African descent. The persistence of segregation, poverty, and hopelessness ensures that the "social death," as Orlando Patterson vividly describes it, experienced by African peoples uprooted and transplanted to slave societies in the Americas retains an archetypal hold over African-American cultural memory. For many such alienation and the struggle against it cannot be relegated to a bygone past. As a result many African Americans understandably look to Africa as the basis for an authentic selfhood to be reclaimed from the dispersal and denigration of diaspora.

The right's continuing invocation of the ethnocentrism of dominant Western myths of white civilization sustains this tendency. You only have to recall the respectful attention enjoyed in some quarters by the racial libel, to borrow Derrick Bell's apt phrase,[5] of Richard J. Herrnstein and Charles Murray's pseudoscholarly apologia for racism, *The Bell Curve.* Nor was it too long ago that Dinesh D'Souza offered up his Orwellian defense of slavery and segregation, *The End of Racism,* as well as his indictment of black "civilizational deficiencies."

Such is to be expected from reactionaries. But even former civil rights allies have turned all too often to blaming the downtrodden and disempowered. To take just one representative case: in 1991 Arthur Schlesinger Jr. argued in *The Disuniting of America* that racial and ethnic identities asserted by African Americans actually endangered national unity. For Schlesinger "multiculturalism," "Afrocentrism," and "bilingualism" stood for group identities that violated norms of individualism, amounting to a divisive "tribalism" that, left unchecked, would lead to cultural fragmentation.[6]

Schlesinger was most dismayed by the curricular reforms that sought to make Afrocentric materials available to youngsters in urban public schools. Maintaining that the purpose of American education was to inculcate in its students what he termed the Western democratic tradition, Schlesinger claimed that "ethnic ideologues" fostered in minority children divisive group identities based on therapeutic myths and a disabling sense of victimhood. Advocates of multiculturalism "have filled the air with recrimination and rancor and have remarkably advanced the fragmentation of American life."[7]

The liberal Schlesinger shares an assumption with many on the right that Afrocentrism constitutes a radical or leftist ideology. But the cruder forms of Afrocentric nationalism are fundamentally reactionary; they are tainted by biological notions of race, sexism, homophobia, anti-Semitism, and resentment against the black middle class.[8] Such provincialism, needless to say, renders coalition politics impossible and thus colludes with, rather than challenges, much that is hostile to human freedom.

Afrocentrism seems an unlikely target for liberal concern. No doubt a calmer, more dispassionate assessment would judge Afrocentrism a symptom of fragmentation rather than its cause. It would be more precise to say that Afrocentrism is a response to that American form of "tribalism" known as whiteness, an identity historically founded on the exclusion of blacks and other people of color from full citizenship.

The growing body of scholarship on whiteness has its origin in W. E. B. Du Bois's account of the violent backlash of white supremacy against the democratic reforms of Reconstruction. Du Bois argued that poor whites in the South preferred the psychological "wages of whiteness" to a class-based alliance with impoverished African Americans against their common oppressors, the white southern oligarchy.[9] It was this ideology of whiteness institutionalized as social policy that offered the children of once-despised working-class immigrants the material rewards of the middle-class American dream. Their success after World War II was predicated on racial segregation and the exclusion of blacks from skilled jobs and from quality housing and education. Today white identity politics, or, as George Lipsitz puts it, "the possessive investment in whiteness," operates in the immediate context of transnational corporations moving production overseas in a race to the bottom of the global labor market alongside a gross upward redistribution of wealth and attacks on American workers through lost jobs and falling wages and benefits. The racial scapegoating of immigrants and the poor justifies slashing social programs that benefit society at large, the replacement of schools with prisons, and attacks on affirmative action, even as many poor and working-class whites stand to gain little from such punitive policies. This was the 1990s context in which racial discord issued less from the likes of Jeffries and Farrakhan than from the distracting demagoguery of Pat Buchanan and David Duke, from right-wing talk radio and from negrophobic attacks on affirmative action.

It is the problem of whiteness, then, the prototypical identity politics, that remains obscure to many, especially when it is made presentable, as when Schlesinger calls "[f]or better or worse, the white Anglo-Saxon Protestant tradition . . . the dominant influence on American culture and society." Schlesinger's insistence on the dominance of this tradition is striking in its defensive antipluralism and in his frank description of it as "white." Notwithstanding his civil rights credentials, Schlesinger's attack on Afrocentrism summons a more distant imperial past:

> There is surely no reason for Western civilization to have guilt trips laid on it by champions of cultures based on despotism, superstition, tribalism, and fanaticism. The West needs no lectures on the superior virtue of those "sun people" who sustained slavery until Western imperialism abolished it (and, it is reported, sustain it to this day in Mauritania and Sudan), who

still keep women in subjection and cut off their clitorises, who carry out racial persecutions not only against Indians and other Asians but against fellow Africans from the wrong tribes, who show themselves either incapable of operating a democracy or ideologically hostile to the democratic idea, and who, in their tyrannies and massacres, their Idi Amins and Bokassas, have stamped with utmost brutality on human rights. . . . White guilt can be pushed too far.[10]

One may grant Schlesinger's point about the naive romanticism of Afrocentrism in the face of the specific horrors and human rights abuses he cites. Nevertheless, one might do better to emphasize that such brutalities and disregard for democracy are human, not African, crimes; in all fairness he might have acknowledged, too, the West's own histories of mass cruelty from slavery to the Holocaust. The very notion of affronted "white guilt" bespeaks a desire to evade moral responsibility, to foist blame on a discredited other.

Such self-righteous diatribes can only reinforce suspicions that the construct of Western culture is irreparably tainted by racial bias. Similarly, white obsession with black identity politics is matched by the extent to which Louis Farrakhan is driven to distraction by his own anti-Semitism. Each undermines civility and the hope of a common culture. Shocking though the discovery would be for them, the exponents of both views are blood brothers in bad faith, united in divisiveness and self-delusion.

We should not be surprised that African Americans' perpetual struggle to forge a positive identity within a hostile society has been a precondition for antiracist struggles for equality. Writing during the 1960s at the dawn of African independence and the civil rights movement, the sociologist St. Clair Drake could easily have been discussing Afrocentrism when he observed that "the myth of negritude," although questionable as a romantic affirmation of African identity by westernized blacks in the diaspora, "can give confidence to the [black] masses in . . . America . . . who smart under the stigma of . . . being of African descent, although the intellectuals hardly need such a crutch."[11]

Of course, the optimism that accompanied the demise of colonialism in Africa and segregation in the South is a distant memory amidst the present crisis among African Americans beset by joblessness, poverty, social dislocation, and alienation, notwithstanding some economic improvement and the easing of the crack epidemic in recent years. The crisis, and the gulf between black intellectuals and their communities, has occasioned much uncertainty among blacks—even among those intellectuals in whom Drake had placed such confidence.

INTEGRATION AND ITS DISCONTENTS

The crisis facing disfranchised and poor blacks, together with the right-wing-led retreat from racial justice, increasingly elicits anti-integrationist sentiment among some African-American spokespersons. Although there is no hard evidence to suggest dwindling support among African Americans for equal housing and education, one frequently hears negative assessments of "integration" on black talk radio, which is perhaps the most vital institution within the black public sphere.

Anti-integrationism is the peculiar product of both the persistence of racism and the generational fading of group memory. Many of those who voice such sentiments have either forgotten or never heard of the 1960s political critique of "integration" as the tokenism employed by white employers resistant to substantive equal opportunity. Nowadays, as we often hear it from college students, journalists, entrepreneurs, and even academics, anti-integrationism tends to blame middle-class African Americans for failing to return home, as it were, for failing to "give back to the community." One is tempted to regard this as little more than the naïveté of idealistic black college students wrestling with the anxious question of their future, but the crises facing black communities foster a broader middle-class anxiety. Anti-integrationist blacks thus struggle to reconcile their own aspirations for economic security with concerns for the race's survival. Often these concerns are accompanied by self-doubt regarding their authenticity and responsibility as middle-class blacks, doubts usually projected onto those—like black intellectuals in public forums—deemed suspect by virtue of their presumed social distance from less fortunate blacks.

Anti-integrationism is not antiwhite, although it sometimes issues from the conviction that when push comes to shove—when, for example, crucial policy making, zoning, and hiring decisions are made—those decisions are largely made by and for whites. The rejection of integrationism is more concerned with *internal* divisions among blacks that find expression in wariness of those who seem to have integrated themselves *outside* the community. In this view their exodus is seen as tantamount to a betrayal of blackness and, more concretely, of those left behind. As the memory of the unifying struggle against segregation recedes, blacks of all walks of life express anxiety at internal differences of class, gender, and sexuality.

Anti-integrationism is in large part the problem of blacks who have "made it," as much as it is heard from the striving lower-middle class and the working poor. It captures an ambivalence born of their uneasy social position, wedged between the poverty and despair plaguing black communities and the acquiescence of most middle-class whites in segregation and its privileges, particularly where housing and schools are concerned. That ambivalence is seen in the achievement gap that finds many African-American students in integrated suburban school districts outperformed by students of other races. (One suspects that here the problem is a combination of several factors, including black alienation in a society founded on racial slavery; the failure, or benign neglect, of teachers and school districts; and the lack of cultural capital among many black families that are recent arrivals to middle-class status.) Integration and its discontents also find expression among black parents who, out of a misplaced desire to protect their children, join forces to ban antiracist literature from the classroom, claiming that it contains offensive language. It has been commonplace for many whites to resist confronting the realities of racism. When African Americans evince such a desire for innocence, one can only expect the shackles of their alienation to tighten.

Sentiment against integration also finds expression in Afrocentrism, which, despite its flaws, strives to revitalize the black community and its ideals against this perceived ideological and social fragmentation. However misguided some forms of it may be, anti-integrationism mainly derives from a continuing struggle for self-determination. It is part of an effort to define the political interests of communities under assault. For those who subscribe to this logic, black progress and social mobility since the civil rights era are not regarded positively but are seen as a threat to the community's health and cohesion.

Sadly, such mythic notions of blackness are often predicated on conservative gender politics of antifeminism and homophobia. Given the continued popularity of patriarchal notions of community, feminism (often merged with integration as a "white-identified" trend) and homosexuality among African Americans are lightning rods for much of the anxiety around social mobility and internal diversity.[12] Gains by black women are contrasted negatively with the economic plight of many black men. Within intellectual life the prominence of such black women novelists as Alice Walker, Toni Morrison, and Gayl Jones during the 1980s, and their frank portrayals of sexual politics, elicited scathing accusations of their racial disloyalty by black male critics. As Ann duCille has written, "for black women, membership (real or assumed) in the sisterhood of feminists is in some circles an unpardonable sin punishable by excommunication."[13] As for those African Americans whose piety makes them susceptible to the religious right's divisive and opportunistic campaign against gay rights, with its insistence of the incommensurability of gay and African-American struggles for human rights, they have nothing to gain and everything to lose. By jumping on the bandwagon of homophobia, African Americans risk their own victimization, as well, with their tacit support for the erosion of constitutional principles of equal protection and antidiscrimination.

ONCE UPON A TIME: NOSTALGIA FOR SEGREGATION

Another motif in the anti-integrationist romance among middle-class blacks and even some intellectuals is nostalgia for the era of segregation. Again, innocence and a selective vision of the past seem to be gaining on the determination of the community's elders to "never turn back." For many African Americans too young to remember the protracted and bloody struggle against Jim Crow, or those reared in northern ghettoes and thus spared the tendency of their fellow Americans to display *their* regional brand of nostalgia with the Confederate flag, the problems facing black communities are perceived as the result of integration. One black scholar contends that "[o]ut of racist segregation and discrimination, the African American neighborhood [under Jim Crow] molded a set of cohesive values, beliefs, legends, customs, and family lifestyles. . . . Racial integration of public schools transformed all of this." Another claims, as part of a critique of the use of social science theories of the damaged black psyche to support desegregation, that "[m]y disagreement with certain integrationist assumptions looms large in my analysis."[14]

This vision of a pre–civil rights golden age is motivated by the seductive fantasy of a thriving community threatened not by socioeconomic dislocations but, oddly enough, by the reforms of the civil rights era. As Adolph Reed has pointed out, such nostalgia for segregated black schools and communities reflects the sentiments of the middle-class survivors of the Jim Crow system, those privileged few who were groomed for success while the majority outside the fold languished in deprivation.[15]

Not the least of the difficulties with such rejections of integration is that they minimize the impact of structural and political changes on black communities. As Douglas Massey and Nancy Denton have shown, deindustrialization, joblessness, and, above all, residential segregation have accentuated the gap between affluent and poor sectors of the black population.[16] But for many commentators on "the black underclass," poverty and social ills are attributed less to harmful policies and power relations than to the exodus of the black middle class. Blaming the troubles of black communities on integration wrongly assumes that integration has failed when it has hardly been achieved in any meaningful sense. The political passivity and inward-turning character of this anti-integrationist position creates a vacuum to be filled by the highly organized and motivated opponents of liberal and progressive policies of racial and economic justice, voting rights, equality in education and housing, access to health care, reproductive freedom, civil liberties, and so on. In the end nostalgia unintentionally reinforces the right's attacks on governmental remedies for structural and institutionalized inequalities, for which sanctimonious preaching of self-help and personal responsibility is a dismal substitute.

BEYOND COMMUNITY VERSUS FRAGMENTATION

No other prominent black thinker offers the contemporary black intellectual a better compass in these difficult times than Richard Wright. Surely no other black intellectual so courageously faced up to the tense encounter between people of African descent and Western modernity. Refusing the easy clarities of self-congratulatory embrace and angry repudiation, Wright's legacy challenges the polarized positions of Schlesinger and the Afrocentrists and separatists.

Wright refused to minimize the racism and exploitation on which the West was founded. At the same time, he cast his lot with all that is exemplary in Western culture: the triumph of artistic expression, science, and secularism over superstition; its affirmations of human freedom against arbitrary power and authority. He envisioned a synthesis within which independent African states would democratize Western culture and perfect its ideals of freedom. To be sure, the West and African independence movements were in conflict, but their ideals and interests were far from incommensurable. To achieve that harmony, however, the West would have to change. "Westerners, high and low, feel that their codes, ideals and conceptions of humanity do not apply to black men. If until today Africa was static, it was because Europeans deliberately wanted to keep her that way."[17]

In relation to Western culture Wright regarded himself as both participant and outsider. He was sustained in that betwixt-and-between state by his contact with African and Asian nationalist leaders who sought to resolve the tension between the traditional cultures of their homeland and the West's modernity. In this ambiguous resolution there was a certain irony: Wright created a community far from home, *in exile*. He therefore would have scoffed at contemporary black nationalist efforts to locate authentic blackness in the concrete space of "the 'hood." For Wright community took a more virtual form: exile, transnational black radicalism, the life of the nomad—these were more than his way of escaping the racism tolerated by cold war liberalism. They were Wright's way toward a higher belonging, toward a different kind of home, which is why he would not have given solace to those who make such a fetish of "community" that they appear willing to turn back the clock to the era of segregation. There is little in Wright's work to lend comfort to such nostalgia. Wright's books powerfully unmask the horrors of segregation, a system of domination that produced casual brutality in oppressors and fearful accommodation and existential struggle in its victims.

According to Cedric Robinson, "Wright dismissed as fraudulent the claims of ethical superiority of . . . the liberal democrats of the West and the Marxist-Leninists of the East."[18] Pursuing his lonely, independent course through the 1950s, Wright set a lofty standard for intellectual responsibility. That spirit of critical detachment remains a standard for contemporary black intellectuals. At least it should for those of us who prefer the larger project of human emancipation to the divisive pieties of black chauvinism and white identity politics.

NOTES

I am indebted to Jonathan Rieder, Martin Kilson, Wilson Moses, Nell Painter, and, especially, Penny Von Eschen for their comments and suggestions.

1. Jim Sleeper, "Toward an End of Blackness: An Argument for the Surrender of Race Consciousness," *Harper's*, May 1997, 35–42; and Sean Wilentz, "Race, Celebrity, and the Intellectuals," *Dissent* (summer 1995). For a similar argument questioning the validity of black solidarity, but in this instance made by an African-American scholar, see Randall Kennedy, "My Race Problem—And Ours," *Atlantic Monthly*, May 1997, 55–66.

2. A textual example of the drama of racial responsibility is Eugene Rivers's indictment of black intellectuals for shirking their responsibility to the social crises facing blacks. See Eugene Rivers, "On the Responsibility of Intellectuals in the Age of Crack," *Boston Review*, Oct. 1992.

3. See Henry Louis Gates Jr. and Cornel West, *The Future of the Race* (New York: Alfred A. Knopf, 1996); Henry Louis Gates Jr., "Black London," *New Yorker*, April 28, May 5, 1997; Kwame Anthony Appiah, *In My Father's House:*

Africa in the Philosophy of Culture (New York: Oxford University Press, 1993); Paul Gilroy, *The Black Atlantic: Modernity and Double-Consciousness* (Cambridge, Mass.: Harvard University Press, 1993); Paul Gilroy, *Against Race: Imagining Political Culture beyond the Color Line* (Cambridge, Mass.: Harvard University Press, 2000).

4. The best analysis of this phenomenon is Michael Eric Dyson, "Melanin Madness: A Struggle for the Black Mind," *Emerge* (Feb. 1992): 2–34, 36–37.

5. Derrick Bell, "Racial Libel as Ritual," *Village Voice*, Nov. 21, 1995, 51–53. For a trenchant analysis of the right's attempt to consolidate its power by seeking to legitimize racism see Toni Morrison, "Racism and Fascism: The Marketing of Power," *The Nation*, May 29, 1995, 760. For a discussion of antiblack practices and sentiment prompted by the Rodney King beating and the Los Angeles uprising see Sylvia Wynter, "No Humans Involved: An Open Letter to My Colleagues," in *Voices of the Black Diaspora* (fall 1992): 13–16.

6. Arthur Schlesinger Jr., *The Disuniting of America* (New York: Norton, 1991).

7. Ibid., 130.

8. Cornel West, *Race Matters* (Boston: Beacon, 1993); Darlene Hine Clark, "The Black Studies Movement: Afrocentric-Traditionalist-Feminist Paradigms for the Next Stage," *Black Scholar* 22 (1992): 11–18; Kwame Anthony Appiah, "Europe Upside Down: Fallacies of the New Afrocentrism," *Times Literary Supplement*, Feb. 12, 1993, 24–25.

9. See, e.g., W. E. B. Du Bois, *Black Reconstruction in America* (New York: Atheneum, 1975); George Lipsitz, *The Possessive Investment in Whiteness: How White People Profit from Identity Politics* (Philadelphia, Pa.: Temple University Press, 1998); David R. Roediger, *The Wages of Whiteness: Race and the Making of the American Working-Class* (London: Verso, 1991); David R. Roediger, ed., *Black Writers on Whiteness* (New York: Schoecken, 1998); Toni Morrison, *Playing in the Dark: Whiteness and the Literary Imagination* (Cambridge, Mass.: Harvard University Press, 1992).

10. Schlesinger, *Disuniting of America*, 128–29.

11. St. Clair Drake, "Hide My Face," in *Soon One Morning: New Writing by Negro Americans*, ed. Herbert Hill (New York: 1963), 94.

12. An insightful discussion of this problem is E. Frances White, "Africa on My Mind: Gender, Counter Discourse, and African American Nationalism," in *Expanding the Boundaries of Women's History: Essays on Women in the Third World*, ed. Cheryl Johnson-Odim and Margaret Strobel (Bloomington: Indiana University Press, 1992), 51–73.

13. Ann duCille, *Skin Trade* (Cambridge, Mass.: Harvard University Press, 1996), 60.

14. Doris Y. Wilkinson, "Integration: Dilemmas in a Racist Culture," *Society* (March/April 1996): 29; Daryl Michael Scott, *Contempt and Pity: Social Policy and the Image of the Damaged Black Psyche, 1880–1996* (Chapel Hill: University of North Carolina Press, 1996), xviii.

15. See Adolph Reed, "Dangerous Dreams: Black Boomers Wax Nostalgic for the Days of Jim Crow," *Village Voice*, April 16, 1996, 24–29.

16. Douglas S. Massey and Nancy A. Denton, *American Apartheid: Segre-*

gation and the Making of the Underclass (Cambridge, Mass.: Harvard University Press 1993).

17. Richard Wright, *Black Power: A Record of Reactions in a Land of Pathos* (New York: Harper and Brothers, 1954), 343.

18. Cedric Robinson, introduction to *White Man, Listen!* by Richard Wright (New York: HarperPerennial, 1995), xix.

PART III

Unity and Division in the Political Realm

CHAPTER 11

Social Provision and Civic Community

Beyond Fragmentation

Theda Skocpol

We Americans find it easy to dwell on what keeps us apart—and perhaps nowhere is this truer than in recent debates about social policies. Reforming the "urban underclass" and ending "welfare as we know it" have preoccupied Americans since the 1960s. Recently, social security programs for the elderly have also become controversial. To judge from the tone and content of public debates—especially those featured in the mass media that feed on dramatic controversy—irreconcilable conflicts of identity and interest are at work.

Conservatives have denounced "welfare queens," and liberals suggest that mass starvation will follow the abolition of federal guarantees to aid the poor. Such disputes have pitted conservatives against liberals and bitterly divided blacks and whites, scapegoating millions of single mothers and their children in the process. Meanwhile, "intergenerational warfare" has been fanned by pundits who claim that overly generous Social Security and Medicare expenditures for retirees are certain to "bankrupt" the nation and undermine the economic future of "our children and grandchildren." America cannot help young families, fiscal conservatives declare, unless it radically trims or restructures social programs tied to an aging population of greedy Baby Boomers. Americans, it appears, are hopelessly divided by—and about—social provision.

Contemporary conservatives blame the situation on modern liberalism. In the conservative imagination liberalism has taxed and spent the country beyond its means in order to fund overly generous "entitlements"

that undermine personal and family responsibility. Liberal-sponsored welfare programs have had an especially scabrous effect, conservatives believe, turning poor people into dependents, penalizing responsible middle-
class taxpayers, and undermining the integrity of families. Liberalism is
portrayed as the enemy of community and an agent of fragmentation,
turning young against old, class against class, and black against white.

Although there may be bits of truth in this indictment, conservative
charges against liberalism are remarkably unhinged from a full understanding of what has been most legitimate and effective in the long haul
of American social provision. So intense have been recent ideological battles that Americans today barely remember our national history of generous social programs that built bridges across groups while opening opportunities for countless individuals. This history transcends today's
disputes between liberals and conservatives because broad and effective
American social programs started long before the New Deal, let alone
the Great Society.

Since the nineteenth century America's most effective and beloved social programs have given benefits or services to millions of citizens in return for their contributions to the nation and local communities. They
have helped individuals and families not in narrowly circumscribed categories but across the lines of class, race, and place. America's most effective systems of social provision have flourished through civic partnerships between government and voluntary associations that enrolled
millions of citizens as active members. State and civil society worked together to support families and communities.

We need to be reminded of this hopeful history for at least two urgent
reasons. Telling the story of some of our successful efforts to help one
another will help us assess what has gone awry in U.S. social politics since
the 1960s, as liberals and conservatives alike have abandoned formerly
successful formulas for social provision in American democracy. And
telling that story will help us imagine bringing ourselves together once
more in pursuit of a shared civic vision of opportunity and security for
all American families.

THE FORMULA FOR SUCCESS
IN AMERICAN SOCIAL POLICY

Although some might quibble, most would agree that common public
schools, Civil War benefits, early-twentieth-century programs to help
mothers and children, Social Security, Medicare, and the GI Bill of 1944

have been among America's finest achievements in social policy. Each of these milestones has made life much better for a great many individuals, families, and communities.

The story starts in the nineteenth century. The United States was the world's leader in the growth of widely accessible public education, as primary schools, followed by secondary schools, spread throughout most localities and states. Much of this expansion occurred in the decades before the Civil War. After that conflict the nation created another set of massive social programs, Civil War benefits, which included disability and old-age pensions, job opportunities, and social services for millions of veterans and survivors of the massive Union armies that fought and won the Civil War. By 1910 more than a quarter of all elderly men, and more than a third of men over 62 in the North, were receiving regular payments from the federal government on terms that were extraordinarily generous by the international standards of that era.[1] Federal spending on these pensions constituted 25 to 40 percent of the national budget in the decades around 1900.

Programs to help mothers and children proliferated during the 1910s and early 1920s. Forty-four states passed laws to protect women workers and mothers' pensions to enable poor widows to care for their children at home.[2] Congress established the Children's Bureau in 1912, and in 1921 it passed the Sheppard-Towner Act to fund health education programs open to all American mothers and babies.

The Social Security Act was passed in 1935; subsequently insurance for the elderly became its most popular part, eventually expanding to cover virtually all retired employees and providing survivors' and disability protections as well. Most employees and their dependents were covered by the 1960s. Modeled in part on Social Security, Medicare was added to the system in 1965.

The GI Bill of 1944 offered a comprehensive set of disability services, employment benefits, educational loans, family allowances, and subsidized loans for homes, businesses, and farms to sixteen million veterans returning from World War II. Smaller versions of the GI Bill also extended aid to veterans of the Korean War and to others who served in the 1950s and 1960s. The families of veterans, as well as the veterans themselves, were greatly helped by GI Bill programs.

These popular and effective programs are highly diverse. Emerging at different times, they covered various swatches of the population. Nevertheless, they have important features in common that constitute a recurrent formula for policy success and social unity in American democracy.

In the first place, those policy milestones and the movements supporting them have aimed to give social benefits to large categories of citizens in return for service to the community (or to help people prepare to serve the community). The most enduring and popular social benefits in the United States have never been understood either as poor relief or as mere "individual entitlements." From public schools through Social Security they have been morally justified as recognitions of—or prospective supports for—individual service to the community. The rationale of social support in return for service has been a characteristic way for Americans to combine deep respect for individual freedom and initiative with due regard for the obligations that all members of the national community owe to one another.

A clear-cut rationale of return for service was invoked to justify the veterans' benefits expanded in the wake of the Civil War and World War II.[3] Less well understood, though, is the use of civic arguments by the educational reformers and local community activists who pioneered America's public schools. They argued for common schools not primarily as means to further economic efficiency or individual mobility but as ways to prepare all children for democratic citizenship.[4] Similarly, early 1900s programs for mothers were justified as supports for the services of women who risked life to bear children and devoted themselves to raising good citizens. Back then, women's groups argued that needy mothers (like all other mothers) served the community and thus deserved pensions just as much as former soldiers.

Social Security and Medicare today enjoy a profound moral underpinning in the eyes of most Americans.[5] Retirees and people anticipating retirement believe they have "earned" benefits by virtue of payroll contributions. But contrary to claims by many pundits and economists, the exchange is not understood as narrowly instrumental. Most Americans see Social Security and Medicare as a social contract enforced by, and for, contributors to the national community. The benefits are experienced as just rewards for lifetimes of contributions through work, not simply as returns-with-interest on savings accounts.

Second, successful U.S. social policies have built bridges between more and less privileged Americans, bringing people together—as worthy beneficiaries and as contributing citizens—across lines of class, race, and region. Even if policy milestones started out small compared to what they eventually became, the key factor has been the structure of contributions and benefits. Financed by broad-based taxes, successful social policies have delivered benefits to more and less privileged Americans at the same time, even if some extra help has been provided to less privileged beneficiaries (as in today's Social Security system). America's most successful social policies have been broad and encompassing and therefore not labeled "welfare" programs.

Public schools, for example, were founded for most children, not just the offspring of privileged families, as was originally the case with schools in other nations.[6] Civil War benefits and the GI Bill were available to all eligible veterans and survivors of each war. Although mothers' pensions eventually deteriorated into "welfare," they were not originally stigmatized in this way.[7] During the early 1900s a great many American mothers who lost a breadwinner-husband could suddenly find themselves in dire economic straits. What is more, early federal programs for mothers and children were universal. The Children's Bureau was explicitly charged with serving all American children,[8] and its first chief, Julia Lathrop, reasoned that if "the services of the [Sheppard-Towner] bill were not open to all, the services would degenerate into poor relief."[9]

Social Security and Medicare are today's best examples of inclusive social programs with huge cross-class constituencies. Although Social Security is the most effective antipoverty undertaking ever run by the government of the United States, its saving grace over the past several decades—during an era of tight federal budgets and fierce political attacks on social provision—has been its broad constituency of present and future beneficiaries, none of whom understand it as "welfare."[10] Were Social Security and Medicare to be divided into residual social safety nets versus individualistic private market accounts, they would soon be on the road to moral, political, and fiscal demise. America would not just be making a technical or budgetary adjustment. Especially in the case of Social Security, even partial privatization would undercut a successful solid program that, with minimal "bureaucratic" hassle, enhances dignified security for millions of working families.

Finally, broad social policies have been nurtured by partnerships of government and popularly rooted voluntary associations. There has been no zero-sum relationship between state and society, no trade-off between government and individuals, and no simple opposition between national and community efforts. America's policy milestones were developed (if not always originated) through cooperation between government agencies and elected politicians, on the one hand, and voluntary associations, on the other hand. These voluntary associations are not confined to nonprofit, professionally run, social-service agencies but include voluntary citizens' groups as well. The associations that have nurtured major U.S.

social programs have usually linked national and state offices with participatory groups in thousands of local communities.

Public schools were founded and sustained by traveling reformers, often members of regional or national associations, who linked up with leading local citizens, churches, and voluntary groups.[11] The movers and shakers behind early 1900s state and national legislation for mothers and children were the Women's Christian Temperance Union, the General Federation of Women's Clubs, and the National Congress of Mothers (which eventually turned into the PTA).[12] Civil War benefits ended up both reinforcing and being nurtured by the Grand Army of the Republic (GAR).[13] Open to veterans of all economic, ethnic, and racial backgrounds, the GAR was a classic three-tiered voluntary civic association, with tens of thousands of local "posts" whose members met regularly, plus state and national affiliates that held big annual conventions.[14]

Social Security has had a complex relationship to voluntary associations. During the Great Depression a militant social movement and voluntary federation of older Americans, the Townsend movement, pressed Congress to enact universal benefits for elders. But Social Security definitely did not meet the specific demands of the Townsend movement (which wanted every retired man or woman to be given an immediate pension of $200 a month on the condition that he or she would retire and open up jobs for younger Americans during the Depression).

Today more than thirty-five million Americans fifty years and older are enrolled in the American Association of Retired Persons (AARP), whose newsletters and magazines alert older voters to maneuvers in Washington, D.C., that may affect Social Security and Medicare. The AARP does not have very many local membership clubs—and this absence is surely a source of some weakness in the association. Still, many elderly Americans participate in locally rooted seniors' groups, including the union-related National Council of Senior Citizens, which has played a key role in advocating for Medicare. Along with unions and religious congregations, federal, state, and local governments have done a great deal in the past thirty years to create services and community centers for elderly citizens. An important side effect has been considerable social communication, civic volunteerism, and political engagement among older Americans.

The final example of government-association partnership in the expansion of inclusive U.S. social provision is perhaps the most fascinating: the crucial role played by the American Legion in lobbying for and shaping the GI Bill of 1944.[15] In return for service, the GI Bill gave benefits, including home mortgages, business loans, and farm loans, as well as training and education benefits and support for families while a veteran studied. The education benefits were designed to maximize opportunities for millions of individual veterans to enroll in any program or institution that would accept them. But the GI Bill became as generous and flexible as it did only because it was championed by a nationwide, locally rooted, voluntary federation, the American Legion.[16] The Legion pressured conservatives in Congress, who were reluctant to give generous educational benefits to returning World War II veterans. The Legion also reshaped the proposals of the wartime Roosevelt administration, whose "planners" had initially wanted to limit college benefits to one year for all veterans, followed by additional years of college restricted to a small minority approved by the colleges and universities. In the end millions of GI Bill beneficiaries did very well in college; the various provisions of the GI Bill ultimately helped about half of the young families in the postwar United States. But if benefits had not been initially opened up to many more than the Roosevelt administration first envisaged, the egalitarian potential of the bill would not have been realized.

AFTER WORLD WAR II: RACIAL DIVISIONS AND GENERATIONAL IMBALANCE

Given the repeated success of broad social provision in American democracy, one might imagine the concept would endure, especially after the civil rights revolution of the 1960s cleared the obstacles to African-American participation in elections and other civic institutions. But for complex reasons both of circumstance and strategic choice, liberals and conservatives turned away from the best tradition of inclusive social provision, fanning instead the flames of racial and generational controversy. The Democratic Party and liberals abandoned a long-standing formula for successful social policy making and became entangled in controversies of race and generation that have increasingly fragmented Americans into camps of black and white, old and young, middle class and underclass.

As these divisions have become bitterly politicized, moreover, socioeconomic gaps have grown, dividing the most economically privileged and politically influential Americans from all others. Contemporary liberalism has been woefully unable to highlight this very real problem or to bring the majority of Americans together to address it.

The contradictions that have gripped American social politics since the 1960s were not immediately foreseeable in the aftermath of World War II. During the Depression and the war many Western nations launched comprehensive systems to guarantee citizens full employment and social provisions. In the United States, too, New Deal reformers battled for broad protections for all citizens or wage earners. But by the 1950s the United States was left with only one relatively universal permanent program—Social Security's contributory disability and retirement insurance. Other attempts to institutionalize broad social programs were defeated, and America was set on the road to a "missing middle" in social provision—the relative absence of protections for working-aged adults and their children that pertains today.

For many younger American families the GI Bill of 1944 and subsequent veterans' legislation temporarily filled such gaps in protection. Hearty postwar economic expansion, coupled with the age-cohort-specific social investments promoted by veterans' programs, ensured the "rising fortunes" of many young American adults after the war. Especially well served were those working- and middle-class whites who entered the labor force, married, and raised children from the late 1940s into the 1960s. But after that the impact of the GI Bill faded, just as the national economy was about to take a turn for the worse for young workers and families.[17]

CONFLICTS ABOUT "WELFARE"

As the generational imbalance in U.S. social provision became apparent with the waning of the effects of the GI Bill, there was an obvious solution: the United States could have done more for *all* parents and children rather than simply expanding preexisting, New Deal–style Social Security for the elderly and "welfare" for a few of the very poor. This might have happened starting in the 1960s, but racialized disputes over "welfare" sidetracked the nation.

A new era of cross-racial politics might have blossomed after African Americans finally achieved civil rights between 1955 and 1965. Briefly in the mid-1960s liberal Democrats gained executive power and majorities in Congress, and some dreamed of "completing" the social and economic agendas left over from the unfinished New Deal reforms of the 1930s and 1940s. Active full-employment programs might have been designed to make sure that every American adult could get job training and a job with wages and benefits sufficient to support a family. Such employment programs would have aided the poor along with other Americans, offering help to all nonelderly adults willing to serve the nation through work. Progressives in the 1960s might also have fashioned new security programs such as universal health coverage—a social benefit vital for any family trying to raise children.

But this was the path not taken. In the immediate aftermath of the civil rights struggles in the South, it proved impossible to unite unions and civil rights activists, despite efforts by leaders like Walter Reuther, Bayard Rustin, and Martin Luther King Jr. National-level policy making went forward in already-well-worn grooves. The legacies from the New Deal era encouraged policy makers to model Medicare on Social Security, thus restricting universal health coverage to the elderly. Existing patterns of macroeconomic management encouraged the Kennedy and Johnson administrations to use "commercial Keynesian" tax cuts to stimulate the national economy.[18] Tiny job-training programs and targeted welfare efforts were all that remained to help the very poor. Between the mid-1960s and mid-1970s millions of needy single-parent families were added to the welfare rolls, becoming eligible as well for Medicaid and other means-tested assistance.[19] This helped countless poor mothers and children but left millions of other poor and less privileged families out in the cold.

A fierce political backlash against liberalism soon gathered force. As many Americans faced declining economic prospects from the early 1970s, and as more and more women entered the wage-labor force, welfare programs directed at poor mothers, who were often stereotyped as black, could easily be portrayed as unfair. Conservatives played this theme for all it was worth, and many ordinary Americans responded. It has hardly mattered that most welfare mothers have had to work part-time off the books simply as a matter of survival.[20] The point is more cultural and political: Aid to Families with Dependent Children (AFDC) benefits, originally conceived as "mothers' pensions," lost their legitimacy in an era of racial conflict, declining wages, and widespread female entry into the wage-labor market.

For more than a generation welfare served as a spectacularly successful conservative political battering ram against "liberals." Republican president Richard Nixon expanded welfare benefits (as well as affirmative action), then turned around and criticized these policies to spark conflicts among Democrats. Ronald Reagan featured antiwelfare appeals as part of his winning campaign for the presidency in 1980. Intellectual and political attacks on welfare subsequently deepened and spread to

Democrats—culminating in the bipartisan congressional majorities that voted to "end welfare as we know it" in August 1996. In U.S. politics it has always been difficult to justify social benefits for the poor alone and never more so than in recent decades.

Liberal Democrats missed opportunities and worked themselves into a political impasse. The long-standing formula for successful American social provision—giving support to people across classes who are seen as "contributors" to the community—was *not* extended after the GI Bill into new programs for the nonelderly. Welfare programs proliferated instead but soon became racially controversial and culturally delegitimated in an era of changing roles for women. After the 1960s nobody in the Democratic base was happy. Welfare efforts failed to reverse economic and family trends that meant poverty for more and more families, and millions of downscale Americans were left without forms of assistance (such as Medicaid) that were available to some of the very poor.[21] All of this placed the Democrats in an untenable situation: they came to be seen as champions of ineffectual poverty programs rather than as advocates of opportunity and security for all families. Republicans, meanwhile, turned more and more toward racially divisive maneuvers and efforts to shrink government and cut taxes on the rich. No one, it has seemed, is able to speak up on behalf of a social politics that would benefit the less privileged while bringing most Americans together.

ADVOCACY DISPUTES OVER "ENTITLEMENTS"

The War on Poverty and Great Society could be dismissed as "mistakes" made by liberals, who failed to replace the fading GI Bill with broad new social programs for all working families, black and white alike. Broad social programs, the core of the New Deal, survived and even expanded. Social Security pensions for the elderly became more generous in the late 1960s and early 1970s, as benefits for the poor were raised and retirement pensions were indexed to inflation. Medicare, moreover, was added to Social Security, offering considerably more access to adequate and affordable health care for virtually all elderly citizens.

But even these achievements, championed by liberal Democrats, became a source of renewed political controversy from the 1980s onward, as conservatives learned to highlight the sharp generational imbalances in U.S. social provision as a whole as part of a broader right-wing strategy, as Stuart Butler and Peter Germanis have shown, to undermine popular support for Social Security.[22] Late-twentieth-century America ended up with generous social supports only for the retired elderly, making it possible for opponents of a strong governmental role in social provision to appeal to young working adults and parents as taxpayers rather than as beneficiaries of public social programs.

Taken together, the War on Poverty, the Great Society, and many of the social-policy initiatives sponsored by moderate Republican president Richard M. Nixon aimed to help poor children and working-aged adults, especially African Americans who had not been fully incorporated into the economic growth or social insurance protections of the postwar era. But when the dust settled, the broadest and costliest achievements focused on the elderly. The most important federal innovations were Medicare, enacted in 1965, and the 1972 indexing of Social Security pensions to inflation. During the "Reagan era" of the 1980s, moreover, cutbacks occurred primarily in welfare programs for the poor and not in these popular social insurance programs, which covered the middle-class elderly along with working poor retirees.

Today grand schemes for reconstructing U.S. social policy are promoted in generational terms. The fiscally conservative Concord Coalition, for example, proclaims loudly that too much is being done for the elderly and calls on the nation to balance the federal budget by slashing "middle class entitlements."[23] At the other end of the political spectrum groups like the Children's Defense Fund insist that more must be done to uplift poor children. The United States stands out among advanced industrial nations today for the prominence of arguments about generational conflict. There is no evidence that younger Americans actually resent adequate provision for their parents and grandparents through Social Security and Medicare. But advocacy groups and partisan politicians can readily create public controversies about the sharp imbalance between America's relatively generous and comprehensive social programs for all of its elderly citizens and its paltry efforts to help only a minority of nonelderly adults and children. The majority of American working-aged adults have a right to wonder how their values and interests are reflected in all of this.

Ordinary Americans have even more reason to wonder about this now because how the United States "does politics" has changed just as much as the nature of the programs liberals or conservatives propose. Partnerships between broad citizen membership associations and government have eroded since the 1960s. Especially at the national level, U.S. politics has become the affair of professionally run, top-down advocacy groups. Once American social policy discussions were carried on by, and through, political parties that had some popular organizational roots and among nationwide membership associations (like the American Legion, or the AFL-CIO trade unions, or farmer or business groups) with a presence in localities and states, as well as in Washington, D.C. No longer. Now American political parties—and especially the Democratic Party—are little more than collections of fund-raisers, pollsters, and media consultants.[24] And the groups active in social-policy disputes—especially on the so-called liberal side of battles—are almost invariably professional offices situated in Washington, D.C., or New York City, concentrating on media relations and congressional lobbying.

Ordinary citizens rarely belong to these groups. At most, they are mailing-list members, periodically asked to send checks to keep the operation going. Certainly, ordinary citizens have few organized venues in which to talk among themselves or talk back to national leaders. Thus, battles over such fundamental matters as the future of Social Security are largely waged among think tanks, foundations, and detached advocacy groups such as the Concord Coalition and the Third Millennium.

In sum, in the period since the 1960s the long-standing formula for successful social policy making in American democracy has vanished. New social programs have not been devised to bridge social divisions; nor have they been justified as returns for citizen service. Surviving broad programs, such as Social Security and Medicare, have been stigmatized as generationally divisive—a message that has had some resonance among younger Americans because there is, indeed, a vacuum in U.S. social provision for working-aged families. Buffeted by ideologically polarized arguments, Americans speak less and less of social programs as rewards for, and supports for, individuals' contributions to the national community. And partnerships of voluntary membership associations and government have been displaced by a national politics increasingly run from the top by professional consultants and advocacy groups.

GETTING AMERICA BACK ON TRACK

Given these troubling recent developments, what can Americans now do to fashion social policies that would bring most of us together and address social inequalities, rather than fuel continuing partisan and racial conflicts? The answer may be that little can or will be done, that current divisions and fruitless battles over revamping U.S. social provision will continue. The country may well be headed toward doing less and less to support most families through government. We may simply encourage citizens to sink or swim in competitive labor and capital markets: working-aged citizens must get ahead through wage-work alone, and elderly retirees must increasingly rely on private savings and investments. Much of what is advocated by conservative Republicans and by "New Democrats" of the Democratic Leadership Council points exactly in this direction.

But it doesn't have to stay this way. There are stirrings among progressives and other Americans who care about broad and equitable social programs that could reestablish the old formula for successful social policy in a new era. Already existing security programs may end up being reformed in ways that retain their shared character and generous guarantees to the retired elderly. And new social supports for all working families may be fashioned in the era after welfare "as we knew it."

Many Americans are bestirring themselves to support Social Security and Medicare, refusing to heed the call of advocacy groups trying to push us into deeper and deeper generational warfare. Social Security and Medicare, argue many liberals and key groups like the AFL-CIO, can be adjusted for the future in cautious ways that preserve their cross-class nature and their moral legitimation as socially guaranteed rewards for lifetimes of work. Social Security and Medicare are the most important "family" supports the United States has right now, and we can be sure that most nonelderly Americans, especially women, are just as aware of their value as are current retirees. The American public remains cautious about major changes in these programs, and, especially given the vagaries of an uncertain world economy, calls for sharp cutbacks in Social Security or for restructuring it into a series of individual market-investment accounts may not carry the day, especially in the wake of the economic downturn that followed the recent economic boom.

Even as they defend and update Social Security and Medicare, Americans who care about equality and social cohesion realize that they need to address the "missing middle" in social provision. Of late, some voices have been raised on behalf of working families and, above all, working *parents*. As Sylvia Ann Hewlett and Cornel West have argued, it is time for the United States to devise a new "GI Bill"–style set of supports not just for poor children but for all families with children.[25] Working parents could be at the center of a new round of inclusive social policy making that stresses vital contributions to the nation and extends support across lines of race and class. And they could also be key actors in institutions and associations that helped to bring about such social supports.

The rationale for a new round of inclusive social supports is powerful. The twenty-first-century United States will have a growing economy able to support pensions and health care for the elderly *only* if the workers of today and tomorrow are healthy, well educated, and productive. Parents must do well at their uniquely important job if a good national future is possible. Families need a sense of security; working adults have to have opportunities to get ahead; and mothers and fathers must be able to afford to spend time at home and in their communities. Children need safe, good schools and supportive activities. Parents are the ones who must take the lead, working with teachers and community associates to ensure good schools and engaging activities. Businesses, in turn, might benefit over the long run from a society more supportive of families raising children, the workers of tomorrow.

Currently, America treats parental work as a kind of private luxury. Higher incomes and glamorous freedoms go to individuals who take off on their own or shirk their responsibilities. Workplaces and the economic rules of the game make life hard for family men and women. Parents end up making disproportionate sacrifices—to do the very work of raising children, on which we all depend! The nation has a stake in fashioning a more family-friendly economy and society. Public social supports and our employment system could honor and facilitate the work of parents, recognizing that parental service to the community and nation is vital.

This is not the place to detail technical policy prescriptions; it is possible, however, to outline the goals of a national partnership with parents that will promote security and opportunity for all American families. Work in the United States should be made more hospitable than it now is to family life. In a nation that values work as highly as the United States does, parents need to provide for themselves and their children through work. Adults must therefore be able to find jobs and take advantage of opportunities for education or training. All jobs must have decent wages and health and pension benefits that make family life viable. There could be rights to paid family leave on terms that make it truly available to all employees. Because parents need time as well as money, we as a nation could work toward the norm of a thirty-five-hour workweek (with pay remaining at least at the level it was before the reduction in hours).

U.S. family structures have changed markedly over the past few generations, and social programs will surely be adjusted in response. Ways could be found to bridge conservative and liberal concerns. Public policies—taxes, benefits, and marriage rules—can be structured to support married parenthood. At the same time, Americans recognize that there are many divorced and single parents doing the best they can. If marriages fail, there can be social supports to help children and the parent who takes responsibility for them, including automatic systems of child support that allow a custodial parent to work less than full time and still provide for children.

Another area of possible partisan convergence focuses on making communities safe and supportive for families and children. Today liberals and conservatives agree that there must be tough crime laws and active measures to make neighborhoods safe, clean, and orderly. Americans want schools that are held to high standards and are able to afford small classes with administrators and teachers free to innovate.

Pursuit of family security through a partnership with all American parents could revitalize the tradition of successful social policy making in U.S. democracy. Americans have long believed in linking national social provision with important individual contributions to community well-being. Responsible parents are critical to the nation's future, yet today their efforts are undervalued and poorly supported. Mobilizing government to work with nongovernmental institutions to better support parents could strengthen Americans' sense of community across classes, races, and places.

The point is not simply the vast mass of potential voters that can be culled from all the individual parents. Not every American adult is a parent (in fact there are more U.S. adults living alone and proportionately fewer families with children than ever before). But demography has never been destiny for social policy. All kinds of Americans will find the themes of responsibility and social support for parents morally compelling. Even retirees—who may not be active parents now and vote against active parents in school budget referenda—are often grandparents who care about their children and grandchildren. Elders also understand the nation's and their own stake in productive workers.[26] It is an odd feature of U.S. politics today that so many pundits are declaring "generational warfare" just as the country faces the prospect of more elders but fewer dependent children per adult worker. Retirees, working-aged adults, and children can all flourish together. An aging society is not a zero-sum game.

Some liberals may feel that it is best to avoid talking about families, lest we exacerbate racially charged divisions between dual- and single-parent families. But family-friendly policies are vital for both sets of families, and public leaders need not adopt a morally relativist stance in discussing them. We can acknowledge that two married parents are best for children, even though most of us are personally acquainted with mothers (or fathers) who have to soldier on outside of this ideal situation. As policies are formulated to help parents and their families, Americans can acknowledge the tension between ideals and second-best necessities, while extending support to all working mothers and fathers.

History tells us that a morally grounded appeal to shared concerns will always do better in American politics than any explicit call for race- or class-based mobilization. The needs of less privileged Americans must be at the center of national concern, but a politics focused on class or racial redistribution alone will not achieve this goal. The entire history of successful social policy making in American democracy suggests that the best way to help less privileged or formerly excluded groups is to include them in broad civic and governmental efforts that encompass the middle class at the same time. Encompassing social policies not only avoids isolating and stigmatizing the poor, but it also builds social legitimation and political support across lines.

Unions, religious congregations, responsible business people, parent-teacher associations, and community groups of all kinds can surely find common ground in support of parent-friendly programs. As concrete victories are achieved, parent-friendly policies can generate new resources and social connections—in local communities, at workplaces, and across the nation. Such resources for parents—and connections for and among parents—would not be overtly partisan. But in real life they would help family-friendly politicians to run for office and, equally important, prompt such politicians to do worthwhile things once they get into office. More civic infrastructure centered on parents can only be good for the future of democratic politics in the United States. This is not a trivial consideration in the wake of dwindling numbers of eligible voters who have participated in recent elections. Institutions and associations involving families and parents and grandparents along with children could conceivably become new civic partners with government in the next round of broad American social provision.

BRINGING OURSELVES TOGETHER

Commentators on American life often stress the ways in which political and policy disputes reflect divisions created by underlying interests of race, culture, class, or partisanship. But this classic assumption must be turned on its head, not simply out of some moral impulse but because American history requires it. Politics and the state are not helpless witnesses to those divisions. Government efforts—especially social policies—can either exacerbate conflict or diminish it. Throughout American history, from schools and Civil War benefits through programs for mothers and children and the elderly, there have been broad, encompassing social policies that furthered social unity even as they helped huge numbers of Americans. And they succeeded because they invoked an enduring moral principle: those who serve the community (or are preparing to do so) deserve the nation's succor in return.

Alas, in the decades after the 1960s Americans lost sight of this wisdom. They forgot what they once knew. Instead of healing the rifts between black and white, rich and poor, old and young, U.S. welfare policies divided Americans. And so in the wake of the 1996 decision by President Clinton and the Republican-dominated Congress to end the federal government's commitment to "welfare as we knew it," we face a fork in the road. Liberals and conservatives can continue to wrangle about narrow programs to help or discipline the very poor, about whether the elderly or poor children deserve public generosity. Or Americans can understand the futility of such debates and turn instead toward a broader conception of support for all American families—devising ways to help all parents, while expecting them to contribute through work and responsible nurturance of the young. Social Security and Medicare can be adjusted for the future and supplemented with broad new protections for working-aged adults and families raising children.

For those of us who want to help the vulnerable while furthering a new sense of national unity, the goal of "Family Security for All" is an excellent beacon on which to set our sights. History shows that this objective holds promise for revitalizing the best possibilities of inclusive social provision known to American democracy.

NOTES

1. Theda Skocpol, *Protecting Soldiers and Mothers: The Political Origins of Social Policy in the United States* (Cambridge, Mass.: Belknap Press of Harvard University Press, 1992).

2. Mark Leff, "Consensus for Reform: The Mothers'-Pension Movement in the Progressive Era," *Social Service Review* 47 (Sep. 1973).

3. See Skocpol, *Protecting Soldiers and Mothers,* 148–51; and Davis R. B. Ross, *Preparing for Ulysses: Politics and Veterans during World War II* (New York: Columbia University Press, 1969).

4. See Mustafa Emirbayer, "The Shaping of a Virtuous Citizenry: Educational Reform in Massachusetts, 1830–1860," *Studies in American Political Development* 6 (fall 1992): 391–419; and David Tyack and Elizabeth Hansot, *Managers*

of Virtue: Public School Leadership in America, 1820–1980 (New York: Basic Books, 1982).

5. Eric R. Kingson, Barbara A. Hirshorn, and John M. Cornman, *Ties That Bind: The Interdependence of Generations* (Washington, D.C.: Seven Locks Press, 1986); Stanley B. Greenberg, *The Economy Project* (Washington, D.C.: Greenberg Research, 1996).

6. Ira Katznelson and Margaret Weir, *Schooling for All: Class, Race, and the Decline of the Democratic Ideal* (New York: Basic Books, 1985).

7. See Skocpol, *Protecting Soldiers and Mothers,* chap. 8.

8. See Skocpol, *Protecting Soldiers and Mothers,* chap. 9.

9. From a letter quoted in Louis J. Covotsos, "Child Welfare and Social Progress: A History of the United States Children's Bureau, 1912–1935" (Ph.D. diss., University of Chicago, 1976), 123.

10. Hugh Heclo, "The Political Foundations of Antipoverty Policy," in *Fighting Poverty: What Works and What Doesn't,* ed. Sheldon H. Danziger and Daniel H. Weinberg (Cambridge, Mass.: Harvard University Press, 1986), 312–40.

11. Tyack and Hansot, *Managers of Virtue.*

12. See Skocpol, *Protecting Soldiers and Mothers.*

13. See Skocpol, *Protecting Soldiers and Mothers,* chap. 2.

14. Charles Stuart McConnell, *Glorious Contentment: The Grand Army of the Republic, 1865–1900* (Baltimore, Md.: Johns Hopkins University Press, 1992).

15. See Ross, *Preparing for Ulysses;* Theda Skocpol, "Delivering for Young Families: The Resonance of the G.I. Bill," *American Prospect* 28 (Sep.–Oct. 1997): 66–72; and Theda Skocpol, "The GI Bill and U.S. Social Policy, Past and Future," *Social Philosophy and Policy* 14 (summer 1969): 95–115.

16. William Pencak, *For God and Country: The American Legion, 1919–1941* (Boston: Northeastern University Press, 1989).

17. Sheldon Danziger and Peter Gottschalk, *America Unequal* (Cambridge, Mass.: Harvard University Press, 1995).

18. Margaret Weir, *Politics and Jobs: The Boundaries of Employment Policy in the United States* (Princeton, N.J.: Princeton University Press, 1992).

19. James T. Patterson, *America's Struggle against Poverty, 1900–1980* (Cambridge, Mass.: Harvard University Press, 1981).

20. Kathryn Edin and Laura Lein, *Making Ends Meet* (New York: Russell Sage Foundation, 1997).

21. Rebecca M. Blank, *It Takes a Nation: A New Agenda for Fighting Poverty* (Princeton, N.J.: Princeton University Press, 1997).

22. Stuart Butler and Peter Germanis, "Achieving a Leninist Strategy," *Cato Journal* 3 (fall 1983): 547–61.

23. Peter G. Peterson, *Facing Up: How to Rescue the Economy from Crushing Debt and Restore the American Dream* (New York: Simon and Schuster, 1993).

24. Marshall Ganz, "Voters in the Cross-Hairs: How Technology and the Market Are Destroying Politics," *American Prospect* 16 (winter 1994): 100–109.

25. Sylvia Hewlett and Cornel West, *The War against Parents: What We Can Do for America's Beleaguered Moms and Dads* (Boston: Houghton Mifflin, 1998).

26. Paul Adams and Gary L. Dominick, "The Old, the Young, and the Welfare State," *Generations* 19 (fall 1995): 38–42.

CHAPTER 12

Stable Fragmentation in Multicultural America

Paul Starr

The complaint is familiar: Americans no longer identify with their nation and its common good but only with their tribe and its particular interests. Conservatives see this "new tribalism" as threatening to devalue America's national achievements and undermine patriotism; some liberals say it undercuts the sense of mutual obligation vital to the welfare state and complicates the formation of broad, progressive political coalitions.

The pattern of social cleavages, however, may be neither as new nor as threatening as those views suggest. No doubt, when Americans disagree about education, moral conduct, and many other issues, they often divide into groups defined by race and ethnicity, religion, gender, and sexual orientation. These groups have distinctive and persistent voting patterns, and politicians and parties cultivate their support today as they did in the past. In recent years such groups as women and gays have been newly assertive, but even their demands for rights and representation generally follow paths well worn by groups that preceded them. The "politics of identity" has had more impact on culture than on politics in the conventional sense. If we take the party system and national elections as the decisive arenas of political change, there is little evidence of rising social fragmentation as driving forces.

Americans, to be sure, are not only diverse—they are divided. The U.S. political system, however, discourages aggravating those fractures as a strategy for winning national elections. Raising the "temperature" of social antagonisms risks not only mobilizing threatened groups but also alarming other people and institutions that are determined to maintain civil peace. Such appeals may draw sufficient response to mount a challenge in the primaries (especially because of low and unrepresentative voter participation), but they are unlikely to build majorities in general elections.

The result is not harmony but stable fragmentation—the political containment of social divisions. The policies affecting groups and their relations with parties and coalitions continue to be the subject of normal political jockeying. But the clashes for change tend to be fought out in highly circumscribed ways, and there are strong pressures to avoid explosive conflict, as the 1996 presidential election illustrates.

COME THE COUNTERREVOLUTION?

As the 1996 election cycle began, four related trends appeared to be shaping the politics of race, gender, and group rights—all of which suggested that 1996 might be the climactic year of social counterrevolution.

First, there was an accelerating decline in legal and political support for race-conscious policies. The courts were steadily restricting, if not totally eliminating, the use of race-conscious remedies in the award of government contracts and jobs *(Adarand v. Pena)*, admissions to public institutions of higher education *(Hopwood v. Texas)*, and design of legislative districts *(Shaw v. Hunt)*. Republicans who formerly supported affirmative action, notably California governor Pete Wilson and Senate Majority leader Robert Dole, reversed themselves and called for colorblind policies; Wilson succeeded in banning race-conscious admissions at the University of California. Early polls forecast a big majority for the California Civil Rights Initiative (CCRI), which was being put to the voters to ban all use of racial and gender preferences in state decisions. Political observers suggested that because of California's critical importance in the presidential election, the mere presence of the CCRI on the ballot could make affirmative action a central national issue in 1996.

Second, there was a continuing shift in political initiative and mobilization away from the organizations that have long advanced the claims of racial minorities. The NAACP was consumed in internal feuds and financial disarray; the older civil rights leadership generally seemed to have less capacity to mobilize energies in the black community than did such figures as Louis Farrakhan and Al Sharpton. Yet this new leadership had no moral authority in the larger society, and its rise created deep unease among liberals and threatened old coalitions. The difference in responses to the verdict in the O. J. Simpson trial highlighted the yawning gap that now seemed to divide even white liberals from black America.

Third, a male cultural and political awakening seemed underway. The archetypal voter of 1994, analysts said immediately after that election, was the now-legendary angry white male. With the biggest talk radio audience in America, said to number twenty million, Rush Limbaugh (and talk radio itself) became the symbol of male backlash. A new movement among Christian men called Promise Keepers was filling large stadiums. Among blacks, Farrakhan's Million Man March also called for masculine discipline, moral improvement, and collective self-affirmation, not for rights or benefits (even when the Republican Congress was curtailing them). Meanwhile, feminist groups, like the older civil rights organizations, appeared to be in disarray, thrown on the defensive by attacks on political correctness and affirmative action and by the revitalized Christian right.

Finally, political opposition to both illegal immigration and high levels of legal immigration was on the rise. California again seemed a harbinger of national trends with the passage in 1994 of Proposition 187, which helped salvage Wilson's flagging bid for reelection. When the courts blocked enforcement of the provisions of 187 denying public education to the children of illegal immigrants, congressional Republicans sought to give the states express authority to do so. Even many Democrats were now calling for restrictions on legal immigration as a strategy to raise stagnant wages.

The eroding legal foundations of affirmative action, loss of influence of responsible black leadership, a male cultural and political awakening, and a backlash against immigration and immigrants all seemed to be powerful trends in the wake of the 1994 election. Some serious analysts wondered whether America might be at a turning point comparable to the end of Reconstruction. But it has not quite worked out that way—at least not yet.

DURABLE LIBERALISM: IDEAS BECOME PEOPLE

President Clinton's political revival and the lost momentum of the conservative revolution in 1996 have many plausible explanations: Republicans overreached by shutting down the government, Clinton artfully repositioned himself, Dole ran a thematically incoherent campaign. Beyond these immediate influences, however, there may be another cause: the 1990s did not see a change in public sentiment that could trigger a full-scale social counterrevolution.

The long-term trends in public opinion show a general rise in liberal attitudes and beliefs during the 1960s and 1970s that has since leveled off but has not been reversed. The principal exceptions to the overall trend have been public views of crime and taxes. But on racial and gender discrimination and equality, the patterns in public opinion established a quarter-century ago have held firm, and on a few issues, such as abortion, some evidence indicates a continued increase in liberal opinion.[1] It is easy to forget that at midcentury nearly all occupations in the United States were racially and sexually segregated; blacks and women were routinely excluded from economic and educational opportunities. Today no significant force in American politics questions the fundamental legitimacy— indeed, heroism—of the civil rights revolution. Even the supporters of the CCRI, for example, represented their cause as a return to the original commitment of civil rights to color-blind decision making and invoked the authority of Martin Luther King Jr. The basic legitimacy of women's rights is also not in doubt. For example, television coverage of America's triumphant women athletes at the 1996 Olympics reminded viewers that it was only in the past two decades, thanks to federal regulation, that schools had to devote their athletic budgets equally to women's sports.

The women at the Olympics are a good illustration of a more general phenomenon. Equality for women was once an idea. Then it became policy. Today it is people—national heroes, as well as millions of girls on soccer fields and basketball courts—who have inherited the benefits of a national transformation. Young women may take that legacy for granted and not think of themselves as feminists, but they won't easily give up what they now believe to be theirs as a matter of right.

Demographic diversity is another source of the social entrenchment of liberal ideas and policies. Since the 1960s, when racism was written out of our immigration laws, America has become irreversibly multicultural. Multiculturalism is best thought of not as a weird educational philosophy but as the latest phase of the expanding conception of American identity and culture. As American national identity changed with the arrival of immigrants from southern and eastern Europe, so it has changed again with Hispanic and Asian immigration. Universalism in immigration policy was once an idea. Then it became policy. Now it's people— millions of newcomers who in the process of becoming American have changed what it means to be American.

Against the enormity of these changes in the American civil regime the trends that began in the 1990s look less formidable. To be sure, the decline of racial preferences in the public sector has had real consequences. But the restriction of race- and gender-conscious legal remedies, which have never enjoyed majority support, touches only a limited aspect of the larger transformation that has occurred. The new system of "status relations" penetrates deep into civil society. The United States may well eliminate the use of race- and gender-conscious remedies in the public sector without reversing the deeper change because Americans have acquired new habits of diversity that will outlast the formal requirements of law.

American society is hard to change, but having changed, it will be hard to change back again. It is this deeper reality that came to the surface as the 1996 election unfolded.

BACK FROM THE WEDGE

Several other influences on the candidates prevented 1996 from becoming the year of the social counterrevolution. On the Democratic side some writers and magazines urged abandoning affirmative action and curtailing immigration, but the counterpressures in the party on both issues were overwhelming. If Clinton had turned against affirmative action, he would probably have faced a divisive primary challenge from the left; he was also so personally identified with affirmative action— hadn't he promised a cabinet that "looked like America"?—that he couldn't have reversed himself without severely aggravating doubts about the constancy of his commitments. And in a general election the potential gains among "angry white males" were counterbalanced by potential losses among women and racial minorities. Moreover, as the debate unfolded among Democrats, even many who disliked affirmative action began to worry that the absolute color-blindness advocated by Republicans failed to address many situations in which taking race into account was reasonable.

To comply with *Adarand,* the 1995 Supreme Court decision that imposed the same strict-scrutiny requirements on the federal government that *Croson* had imposed on lower jurisdictions, the Clinton administration had to reassess federal programs using race-based criteria. The administration's reassessment, directed by George Stephanopoulos and Christopher Edley Jr., largely confirmed existing policy.[2] "Mend it, don't end it," became the party consensus, without any protest from moderate and conservative Democrats. Yet support for maintaining affirmative action did not run deep; despite his many visits to California, for example, Clinton did not campaign against the CCRI, although in the final week he did speak out against it.

On the Republican side the failure of the candidacies of Wilson and Pat Buchanan reduced the likelihood that affirmative action and immigration would become central issues in the 1996 campaign. Similarly, the grassroots Republican support for the leading Republican defender of affirmative action, Colin Powell, suggested that the issue was not that potent even among Republicans, and Powell's unchallenged standing as a man of principle complicated any effort by Dole to make race and "quotas" central issues of his candidacy. The gender gap also inhibited full exploitation of wedge issues. If Dole had pursued a hard-edge, Limbaugh-style campaign, he would have had even less chance of bringing back the moderate women voters that he was losing.

To be sure, Dole reversed himself on affirmative action as he did on supply-side economics, and in the home stretch, desperate to win California, he tried to link his fortunes to the CCRI. But it was too late to redefine his candidacy. Just before the Republican convention, Dole made his defining decisions: the endorsement of the 15 percent tax cut and the selection of Jack Kemp. With those choices he opted for the growth-oriented, sunshine conservatism of the supply-siders over the midnight-in-America, culture war conservatism of the Buchananites. Kemp had opposed Proposition 187 and supported affirmative action; like Powell he obstructed Dole from fully exploiting immigration and affirmative action, and he himself refused to take on the offensive role. If Dole had struck Buchanan's themes from the start, he probably would have fared no better than he did—not only because, luckily, he lacks the talent of a true demagogue but also because of deep public resistance to polarizing appeals that threaten the national civil accord.

On election day Dole nonetheless paid an enormous price for his policies on affirmative action, immigration, and other wedge issues, losing among women and Hispanics by historic margins. The patterns in congressional races were the same, although less accentuated. The Hispanic vote was both larger than in earlier elections and more sharply Democratic, thanks in part to Republican policies denying benefits to legal immigrants that had encouraged immigrants to naturalize and then to show up at the polls. One striking upset was the triumph of Loretta Sanchez, the Democratic challenger to the right-wing congressman Robert Dornan in a district in Orange County, California, that was long a bastion of conservatism but has now become 30 percent Hispanic.

Clinton's turnaround victories in Florida (the first win by a Democrat since 1976) and in Arizona (the first since 1948) also benefited from significantly improved percentages among Hispanic voters. In Florida Clinton won only about half of the predominantly Cuban Hispanic vote, but this was a marked improvement among a traditionally Republican constituency. In Arizona Clinton won the Hispanic vote by a ten-to-one margin. In California Hispanics also voted as a Democratic bloc in numbers that previously were characteristic only of African Americans.[3]

Twenty years ago there was much discussion of a "power shift" to the conservative Sun Belt, in part because of its rapidly growing population. What the theory of Sun Belt conservatism failed to anticipate, however, was the emergence of what might be thought of as the Latinized South—the strip across the southernmost rim of the United States running from Florida through Texas, New Mexico, Arizona, and California, where Hispanic voters constitute a growing share of the electorate. Clinton's victory in all those states except for Texas may foreshadow a Democratic revival in the congressional races of the Latinized South, as the southern votes for Goldwater in 1964 and Nixon in 1968 anticipated later Republican gains by southern congressional delegates. To be sure, Clinton's victory in 1996 did not translate into significant Democratic gains in the congressional seats for the Latinized South, but that is the historic pattern: the advantages of congressional incumbency delay the impact of social and political change.

Thus the more immediate relevance of these changes may be to presidential elections. Republicans have always counted on heavy majorities in Orange County to win California; the supposed "Republican lock" on the electoral college in the 1980s depended on an edge in three big states—California, Florida, and Texas—all of which may now be in play because of the southern-rim demographic trends. Of course, neither the gender gap nor the Democratic hold on Hispanic and other minority voters need be fixed in eternity. The Republican Party may respond to these patterns by choosing more female and minority candidates and by modifying its policies. If it moves toward more liberal views, it might further reduce social tensions. But, given the influence of the right in Republican primaries and local and state parties, another line of response seems more likely.

THE POTENTIAL FOR "SOFT" FRAGMENTATION

Some conservatives have suggested a direction for national policy, a kind of synthesis of privatization and separatism, that may be the basis of future support from minority groups. Michael Lind has referred to this strategy as "right-wing multiculturalism."[4] I think of it as "soft fragmentation." The basic idea is to extend opportunities for privatization to minority groups, encouraging them to go their separate ways in schools, charities, and other institutions. Conservative advocates of school choice, for example, now appeal to blacks and Hispanics for support on the proposition that they too should be able to have private or charter schools, even those established on the basis of ideals, such as Afrocentric education, that the public as a whole doesn't approve of. Historically, the "common school" played a central role in establishing a common culture, but despite concern about the new tribalism, conservatives overwhelmingly favor vouchers or other proposals for choice that would erode the common-school tradition. In California and other states, referenda to establish voucher plans have repeatedly lost, but the charter school movement is making rapid progress and may represent a kind of early-stage soft fragmentation of the public educational system.

A second example of soft fragmentation is the attempt to move social programs from the government to private and religious groups. For example, Senator Dan Coats, who in the 1990s introduced a comprehensive Charity Reform Act that would let individuals assign $500 of their tax liability to a private organization, joined with William Bennett in organizing a Project for American Renewal aimed at a large-scale devolution of functions from government to churches and other private groups. Coats contends, "Every dollar spent by families, community groups, and faith-based charities is more efficient and compassionate than any dollar spent by the federal government."[5]

If public institutions continue to deteriorate, representatives of minority groups may be increasingly tempted to take these offers of financing for private and separatist programs. But the dangers are obvious. The secession of the poor would only reinforce the secession of the successful that Robert B. Reich has warned against.[6] The more affluent members of a community would have even less sense of responsibility for the education of poor children or amelioration of poverty than they do today if those functions are devolved to private and religious institutions. If taxpayers can assign some of their tax payments to private organizations, they are likely to follow current patterns of giving and contribute

to churches and other organizations that primarily serve their own social strata or ethnic or local community.[7] The result would drain resources
from the low-income minority communities with greatest needs. Republicans' confidence in the efficiency and fairness of private giving is,
one might say, more "faith based" than evidenced based.

Soft fragmentation also comes dressed in a theory of social evolution.
Many conservatives, most prominently Newt Gingrich, have promoted
Alvin Toffler's thesis that the trend of the new information age is toward
"demassification"—the replacement of mass production and distribution
systems by more specialized and fragmented institutions.[8] Supposedly,
the efforts to introduce markets into public education and to devolve social programs on churches and private organizations reflect the same
broader trend evident in such industries as communications (the decline
in market share of the television networks, for example). But the analogy breaks down. Schools are primarily a local responsibility; vouchers
and charter schools erode the authority of a local democratic institution,
the elected school board. Private and charter schools diminish the likelihood that members of different groups in a community (and their children) will be obliged to work together. Similarly, substituting private and
religious welfare activities for public programs eliminates public deliberation on problems of distributive justice. If only the operations of programs were being privatized, that would be one thing. But what is being
privatized is also the discussion about what schools and public policies
should be.

The conservative hostility to public institutions and preference for
"empowerment" and "choice" may be intended as a reaffirmation of individualism, but choice permits self-sorting by groups. And the kind of
sorting most likely in our society would mean fewer occasions for Americans to meet and work together with people who are different from them.
What started out as soft fragmentation could end up generating much
harsher antagonisms.

THE SOURCES AND LIMITS OF HARMONY

Looking at tribal violence elsewhere, we Americans take pride in our
peaceful diversity—and well we should. We owe our civil peace, however, not only to tolerant attitudes but also to institutions that have recently, if not always in the past, kept appeals to tribal passions in check.
The violent ethnic, racial, clan, and religious conflicts that tear so many
societies apart do not simply spring up from irrational ancient blood

feuds, like spontaneous wildfires. The matches have often been lit by groups and parties, sometimes governments, strategically pursuing political objectives—as in the former Yugoslavia, where Slobodan Milosevic sponsored greater Serbian nationalism to preserve his regime; and in Rwanda, where the Hutu government deliberately planned the massacre of the Tutsis in the spring of 1994. Hatred, like money, is a resource mobilized for power.

In America today, fortunately, there are strong deterrents to the mobilization of hatred. The electoral system inhibits aggressive expressions of tribal identity. Virtually all dominant institutions in the society—corporations, the military, the universities, community organizations—have a stake in preserving a peaceful civil regime. Americans may not always like each other; we may not want to be like each other. But few of us want to put at risk the communities, businesses, and nation that we have made together.

The American founders worried about the difficulty of preserving a large and heterogeneous republic. How impossible a task it might have seemed to them if they had anticipated the scale and diversity of our society today—yet it works. We have evolved into a stable half-integrated society: diverse in the daylight, divided at night. Sporadically, some event underscores the divisions, and we realize how far we are from coming together in the great American family of political speeches. It is a great achievement that we are more diverse and more equal in our rights than we were only a few decades ago. It is extraordinary that we welcome strangers into our midst as readily as we do. But we go home to many separate worlds, and as long as politics keeps those worlds from colliding, most of us would just as soon live without any deeper communitarian harmony.

NOTES

This article was written in December 1996.

1. Tom W. Smith, "Liberal and Conservative Trends in the United States since World War II," *Public Opinion Quarterly* 54 (1990): 479–507. See also Benjamin I. Page and Robert Y. Shapiro, *The Rational Public: Fifty Years of Trends in Americans' Policy Preferences* (Chicago: University of Chicago Press, 1992).

2. *Affirmative Action Review: Report to the President* (Washington, D.C.: White House, 1995).

3. Patrick J. McDonnell and George Ramos, "Latinos Make Strong Showing at the Polls," *Los Angeles Times,* Nov. 8, 1996.

4. Michael Lind, *The Next American Nation* (New York: Free Press, 1995).

5. Dan Coats, "Re-funding Our 'Little Platoons,'" *Policy Review* 75 (Jan.–Feb. 1996).

6. Robert B. Reich, *The Work of Nations* (New York: Alfred A. Knopf, 1991).

7. See Teresa Odendahl, *Charity Begins at Home: Generosity and Self-Interest among the Philanthropic Elite* (New York: Basic Books, 1990); and Julian Wolpert, "Delusions of Charity," *American Prospect* 23 (fall 1995): 85–88.

8. Alvin Toffler, *The Third Wave* (New York: Morrow, 1980).

CHAPTER 13

The Moral Compassion
of True Conservatism

John J. DiIulio Jr.

The final decades of the last century are rightly considered a period of
conservative ferment. From the Reagan years through Clinton's declaration that the era of big government is over, and beyond into the new
century, in many respects the nation's ideological center of gravity
shifted. But for all this ferment, there have been a lot of false prophets
and pretenders claiming the mantle of conservatism.

Our image of conservatism has been obscured most obviously by the
insistence of liberals that conservatism is by its nature divisive, ethnocentric, bigoted, mean-spirited, selfish, irrational, and anti-American.
More critically, many self-proclaimed conservatives have given credence
to that liberal charge, in part by failing to fulfill the precepts of true
conservatism. Decades ago Clinton Rossiter observed that, compared to
their European cousins, American conservatives were bound to be "anti-
statist." But that did not mean they had "to go blithely to the extreme
of rugged individualism" or dwell so "exclusively on the points of conflict
in the relationship of individual and society, ignoring man's need for the
sheltering community."[1]

It would be totally incorrect and grossly unfair to tar all positions held
by self-described contemporary conservatives—paleo-, neo-, cultural,
religious—with this brush. To cite just a few diverse examples out of
dozens over the past years, William Bennett has shamed the music industry for promoting violent and vulgar lyrics among children, challenged
the alcohol industry for concentrating crime-and-disorder-producing out-

lets in poor neighborhoods, and cautioned against the excesses of welfare "reform." James Q. Wilson has dramatized the socioeconomic inequalities and conditions that have produced two nations; and a number of senators—and now the current administration of George W. Bush—have worked to refine new federal policies that permit nondiscriminatory religious organizations to access government funds for social and antipoverty services.

These thinkers have been on to an important truth, which all too often so-called conservatives have forgotten: as a public philosophy conservatism is a moral and moralizing social force. Distance conservatism from its moral roots; strip it of its collective responsibilities—familial, local, and national; reduce it to an intellectual or political hired gun for individualistic, materialistic, utilitarian, and commercial interests; and you are left with an irreligious, just-leave-me-alone, reflexively antigovernment libertarianism at home and an unpatriotic, globe-trotting, corporate welfare culture both at home and abroad.

True conservatism flows from a single unifying belief: God. In private life and in the public square good liberals can take Him or leave Him, but true conservatives must always seek Him and strive to heed Him. In the conservative creed human beings are moral and spiritual beings. Each of us has God-given personal rights and God-given social duties, God-given individual liberties and God-given moral responsibilities. In "the conservative mind," as Russell Kirk described it, "a divine intent rules society as well as conscience, forging an eternal chain of right and duty which links great and obscure, living and dead. Political problems, at bottom, are religious and moral problems."[2]

True conservatives truly believe in the God of Abraham. They may agree that religion reduces social deviance or that religion tempers popular passions, but they never profess religion for purely prudential purposes. There are no atheists, Straussians, or social engineers in truly conservative foxholes.

CALLING "LARGER COMMUNITIES"

True conservatism follows an ancient religious teaching about family, community, and government: subsidiarity. The faith-anchored formulation of subsidiarity that I love best is that of my own Roman Catholic catechism. The Church's catechism defines the family as "the original cell of social life," the "community in which" we first "learn to care and take responsibility for the young, the old, the sick, the handicapped, and the poor." Following the subsidiarity principle, we must "take care not to usurp the family's prerogatives or interfere in its life." Following the exact same principle, however, when families cannot fulfill their responsibilities, "larger communities" have "the duty of helping them."

But which "larger communities" are to help distressed families, how, and under what conditions? "Excessive intervention by the state," the Catholic catechism cautions, "can threaten personal freedom and initiative. . . . The principle of subsidiarity . . . sets limits for state intervention." That, however, is only half of the principle. The other half is that "larger communities," up to and including national political communities of citizens acting through their democratic governments, must support the family "in case of need and help co-ordinate its activity with the activities of the rest of society, always with a view to the common good." Fidelity to the "common good" requires that each of us work to bring about a condition of "social well-being" in which we "make accessible to each what is needed to lead a truly human life: food, clothing, health . . . and so on."

MINISTRY *AND* MEDICAID

As Dan Quayle has argued, "When families are happy and healthy, communities thrive."[3] The family is our best department of health, education, and welfare. Granted, but how should a true and truly subsidiarity-minded conservative respond, say, to the plight of the estimated 1.3 million children in America today whose fathers are imprisoned, whose families are often broken and impoverished, and whose own life prospects, as all the research shows, are thereby badly diminished, facing illiteracy, violence, joblessness, and even premature death? How should he or she respond to the plight of millions of children and families in poor neighborhoods from North Central Philadelphia to South Central Los Angeles? How should a true conservative manifest effective social compassion for the innocent inner-city toddlers and teenagers who this very night could lift their eyes to heaven and with complete justification cry, "My God, my God, why have you forsaken me?"

In all such cases a true conservative should respond by giving at least some of his or her time and money to family-supporting communities—national and local, public and private, religious and secular, in the suites and on the streets. I am talking about national secular nonprofit organizations like Big Brothers and Big Sisters of America; national religious nonprofit organizations like Prison Fellowship; charity dollars for grassroots volunteers who know the low-income inner-city children whom they serve; tax dollars for government employees who, without knowing these same children, serve them by faithfully implementing democratically enacted programs like Medicaid for children of low-income parents; and many more.

Metaphorically speaking, a true conservative's first call for larger communities is always a local call, starting with a house call. Charity begins at home, and so does social compassion. We do our utmost to honor our social obligations through families, voluntary associations, churches, and charities. We prefer social cooperation to social engineering; the veneration of subsidiary norms to the proliferation of bureaucratic rules; and the cultivation of civic virtue to the exercise of public authority.

But true conservatives are also obliged to call long distance when local lines are down or busy and help from families, churches, and neighborhood groups proves to be a nonworking number. As happened massively during the Great Depression, private initiatives and civil institutions are sometimes unable to help the needy and neglected in their midst. We should then call on ourselves as members of one or another political community, enlisting to the cause of effective social compassion our representative political institutions and the federal, state, and local government bureaucracies that translate legislative decisions into administrative actions.

POLITICAL COMMUNITY

True conservatives are not the least bit allergic to government. Government can be a legitimate and effective means of promoting a humane social order within which ordinary men, women, and children can lead peaceful and productive, if not uniformly prosperous, lives. We are, however, always wary of becoming addicted to government and are ever mindful that public laws can enervate families and smaller communities even when that is no one's intention. For example, state and local governments weakened the black family and stifled its socioeconomic progress through Jim Crow laws. After new federal civil rights laws were enacted, Washington's well-intentioned welfare laws undermined another generation of poor black families from coast to coast.

True conservatives are about the business of pruning government policies that enervate civil institutions and planting ones that make it easier for government at all levels to bolster these institutions, including grassroots, family-supporting, community-serving religious ministries. As a rule we prefer civil society action to local government action, local government action to state government action, and state government action to federal government action.

But we need to apply our subsidiary principle to an America that is today a demographically diverse society of nearly three hundred million souls living in fifty states and tens of thousands of local jurisdictions. We need to understand that the era of "big government" is over because, in this great nation, it never actually began. Instead, over the last seventy years, as Washington's taxing and spending exploded, America developed what Donald F. Kettl has aptly termed a system of "government by proxy."[4] Not a single big-budget domestic program enacted by Washington since 1950 has been set, implemented, and financed solely by the national government. Not Social Security. Not Medicare or Medicaid. Not the defunct Aid to Families with Dependent Children program or the new Temporary Assistance to Needy Families program. Not a one.

What American government at all levels now does to help our society's distressed families, our deserving poor, our disabled, our infirm elderly, our abused and neglected children, and others, it does through all manner of intergovernmental, public/private, and other partnerships. This uniquely American hybrid of public administration and public finance puzzles our European cousins, but it often works remarkably well, and it is a tribute to the conservative insistence that government power be as decentralized as possible.

Thus, a true conservative sitting in Philadelphia, Pennsylvania, is glad when not just local charities and local governments but also federal disaster relief agencies respond to the plight of fellow citizens in San Francisco who suffered a terrible earthquake and to the plight of fellow citizens in Oklahoma who suffered a terrible bombing. He or she is likewise pleased when a Republican-led Congress and a Democratic White House enact a new federal law that extends federal-state Medicaid coverage (begun in the year 2002) to all needy persons aged nineteen or younger, including low-income kids who live in Philadelphia, Mississippi. And he or she is heartened when partnerships between inner-city preachers and local law enforcement officials, in conjunction with intergovernmental social welfare and public health programs, help to reduce youth fatalities in Boston and other cities.

POOR COMPASSION

But wait. For a sixteen-year-old girl in a poor inner-city neighborhood who has lived without anyone—no parent, no teacher, no preacher, no

social worker—seeing to it that she has adequate food, money, and medicine, or that she is protected from street violence and sexual predation,
or that she feels consistently loved and cared for by at least one socially
responsible adult because she is, in fact, loved and cared for by at least
one socially responsible adult, subsidiarity is a false gospel, social compassion is a social fiction, and true conservatism is truly meaningless.

I have no idea whether Jesus would have conservatives support a capital gains tax cut, but I am certain that He would not want us to ignore
that girl or to deny what He called "the least" of His "family": "I was
hungry and you gave me food, thirsty and you gave me a drink . . . in
prison and you visited me. . . . Amen, I say to you, whatever you did for
one of these least . . . you did for me" (Matt. 25:35, 40 New American
Bible). As the Bible also admonishes us, God has "chosen the poor in the
world to be rich in faith and to be heirs of the kingdom that He has promised to those who love Him," but we have too often "dishonored the
poor" (James 2:5–6 NAB).

Because America's poor are so much better housed and better fed than
the poor of any previous generation; because poverty often results from
an individual's own bad choices (for example, dropping out of school,
using illegal drugs, committing street crimes, having children outside of
marriage); and because welfare reform seems like an unqualified success,
many self-described conservatives now openly doubt that we still have
a serious domestic poverty problem. Liberal cynics can be forgiven for
concluding that conservatives start preaching compassion only when they
think there is no one left who actually needs it.

Why is there relatively little grinding poverty in America today? The
answer is a portrait in subsidiarity framed by the government antipoverty
programs that too many conservatives have disparaged. The civil sector
has done its share. For example, the average big-city religious congregation, during the course of a year, now provides over fifty-three hundred hours of volunteer support to needy neighbors and a total of about
$144,000 a year in community programs that primarily serve the poor
and "unchurched" children. The public sector has also done its share.
Food Stamps, Medicaid, and other government antipoverty programs
provide billions of dollars annually in cash assistance and social services
for the poor.

Thanks to the combined efforts of these larger communities, in 1996
only 14 percent of all American families with children were in poverty,
and poverty among blacks reached new lows. And thanks to the so-called
Charitable Choice provision of the 1996 federal welfare reform law, it

is possible that in the first decades of the twenty-first century we will witness greater cooperation between government and faith-based social service delivery and antipoverty efforts.

Why is welfare reform working? The answer is that, contrary to how some conservatives described welfare recipients during the debates over welfare reform, most poor adult Americans are decent, law-abiding citizens who, if given half a chance, will work. The total number of people on welfare in America fell from 14.1 million in 1993 to 8.9 million in March 1998 (a 37 percent decline). Many states have reported promising trends in the percentages of former welfare recipients who are finding jobs. Between 1994 and 1998 the welfare rolls in 30 of the largest American cities declined by 35 percent.

But are we now living in a postpoverty America? Conservatives who think so should try living with their family on under $17,000 a year, as one in five black children still do. They should plan their next summer vacation in one of the inner-city public-housing complexes where, legend has it, everyone is maxing out on government benefits and air conditioners are buzzing in every window. They should stop by a city social services agency that is both placing more formerly dependent adults into jobs and coping with a rising tide of child-only welfare cases. They should next visit a maximum-security prison and learn about the abject material and moral poverty from whence so many of its inmates came.

TRUTH AND DEED

Millions of America's "least of these" still need help from the rest of us and our larger communities. In the twenty-first century true conservatives should lead a charge for social compassion, but will they? To invoke Clinton Rossiter once more: however they begin, conservative sentiments in America tend in the end to be materialistic and individualistic to a fault. Nothing, wrote Rossiter, can relieve American conservatism of "its chief intellectual sin: the glad, unthinking zeal with which it first embraced and still cherishes the principles of economic Liberalism," measuring "all things—even the morals of Jesus—with the yardstick of economic fulfillment."[5]

America's libertarian conservatives, one often hears, have been increasingly at war with religious and cultural conservatives on abortion and other issues. Maybe so, but both libertarians and the so-called religious right remain reliable Republican Party constituencies, and many religious conservatives continue to parrot libertarian ideas about social policy and economic policy. Thus, the Christian Coalition is strongly prolife but not steadfastly propoor.

In the next decades it is possible that calls for conservative social compassion will be squeezed into intellectual and political insignificance by an irreligious, leave-me-alone, reflexively antigovernment conservatism at home, and an unpatriotic, globe-trotting, commerce-first conservatism abroad. But as President George W. Bush's oratory during the 2000 campaign and since suggests, there remain countless leaders who are working to make American conservatism synonymous with subsidiary and social compassion. "If someone who has worldly means sees a brother in need and refuses him compassion, how can the love of God remain in him? Children, let us love not in word or speech but in deed and truth" (1 John 3:17–18 NAB).

NOTES

1. Clinton Rossiter, *Conservatism in America*, 2d rev. ed. (Cambridge, Mass.: Harvard University Press, 1982), 11.

2. Russell Kirk, *The Conservative Mind: From Burke to Santayana* (Chicago, Ill.: Henry Regnery, 1953), 7.

3. Dan Quayle with Diane Medved, *The American Family* (New York: HarperCollins, 1996), 2.

4. See Donald F. Kettl, *Government by Proxy* (Washington, D.C.: Congressional Quarterly Press, 1988).

5. Rossiter, *Conservatism in America*, 211.

CHAPTER 14

Shaking Off the Past

Third Ways, Fourth Ways, and the Urgency of Politics

E. J. Dionne Jr.

Long before the 2000 presidential election, Steve Goldsmith, one of George W. Bush's top campaign policy advisers and the former Republican mayor of Indianapolis, was explaining the inner balances and tensions within compassionate conservatism. After he had described the importance of both the government and the market to this putatively new philosophy, Goldsmith was asked the obvious question: Didn't it all sound a lot like the "Third Way" of which Bill Clinton and Tony Blair were so fond?

"No," Goldsmith replied firmly but with a chuckle. "It's the Fourth Way."

The notion of cross-ideological larceny was not entirely new. "The good news is that we may elect a Republican president this year," Republican consultant Alex Castellanos had declared before the 1996 election. "The bad news is that it may be Bill Clinton."

Clinton held no secret GOP party card, but Castellanos had vented what was a constant charge in the 1990s. Frustration with Clinton's success in co-opting stances associated with Republicans, blurring issues, and adopting aspects of Reagan's rhetorical style penetrated deep on both the right and the left. It's been convenient for both ends of the spectrum to brand Clinton an apostate. One of the first people to broach the notion of Clinton as Republican was Bill Clinton himself. "Where are all the Democrats?" Clinton cried out at a White House meeting early in his administration, according to Bob Woodward's account of those days.

"I hope you're all aware we're all Eisenhower Republicans. We're Eisenhower Republicans here and we are fighting the Reagan Republicans."

Then came the grandson of a genuine Eisenhower Republican, George W. Bush. Bush was not an Eisenhower Republican. He was a thoroughgoing conservative. Yet he understood that times had changed, that Clinton, for all the attacks Bush and other Republicans had leveled at him, had genuinely altered the dynamics of the American political debate. Thus, Bush did not repeat Ronald Reagan's famous declaration that government is not the solution, that government is the problem. Bush said instead: *"Government if necessary, but not necessarily government."* Bush might pursue an agenda more conservative than Reagan's, but his rhetoric was resolutely more moderate. Agendas, he understood, had to go forward under partial disguise.

These convolutions reflect a sea change in American politics. Over the last decade it has become increasingly difficult to label political events and actors. Sometime in the mid-1990s, new-breed types emerged across the spectrum, as "civic liberals" began to square off against "compassionate conservatives." This linguistic squirming has been going on for some time now.

There is a temptation—one that should not be reflexively denied—to think of this play of nomenclature as unfolding only on the cosmetic surface of politics. In this rendering media-savvy politicians seek to repackage potentially unpalatable ideas in more attractive wrappings. And surely the early course of the Bush administration gave ample evidence of that decorative instinct. Bush himself displayed a great talent for using Democratic rhetoric in support of conservative Republican programs. Recall that in late 2001 Democrats wanted an economic-stimulus package tilted heavily toward benefits for the unemployed. Bush wanted a package tilted heavily toward tax cuts, especially for the well-off and business. How did Bush sell his program?

"I proposed help for those who need it most, immediate help in the form of extended unemployment benefits and cash grants for workers who have been laid off," the president said in an early December radio address. As for the tax cuts for the wealthy and large companies, he described them as "a long-term strategy to accelerate economic growth to create more opportunities and more jobs." His tax cuts wore a disguise: they were simply "a long-term strategy."

But the truth is that something deeper is at work than a search for tactical rhetorical advantage. The confusion of tongues reflects a changing reality, really a set of realities—in the global economy, in the perception of government, in the structure of families, in foreign affairs. These circumstances have not yet called forth a new set of theories and ideologies to explain them and the politics they encourage. And whether it will be a Third Way, after the fashion of Clinton, some not yet clarified Fourth Way, as Goldsmith suggests, or still something entirely different is not yet clear. But we are decidedly in a transition period, a time in which neither left nor right dominates in politics. Republicans and conservatives kept control of both houses of Congress in 2000, barely, yet to do so, many of them ran on liberal and Democratic issues—a patients' bill of rights, a prescription drug benefit, more spending on education. Once Bush was in office, most Democrats stoutly resisted the size of his tax cut and its tilt toward the very wealthy. Yet they proposed sizable tax cuts of their own, not wanting to seem unsympathetic to the desire of taxpayers for a break. Republicans wanted to seem more progovernment than they were, Democrats more sympathetic to the average taxpayer.

And Senator Jim Jeffords of Vermont may have been the perfect symbol of how closely divided American politics has become and of how an uncertain political center can drive politics in unexpected directions. By moving from the Republican Party to independent status, and by throwing his vote to the Democrats on the matter of who would lead the Senate, he shifted party control of one house of Congress and radically altered the distribution of power in Washington.

It's an odd time. In some ways voting has become more partisan—there are fewer split tickets these days—yet the role of Independents in politics looms large. We are divided sharply along ideological lines—such is the lesson of polarization around the Clinton impeachment and the Florida election fiasco of 2000—yet there is that rush to the political center. What is the historical context of these changes?

CULTURE WAR CONUNDRUMS

It is fair to say that a significant portion of the electorate in the past decade has grown angry, frustrated, and disappointed over what they see as the irrelevance of the political debate to their immediate concerns. Part of the problem lies with the fragmentation of our political life and the vitriol and recrimination that have characterized it in recent decades.

The divisiveness is more than personal distemper and sour mood; its roots lie deep in the cultural civil war that split America in the 1960s. Ever since, the American political system has been reeling from novel threats to the old partisan structure that channeled conflict in a predictable manner for some time. Just as the Civil War dominated American political life for decades after it ended, so has the civil war of the 1960s—with all its tensions and contradictions—shaped our politics today, although in complex and diminishing ways.

Although political scientists have shed a lot of ink trying to figure out whether the unraveling of this system was a realignment or merely a dealignment, the more urgent question is not technical but substantive. Through the 1980s and 1990s the country was still struggling with major questions left over from the old cultural battles: civil rights and the integration of blacks into the country's political and economic life; the revolution in values involving feminism and changed attitudes toward child rearing and sexuality; and the ongoing debate over America's role in the world that began with the Vietnam War and that the ending of the cold war has only intensified.

These so-called wedge issues hit the Democratic Party especially hard, splitting it into myriad factions. Over time they gave new divisive bite to partisan differences, as both parties realigned on these disagreements of race, family, and foreign policy. Whatever else was going on in the electorate at large, these issues provided a divisive clarity to partisan party struggle, which only intensified as Ronald Reagan courted moral conservatives, especially evangelical and fundamentalist Christians and the prolife movement, and gave them a powerful presence within the Republican Party.

Already by the early 1990s these wedge issues had a powerfully unhappy consequence. They and the politicians who championed them posed complex matters of moral and social conflict in race, in family life, and in sexuality as false polarities, in either-or terms that did not speak to the amorphous center where the majority of American voters dwell.

In truth, America's cultural values are a rich but not necessarily contradictory mix of liberal instincts and conservative values. Americans believe in helping those who fall on hard times, in fostering equal opportunity and equal rights, and in providing access to education, housing, health care, and child care. At the same time, Americans believe that intact families do the best job of bringing up children, that hard work should be rewarded, that people who behave destructively toward others should be punished, that small institutions close to home tend to do better than big institutions run from far away, and that private moral choices usually have social consequences. Put another way, Americans believe in social concern and self-reliance; they want to match rights and responsibilities; they think public moral standards should exist but are skeptical of too much meddling in the private affairs of others.

A similar search for balance can be found in the politics of family and sexuality. Overwhelmingly, the country accepts the entry of women into the workforce. The vast majority of Americans see their presence as, at least, an economic necessity and, at best, a positive good. Americans know that for all the conservatives' talk about the "traditional" family, the world of the 1950s is gone forever.

Yet, once again, if Americans on balance agree with liberals that women are in the workforce to stay, they agree with conservatives that not all the effects of this revolution are positive. They worry especially about what will happen to children in the new world we have created. They are concerned that in women's rush to the workforce, the children are being left behind, given that men do not seem eager to take up the slack. The debate the country has always wanted to hear—and, in truth, finally began hearing in the 1990s from thoughtful feminists and thoughtful traditionalists—is not one involving false choices between an ideal "feminism" and an idealized "traditional family" but one about solving the practical problems faced by families, and especially by overburdened working women.

Americans have declared their preference for moderate (or, perhaps more accurately, ambivalent) positions on countless other issues, including abortion. Nonetheless, it was easy to understand, at least until the 1990s, why Republicans had a large stake in culture war. The *Kulturkampf* of the 1960s made Republicans powerful. Conservatives were able to destroy the dominant New Deal coalition by using cultural and social issues—race, the family, permissiveness, crime—to split New Deal constituencies and to woo what had been the most loyally Democratic group in the nation, white southerners, and to peel off millions of votes among industrial workers and other whites of modest income. Simply put, the cultural civil war replaced the old axis of class division with the passions of moral vendetta.

Conversely, the broad political interests of liberals lay in settling the cultural civil war, but many liberals were loath to give up the old polarities. They too had an interest in its endurance. The politics of the 1960s shifted the balance of power within the liberal coalition away from working-class and lower-middle-class voters, whose main concerns were economic, and toward upper-middle-class reformers mainly interested in cultural issues and foreign policy. All of this made the upper-middle-class reformers the dominant voices within American liberalism.

If the wedge issues have worked to the Republicans' advantage, they have not done so in any mechanical or inevitable fashion. In all their over-reaching, the congressional Republicans who spearheaded the program of radical reconstruction missed the essential moderation of the American electorate. The embrace of George W. Bush, with his "compassion-ate" disavowal of meanness, reflects in part a fear of the potential dan-ger of such issues to the forging of a Republican majority.

At the heart of this skittishness lies not just the ambivalence of the anxious middle of the electorate but also powerful schisms within the Republican Party. As Republican pollster Tony Fabrizio showed in a re-markable study a few years ago, the hot cultural issues had the power to split the Republicans, as well, and not simply along the lines of social and economic conservatives, as people ordinarily describe it. Actually, five Republican factions have been vying with each other. Economic con-servatives divide into deficit hawks and tax cutters, each claiming roughly one-fifth of the party's supporters. A small group of "progressives" en-joy no more than a tenth of the party. The remaining two are different camps of social conservatives, each claiming roughly one-fifth of the Re-publican voters. One of them Fabrizio calls moralists—think of them as Ralph Reed/Pat Robertson Republicans—and they are primarily con-cerned about issues such as abortion and homosexuality. The cultural populists—think of them as Archie Bunker/Pat Buchanan Republicans—are more worried about what Fabrizio calls the hard-edged issues: crime, immigration, drugs, affirmative action, and welfare. The cultural pop-ulists are divided on abortion and are more secular than the religiously inclined moralists. Interestingly, both groups of social conservatives are disproportionately female.

This split caused the Republicans no end of problems during the Clin-ton years. For the truth, as Ruy Teixeira and John Judis have shown,[1] is that the rise of a large, suburban middle class means that cultural mod-eration and liberalism may now be a force working for the Democrats, not the Republicans. One of the most striking aspects of elections from 1992 to 2000 was the growing Democratic vote in the suburbs. Teixeira and Judis offer the intriguing theory that the middle-class, socially lib-eral, constituencies that George McGovern activated in 1972 have now become important and influential parts of the electorate. If Democrats once had an interest in ending the culture wars, Republicans may now have an even more urgent need to do so.

THE CLINTON INTERREGNUM: TOWARD CIVIC LIBERALISM

Clinton's victory in 1992, combined with Ross Perot's showing, was a sharp repudiation of Reaganism. The 1994 Republican congressional rout does not refute that point. Indeed, the Gingrich revolution ultimately failed because the Republicans misunderstood the victory as an ideological mandate. It was as much a commentary on the failure of Clinton in his first two years to enact the core, popular parts of his program: health care reform, campaign finance reform, welfare reform, and changes in education and training policies aimed at lifting up Americans battered by economic changes.

The increasing numbers of Republicans contemplating the now ambiguous effect of the social issues included Ralph Reed, who served as executive director of Pat Robertson's Christian Coalition and later became Republican state chairman in Georgia. Reed suggested that the cultural right needed to move beyond the core moral issues dear to religious conservatives to embrace the full range of fiscal and economic concerns of middle-class families. In the midst of the argument over the California Civil Rights Initiative, which ended affirmative action in that state, California Republican assemblyman James Brulte worried that simply as a practical matter the initiative might bring more African-American voters to the polls—to oppose it—than it would mobilize whites in enthusiastic support.

His comments reflected a general Republican mood that the party needed, well, a kinder, gentler, *compassionate* face. The Republicans' loss of Florida in 1996, attributed in part to anti-immigrant rhetoric that offended even conservative Cubans, would add a chastening note. Even on the issue of government itself, Republicans were softening. The 1996 convention issue of the *Weekly Standard,* the influential conservative magazine, included an article by David Brooks warning that Republicans had attacked government more than they needed to, or should.

Brooks was very direct: "The political reality at the moment is that American voters, while critical of some of the government programs we have, have not given up on government itself. Politicians who preach the harsh line of cut, cut, cut end up where Phil Gramm did when he ran for president."[2] Such thoughts in a conservative magazine! No wonder Republicans didn't boo Colin Powell when he defended government, and affirmative action in particular, in his speech to the convention.

Brooks was echoing Fabrizio's warning to the party: many of the stands it has taken for granted as winners are in fact losing wedge issues

that split the party. Opposition to gun restrictions? Large segments of all
five groups support them, and never more than in the wake of a string
of school shootings in white middle-class neighborhoods deep in the heart
of gun-show territory. The flat tax? Only the deficit hawks and supply-
siders support it strongly. The populists and the progressives oppose it,
and the moralists are split.

Cutting entitlements won't unify the party either. A third or more of
each group in the party says it would favor fully funding Medicare and
Social Security, even if it means higher taxes. Even free trade, which has
become Republican doctrine, splits the party's constituencies. Fabrizio's
moralists and populists especially are worried about jobs going overseas,
but so are many in both groups of economic conservatives who are usually assumed to be against protectionism. And general themes that unite
the party in the abstract—cutting government, devolving power to the
states, deregulation—become problematic as soon as you get to specifics.
Thus, talk about regulations to protect the air and water, and sentiment
against regulation dissipates. Cutting government spending is popular—
except for the largest parts of it, such as Medicare, Social Security, and
preserving a strong military.

Clinton's genius, albeit imperfectly realized, lay in his instinct for re-
covering the American center. Suddenly the anxious middle—the same
center Reagan did such a good job of wooing with his reassuring mien,
the same center that Republican cultural warriors seemed intent on
abandoning—was up for grabs.

Clinton's personal foibles—one need only mention the Monica Lewin-
sky scandal—clearly derailed his project of building a broad coalition of
the center-left. As William Galston, one of the architects of the Democratic Leadership Council's agenda, argued, only by gaining "credibility
on defense, foreign policy and social values" could the party get a hearing for "a progressive economic program."[3] Clinton did that. That this
project was serious and had great potential can be seen in the success of
European politicians, Tony Blair in Britain and Gerhard Schroeder in Germany notably, who pursued a similar path. That Clinton forced Republicans to change their rhetoric, if not their policies, is also obvious.

Clinton did not jettison everything liberals ever thought, as some on
the left charged. Rather, he sought a synthesis of liberal goals, pragmatic
means, and values to which most Americans related. The synthesis was
visible in all of Clinton's most popular proposals. And popularity was
part of the point. Clinton was trying to convince the country that active
government need not be its enemy.

His original proposals for welfare reform were designed to lift the poor from dependency and send a clear message that the government's goal is not to make it easier for people to escape the workforce. Clinton's plan for universal college loans that could be paid back with national service was an unapologetic mirror image of the GI Bill: the community, through government, could give individuals a hand, but the community could also expect something back. The commitment to better job training and continuing education was a way of saying government can help individuals through difficult transitions but cannot replace individual effort. On occasion, government really can, to use the overworked phrase, "empower people."

Clinton's talk about "reinventing government" not only responded to popular anger about the state's lumbering inefficiencies but also asserted that Democrats could be open minded and innovative about how they would seek their goals. Sometimes vouchers are better than new bureaucracies—and also more effective in redistributing money and opportunity to the needy. Sometimes market incentives can move us where we want to go faster than government commands.

Clinton effected a similar consensus in the cultural realm. Here, too, his ability to plow under old issues that had divided Democrats was central to his endeavor. Especially on crime and—ironically, in the light of the Monica scandal—family values, Clinton helped Democrats overcome a quarter century of squabbling and setbacks. His initiatives on guns and more cops were accompanied by falling crime rates. Notwithstanding the controversy over gays in the military, Clinton signaled this cultural moderation in many moments, perhaps most memorably in his address to a group of black ministers in Memphis, in which he sounded the traditionalist themes of family breakup, violence, and personal responsibility. Invoking Martin Luther King Jr. to assure his audience that an appeal to white backlash did not lurk beneath his words, he told the ministers that King had not died "to see the American family destroyed" or "to see thirteen-year-old boys get automatic weapons and gun down nine-year-olds just for the kick of it."

Clinton's co-opting of socially conservative themes, especially his direct appeal to suburban working couples worried about how to raise decent children, drove conservative Republicans mad no less than did Clinton's co-opting of their antigovernment rhetoric. The Republicans were eager to associate the noninhaling Clinton with the permissive values of the 1960s. Instead, he talked about 1990s-style families.

Republican Castellanos shrewdly captured what Clinton was up to in pushing such initiatives as school uniforms, teen curfews, crackdowns on truancy, gun restriction, and the V-Chip to block obscene programming on television. The president, following the advice of consultant Dick Morris among others, was reaching out to "soccer mom": the overburdened middle-income working mother who ferries her kids from soccer practice to scouts to school. Clinton's message to her was that the government will do what it can to help her raise her kids and establish some order in her family life.

Castellanos added that Clinton's specific and putatively liberal spending commitments to Medicare and Medicaid for the parents of a soccer mom and student loans for her children reinforced the message that Clinton, and, by extension, the federal government, is the "protector of the family." Conservatives, said Castellanos, had always argued in favor of "protecting the family from government." Clinton, for all his rhetoric against big government, proposed to "protect the family *with* government."

If this all sounded new, it was less new than it seemed. Many of these ideas grew out of Franklin Roosevelt's liberalism. For the New Deal, coming as it did before the time of the counterculture and the revolt against "traditional values," was always singularly concerned with using government to protect families: through family wages, through the Works Progress Administration (WPA) jobs for breadwinners, through Social Security, and, yes, through the Aid to Families with Dependent Children (AFDC) program, which, after all, was originally designed for widows with children.

Senator Daniel P. Moynihan made the point powerfully that family had long been central to federal social programs in his book *Family and Nation*. The loss of this emphasis, he argued, was a grievous blow to sensible policy (not to mention politics). That analysis, ironically, would help lead Moynihan to his vehement and courageous opposition to the repeal of the AFDC program and put him on a collision course with Clinton. It was an unfortunate estrangement because it could be argued that so many other Clinton policies might be seen as coming from a careful reading of Moynihan and a reengagement with the older social policy tradition Moynihan admired.

Thus the Clinton gambit: fiscal caution, free trade, social moderation, and a probusiness orientation to pull in moderate Republicans and suburban independents; and a family orientation in social policy that jumped back over the 1960s and looked to the New Deal for inspiration. Ironically, it was in this second area that Clinton used his most conservative rhetoric to revive support for the activist government whose era is supposed to be over.

For those who welcomed this realignment of policy, politics, and ideas, the Clinton scandal and impeachment controversy was a huge blow. It undercut what had been one of his greatest achievements, the revival of Democratic strength among Reagan Democrats who never fully abandoned their commitment to activist government. Many of these voters were also socially conservative, rural, and southern. Al Gore, partly because of his own failures but also because of Clinton's, suffered serious defections from their ranks.

THE 2000 ELECTION AND BEYOND

Throughout the 1990s it was possible to argue that Clinton had fashioned a new kind of center-left coalition that might establish a majority regime in American politics. This was true even though Clinton's efforts to recast the terms of public policy were uneven, marked by the rhythm of bold adventure and hasty retreat, by failure of nerve and more chastened steps forward. Indeed, the precise emphasis varied with various phases of his administration. Early on, conflicts between the Democratic Leadership Council (DLC) on the one hand and more liberal Democrats on the other exploded. They came to the fore in the health care initiative. Its failure forced Clinton to declare, whether he fully believed it or not, that the era of big government was over.

Given the preoccupation with sex and lies, the drawn-out impeachment melodrama, and the sordid finale of the pardons, it's easy to forget that Clinton-style civic liberalism reflected a broader, in part global, dynamic. Clinton was at the forefront of an important transformation that took place in the wealthy democracies of Europe and North America. On both sides of the Atlantic politicians and intellectuals were debating what sort of politics should replace the traditional liberal and social democratic doctrines of the left and the free market ideas of the right. For most of the 1990s the parties engaged in that quest were winning elections in the United States, Britain, France, Italy, Portugal, Holland, and Germany. The new ideas—at least the quest for them—were coming to be known as the politics of *The Third Way*.

Those three words arouse instant suspicion, and skeptics have raised fair questions. They asked whether the Third Way was a set of real ideas or an advertising slogan. They wanted to know if it represented a serious effort to create new forms of progressive politics or was, instead, a capitulation to the right, the final triumph of Ronald Reagan and Margaret Thatcher. Ultimately, they asked whether the Third Way was simply a ploy that shrewd politicians such as Clinton and Blair could use to distinguish themselves from some terrible "them" (the "far right," the "old left") without ever having to define who "we" are.

Today the momentum toward a progressive Third Way seems somewhat stalled. Still, notwithstanding the Bush "victory," it is plausible to argue that a new progressive majority was in the making. Even putting aside the controversy around the Florida recounts, Gore did defeat Bush in the popular vote by over a half million. Between them, Gore and Green Party candidate Ralph Nader secured a clear majority of the vote. Whatever the voters did in November 2000, they did not provide the center-right with a presidential majority. The Democrats also gained seats in the House and Senate, producing a virtual tie in the House and a literal tie in the Senate, later to be overturned by Jeffords. And of course, there is growing evidence that absent machine errors—and, perhaps, with a full recount—Gore would have won Florida, the electoral college, and the presidency.

It is also easy to overplay the role of issues and philosophy in the election of 2000. Three factors played a large role in keeping Gore from winning a clear triumph: Al Gore himself, Bill Clinton, and the relationship between the two of them. In an election this close factors of personality and performance can, all by themselves, explain the outcome. If Gore had not sighed so much in that first debate with Bush, he might be president. More generally, Gore allowed the election to be as much a personality struggle (Bush won this) as a contest over who was better prepared to be president (a competition that favored Gore). The Clinton scandals were also critical. The Bush campaign shrewdly played on Clinton's problems with veracity to highlight Gore's "little lies" and exaggerations. In normal circumstances these would not have been an issue, or not much of one.

Yet Gore and his strategists were so spooked by the Clinton drag on the ticket that they failed to take full advantage of the broad satisfaction in the electorate with the state of the country after the eight Clinton-Gore years. During the Democratic National Convention a Gore strategist outlined what looked then—and looks now—like a shrewd strategy. Gore would emphasize populist themes and distance himself from Clinton during the early stages of the fall campaign. He'd then turn in October to an embrace of the Clinton prosperity and to warnings about the risk of Republican policies to these achievements. The first half of the strategy would secure the Democratic base and bring left-of-center voters home to Gore after their flirtation with Nader. The second half would secure the ballots needed from middle- and upper-middle-class voters who did very well under Clinton.

The problem with the strategy is that Gore didn't get to stage two until the last week of his campaign. There is a consensus across the Democratic Party, from left to center, that Gore—because of his understandable frustrations with Clinton—never took full advantage of what the Clinton record might have achieved for him.

Still, even if civic liberalism remains a plausible option, the progressive majority that looked so promising only half a decade ago no longer seems as inevitable as it once did. One can also see the possibilities for a center-right majority. Since the election, New Democrats associated with the Democratic Leadership Council have argued that Gore's embrace of "populist" themes actually hurt him. The populism, they say, turned off potential middle- and upper-middle-class allies and distracted attention from the themes of peace and prosperity. As several commentators have noted, Gore's slogan seemed to come down to "You've never had it so good—and I'm mad as hell about it."

There may be an instructive lesson, both for parties of the center-left and the center-right, in Gore's dilemma that transcends this particular election or the happenstance of the candidates and circumstances bequeathed them. The essence of Third Way politics has been defined in largely negative terms. It was not "the old left" or "the new right." It was not about unlimited confidence in the state, and it was not about unlimited confidence in the market. As common sense goes, it's not a bad formula. The electorates in most of the wealthy democracies have doubts about the old left and the new right, and they do not fully trust either the government or the unfettered market. But this third-way formula has proven better as a critique of the past than as a road map to the future. The surprising failure of moderate socialist prime minister Lionel Jospin to reach the runoff in France's 2002 presidential election underscored the difficulty of center-left politicians who try to balance state and market. The rise of the far right in Europe—its successes should be neither exaggerated nor ignored—suggest problems for the moderate right.

In the American case Democrats are still badly divided over the proper response to the global economy. In principle both sides of the internal debate agree that the global market is here to stay but that some forms of regulation (on the domestic side, certainly, but also at the international level) are needed—especially where the environment and labor and human rights are concerned. In practice, it's not at all clear what this formula means.

Similarly, both ends of the coalition agree on a role for government in assisting those left out of the current prosperity. Both sides mouth the same slogans about the need for "new," "more efficient," and more "market-friendly" approaches to social insurance, job training, and education. In practice there are clear differences over what that means. Democrats have been split over whether and how private investments should be part of the Social Security system, or how private insurance should play a role in the Medicare program. It is significant that as time went on both Gore and Clinton became more skeptical of proposals to "privatize" parts of Social Security. Their substantive conclusion—correct, I think—was that most privatization plans would endanger benefits, especially for lower-income workers. Their political conclusion was that the core Democratic vote came from those also skeptical of dismantling Social Security. Given that Gore made large gains in the closing days of the campaign with warnings about the dangers of Bush's privatization plans, this conclusion seems right too.

The trouble, then, is that center-left parties, no matter how often they use the word *new,* find themselves inevitably cast as defenders of older forms of social provision. They become the parties of status quo because they are willing neither to do much to expand current forms of social provision nor to cut them back in serious ways. (This, by the way, is why they face a constant struggle to mobilize their core constituencies. The base is often looking for more change than the moderate center-left wants to offer.) They support market capitalism more or less as it is—and are wary that even their own reforms might upset it. As a result, although parties of the moderate left have done well in shedding politically damaging baggage, they have not created a sense of excitement or commitment. As the former president George Bush Sr. might put it, the moderate left has a problem with "the vision thing." The trouble faced by Blair, Clinton, and their colleagues on the moderate left is that in abandoning old progressive dreams, they seem to have created what Philip Collins, director of the London-based Social Market Foundation, calls "politics without a lodestar."[4]

These vulnerabilities at the core of the Third Way provide hope and inspiration to partisans of a center-right Fourth Way. As we will see, such a Fourth Way is not without its own ambiguities, as Bush continues to discover. Nonetheless, the Bush project should be taken seriously because it does contain elements that are genuinely new—even as it uses innovation to support an older market conservatism, buttressed by an even more ancient traditionalism.

Throughout the election Bush tacitly honored the logic of the Third Way. Most obviously, the rhetoric of compassion was a pointed break with the conservatism of the 1980s and mid-1990s. The characteristic of Anglo-American center-right politics during the years when Margaret Thatcher, Ronald Reagan, and, later, Newt Gingrich were in the ascendancy was a hard antigovernment, antistate rhetoric—a rhetoric that was often harder than the programs embraced by the protagonists. The classic formulation was Reagan's statement that government isn't the *solution;* government is the *problem.*

Pure antistatism ran out of steam—and Bush and his advisers knew it. The strategic correction Bush introduced was to embrace, Third Way–like, a rhetoric declaring that conservatives, too, understood the limits of both state and market. Bush, like the Third Wayers, went out of his way to criticize his own side. "Too often," he declared, "my party has confused the need for limited government with a disdain for government itself."

Bush also distanced himself from a pure embrace of the market—but he used conservative, traditionalist, and religious rhetoric to this end. "The invisible hand works many miracles, but it cannot touch the human heart," he declared in a speech in July of 1999. "We are a nation of rugged individuals. But we are also the country of a second chance— tied together by bonds of friendship and community and solidarity." For good measure, he added: "There must be a kindness in our justice. There must be a mercy in our judgment. There must be a love behind our zeal." Bush returned to these themes in the spring of 2002 in a speech in California. "We are a generous and caring people," he said. "We don't believe in a sink-or-swim society. The policies of our government must heed the universal call of all faiths to love a neighbor as we would want to be loved ourselves. We need a different approach than either big government or indifferent government." This is the Fourth Way at its purest.

Bush's rhetoric on the limits of markets was not about changing the market system but about strengthening nonmarket institutions, especially religious institutions. In a long conservative tradition Bush was arguing that the cool calculations of the market would be tempered by those havens in a heartless world, the family and the church.

Although Bush's Fourth-Way synthesis should not be dismissed, the ultimate victory of a center-right coalition is no more inevitable than Third-Way progressivism. Bush has linked this rhetoric to a more ener-

getic assault on the old New Deal–Great Society state than Reagan himself dared pursue. Bush was the first presidential candidate ever to propose the partial privatization of Social Security, that supposed "third rail"
of American politics that no conservative politician would dare to touch.
He spoke of a Medicare program more implicated in the private insurance market than the current system. And of course, like Reagan, he proposed a large income tax reduction, tilted inevitably toward wealthier
taxpayers. Bush gave wonderful speeches about compassion for the poor
but put far more money into tax cuts for the best off—and, after September 11, into the Pentagon. It's clear that the election of 2002 was not
a mandate for assaults on government social programs that were never
telegraphed in Bush's electoral rhetoric. In his speeches, if not in his policies, Bush recognized this.

In the meantime the rhetoric of the center-left emphasizing government's role in protecting average citizens still had power. Defenders of
Gore's populism point out that his most successful period came in the
weeks after his populist turn at the August Democratic Convention. If
the election had been held at some point in September, Gore would have
won a victory in the range of seven percentage points (or so, at least, the
polls suggest). Gore's populism was of a highly tempered sort. His targets were large insurance companies, health maintenance organizations,
"big polluters," and "big oil," the last an inevitable attack given the business ties of the Republican candidates for president and vice president.
"Big polluters" fare very badly in the polls, and "big oil" (outside the oil
patch) doesn't do too well either. And Gore's assault on insurance companies and health providers was harnessed to popular causes—notably
a prescription drug benefit for elderly Americans under the Medicare program and a patients' bill of rights.

In short, Gore's populism worked well as far as it went. His failure
was not to integrate the populist appeals into a self-confident, forward-
looking program that promised to build on past achievements. Gore had
good issues but not enough lift. He had more program than theme. He
made a series of reasonable, individual promises that did not quite add
up to a broader promise for the country.

Bush and the policies he has championed remain out of line with popular opinion on the environment, energy, health care, and several other
issues. Consider Bush's big success, his tax cut. The president liked to
say that his stand on taxes was principled, because he was not following the polls. He was right about the polls. A big tax cut, tilted toward
the best off, was never what the public wanted most. Throughout the

2000 campaign and after, majorities cared more about fixing Social Security and Medicare and improving education. In a sense, once elected, Bush was forced to choose between what Democratic consultant David Doak called "expansive, big tent rhetoric,"[5] which Bush used to gloss over his frankly conservative policy proposals, and the proposals themselves. He chose the policies. David Winston, a Republican pollster, has pointed out that "[t]he focus of compassionate conservatism should not be about being more green or appealing to specific groups. . . . [It] was about understanding people's problems. That's what his strength was in the campaign."[6] But in his approach to governing in the period before September 11, as Robert Shrum, an adviser to Gore in 2000, observed, Bush was "off the wavelength and strategy of his own campaign."[7] Shrum knew what he was talking about. He spoke shortly after he had advised the British Labour Party in its landslide 2001 victory. Labour's Conservative Party foes made the mistake of imitating Bush's behavior in office rather than his strategy during the campaign. In the process they ensured the triumph of Blair's Third Way.

All of this brings us back to the possibilities for a progressive regime. The center-left has solved many of its old problems. In most countries (and certainly in Britain and the United States) it is no longer seen as fiscally irresponsible. It is not seen as hostile to the market. It is not viewed as hopelessly defensive of every failed policy innovation in its history. But it now lacks the energy that inspired the older movements around social democracy, New Dealism and Labourism. Its "negative" innovations—better labeled, perhaps, as "strategic corrections"—have largely been achieved.

The plight of the center-right is somewhat different. It enjoys, and can draw on, the sense of solidarity that can be found in abundant supply among traditionalist movements. It profits from two decades of public argument in which market-oriented ideas were dominant and *statism* became a very dirty word. Despite the general popularity of tax cuts, however, it has not yet overcome the suspicion that its rhetoric of compassion is a cover for a program of redistribution of wealth upward. And in the United States the growing constituencies—especially Latinos, but also the socially moderate middle class—are those *least* likely to form the base of a new Republican majority. If demography is destiny, the demographics favor the center-left.

In sum, one could argue that on the eve of September 11 the contemporary center-left had succeeded in jettisoning failed dreams, but it has not yet generated new ones. The contemporary center-right has learned a great deal from the rhetoric of the center-left, but its program still looks back to the dreams of Ronald Reagan and Margaret Thatcher.

AFTER SEPTEMBER 11

We say that September 11 changed everything. But in politics we do not know yet exactly what September 11 changed or how much it changed us. Will the profound seriousness that overtook the country after the assaults of that day cause a more permanent change in politics as practiced in the past decade? It is already clear that the bipartisan mood that characterized the immediate aftermath of the attacks cannot be the way of politics. The divisions between center-left and center-right on the role of government—witness the early battles over airport security and the economic stimulus packages and later fights over budgets and health care—are too deep.

Yet there can be little doubt that something important happened in the wake of September 11. The tough guys of politics—the political consultants whose first, second, and third jobs involve winning elections—were among those who thought politics had turned a corner. At the very least, they began advising their clients to be prudent in picking their fights. "One of the things you've seen is a desire for a very different kind of discourse,"[8] said Winston, the Republican pollster. Americans, he said, wanted to know that leaders (and preachers and even comedians) understood how much the world had changed. He argued that criticisms of statements by the Reverend Jerry Falwell and Bill Maher of TV's *Politically Incorrect* in the aftermath of the assaults were not so much an attack on free speech as an assertion of new public norms. For at least a few weeks after September 11, he said, the public saw "a different political debate" carried out—more civility. As a result, he said, "politicians are going to do tit-for-tat at their own risk."

Some of this was, and will remain, purely tactical—a moderate-sounding style overlaid on the moderate-sounding rhetoric that became the rule in the late 1990s. Democratic pollster Guy Molyneux predicted that politicians would define their positions as "the sensible bipartisan solution" and define their opponents as the ones "breaking the bipartisan coalition."

Some things were obvious. Polls showed a reversal in the antigovernment sentiment that had been so powerful for so long. That may prove a favorite adage of former defense secretary Senator William Cohen: "Government is the enemy until you need a friend." And, paradoxically at a time of increased anxiety, many more Americans thought the nation was on the "right track" than did so before the attacks.

Winston argued that those polling results showed that Americans, although worried about the future, were gratified by the country's new sense of community. "People saw this as a horrible event," he said. "They think the economy is going to get worse. They think life is going to be tougher. But they also saw these firefighters stepping up to the plate. These were good people. They saw millions of Americans reaching into their pockets to make contributions. They saw people crashing that plane into the ground in order to save the lives of others. They saw people who acted as Americans who made them feel proud."[9] If a new fear was one product of September 11, a new solidarity was the other.

The very seriousness of the problems the country confronted shoved old scandals off the front pages, the talk shows, and cable television. Old slogans, left and right, seemed painfully stale. Only the most contorted analysis could lay the blame for the slaughter of innocents on "American imperialism." The rhetoric of free-market omnipotence, so dominant for so long, became a bit less believable when Republicans and Democrats in Congress agreed that the marketplace couldn't keep the airlines flying; only the government, however clumsily, could do that. Later, the Enron scandal would challenge the fashion for deregulation. Capitalism without clear rules, seriously enforced, could lose a lot of people a lot of money for reasons that had little to do with genuine success or failure in the marketplace. The scandal, and the spate of similar corporate scandals that followed, showed clearly that the interests of outsiders—both employees *and* shareholders—needed to be protected against the greed of insiders.

September 11 had another effect: complaints about America's alleged "moral bankruptcy" or "hedonism" were laid low by the community spirit and selflessness of countless firefighters, rescue workers, and volunteers. Our celebrities, suddenly, were not high-tech wizards, Hollywood beautiful people, or hotshot investors. The heroes were public employees who soared in our esteem by simply doing their jobs—and ordinary citizens who simply behaved as citizens should.

Patriotism was suddenly spoken of without any irony. The American flag, a politically contested symbol in the forty years war that began in the 1960s, was restored as the banner representing the entire American community. This was not a trivial change. Nothing more perfectly symbolized the end of the culture wars. And it suggested we might begin believing again in common endeavor. Politics, public life, and public service were suddenly too important to be trivialized or denigrated. If we don't come to believe that after September 11, we never will.

To predict with any certainty how these changes affect the political future would be foolhardy, especially given that the signs remain contradictory. President Bush's soaring popularity in the wake of the attacks—and the widespread view, held even among his critics, that he handled the early months of war with great skill—pointed to a Republican future built around patriotism, military virtues, and a yearning for security.

And in the elections of November 2002, Republicans used every single one of these issues—and Bush's frenetic campaigning—to oust the Democrats from control of the Senate and to expand their majority in the House of Representatives. It was a close yet still stunning result, better than many Republicans expected. At mid-summer, the election seemed likely to point to the limits of the September 11 effect. A sagging economy and the scandals that wracked corporate America crowded terrorism out of the news.

But the Bush political team shrewdly turned the country's attention back to national security issues. At the end of August Vice President Dick Cheney fired the first rhetorical guns in a new debate over whether the United States should invade Iraq to overthrow Saddam Hussein. The president went to the United Nations on Iraq in early September. Despite the administration's best efforts, it could never provide a clear link between Saddam and Al Qaeda—and thus September 11. But in the end, this didn't matter. One does not have to believe that the Iraq debate was driven by primarily partisan and political imperatives to see that it displaced economics, split the Democratic party, and left the Democrats struggling (unsuccessfully, as it turned out) to move the nation's political dialogue back to what might be seen as "normal" domestic issues such as health care, social security, and economic growth.

For good measure, the administration took what might be seen as a bureaucratic issue—the reorganization of the government to create a Department of Homeland Security—and inflated it into a major cause. Democrats resisted a provision sought by Bush to give the president more freedom to hire and fire through a weakening of union rules and civil service protections. But Bush scored when he argued that Democrats preferred protecting their union allies to passing the bill he said he needed.

This was classic, divisive wedge politics. Democrats had a choice of capitulating to Bush and thereby angering some of their most important allies or going on the offensive with an aggressive defense of the rights of unionized civil servants. (They might have reminded the country of the heroism of those unionized firefighters and police officers.) The Democrats chose neither to capitulate nor to fight back effectively, and Bush bludgeoned them with the homeland security club.

Here lies a cautionary tale about the hopes for greater civility in a post-9/11 world. In principle, the homeland security bill was bi-partisan. Bush had, in fact, resisted the idea at first and then picked it up from the Democrats. And when it came election time, the administration was willing to use a minor provision in the bill to bash its twin opponents in the unions and in the opposition party. A relatively minor dispute was turned into Republican television advertisements charging that Democrats—even including Senator Max Cleland of Georgia, a disabled Vietnam War hero in a wheelchair—were somehow soft on homeland security. More generally, Bush engaged in what conservative writer Jeffrey Bell called "fierce, relentless, highly effective partisanship."[10] Yet Bush succeeded brilliantly in hiding partisanship and ideology behind the determined face of national unity. To Republicans and many suburban independents, it was Democrats who seemed to be the partisan aggressors, even though Democrat after Democrat swore fealty to Bush in the war on terror.

Seen in this light, the 2002 elections may have buried Goldsmith's Fourth Way and—if one dares go on like this—marked the beginning of a Fifth Way, yet another attempt at realignment. This try would be rooted not in compassionate conservatism but in the quest for national security. The old tax-cutting conservatism would be harnessed to a new toughness on security and a new patriotism cast in terms set down by a politically savvy White House. With the Republicans enjoying ever growing advantages in fundraising, and a mass media increasingly tilted to the right through the power of conservative voices on radio and cable television, a Republican realignment seemed a possibility. Yet the inexorability of such a realignment was almost immediately called into question. First, there was the re-election of Democratic Senator Mary Landrieu in Louisiana's runoff election in December of 2002, despite prodigious efforts by Bush and his administration to turn the seat Republican. Republican toughness in November called forth a tough Democratic response in December. At around the same time, the widespread reaction against Senate Republican Leader Trent Lott's suggestion that the country would have been better off if Strom Thurmond's segregationist presidential ticket had triumphed in 1948 suggested that wedge issues are two-sided. So embarrassing was this explicit reach back to segregation that the president himself was required to condemn it. Whether the Fourth

Way or the Fifth, a new Republican realignment would certainly fail if it became ensnared in old-style right wing politics. As John Judis and Ruy Teixeira argue in *The Emerging Democratic Majority,* not only are minority voters a growing part of the American electorate, but so, too, are members of the professional middle class. Neither group is likely to be attracted by a call to the pre–Civil Rights Era.[11]

And so even in the wake of a Republican victory and in a political environment unsettled by terrorism, Americans were still rejecting the old wedge politics and the reopening of such settled questions as the equality of the races and the genders. Despite the president's embrace of a libertarian economics around taxes, the new spirit of community and solidarity that was bred by the events of September 11 pointed away from a politics of radical individualism. This was a continuation of 1990s trends, not, as some thought, a reversal. The President's embrace of national service as an ideal suggested that he was as aware of this as anyone. And the new, more positive attitude toward government suggested that at a time when Americans decided they had real enemies, government was unlikely to be one of them. Both trends pointed more toward the left than the right. One of the earliest tests—over whether airport security should become a task for federal employees or private sector companies—the government won, to the chagrin of conservatives in the House of Representatives.

The new patriotism, the new seriousness, and the new solidarity pointed to a style of politics more akin to the ethos of Harry Truman and Dwight Eisenhower than to the ideological styles of either the 1960s or the 1980s. This does not imply a return to the 1950s. Few things were more striking during the war against the Taliban than the triumph of certain ideas from the 1960s, especially the equality of men and women. A conservative administration used feminist values—including a strong speech by First Lady Laura Bush—as part of its argument for the morality of the struggle against terrorism. The arguments against the Taliban were arguments for not only political but also religious liberty. A hard right religious politics rang hollow, as both Jerry Falwell and Pat Robertson learned.

The wars of the past—over culture in the 1960s and over government's role in the 1980s—seem profoundly irrelevant to the new moment. That is why Third Ways and Fourth Ways, and, perhaps Fifth Ways—however imperfectly they are realized—will continue to set the tone of politics. Americans spent the 1990s trying to heal the wounds of the old culture wars and to shake off the politics of the past. In the first decade of this century, propelled by crisis and a sense of the urgency of politics, we might actually succeed.

But there are no guarantees. The old habits of partisanship and wedge politics die hard. A new politics will arise only if the assorted new "ways" become more than short-term gimmicks. And in contemporary politics, overcoming the pressures to think only in the short-term requires courage, commitment, and a faith that democracies ultimately reward achievement and vision. Paradoxically, all the new ways have arisen precisely because that faith remains in such short supply.

NOTES

1. See John B. Judis and Ruy Teixeira, *The Emerging Democratic Majority* (New York: Scribner's, 2002).

2. David Brooks, "Up from Libertarianism," *Weekly Standard,* Aug. 19, 1996.

3. William Galston addressing the Democratic Leadership Council in January 1989, as quoted in John B. Judis, "From Hell," *New Republic,* Dec. 19, 1994.

4. Philip Collins, as quoted in E. J. Dionne Jr., "The Role of Vision in Politics," *Washington Post,* May 19, 2001.

5. As quoted in E. J. Dionne Jr., "A 50 Percent Presidency," interview by the author, *Washington Post,* July 6, 2001.

6. Ibid.

7. Ibid.

8. Quotes in this and the following paragraph are from E. J. Dionne Jr., "Seriously, a Political Turn for the Better," interview by the author, *Washington Post,* Oct. 7, 2001.

9. Ibid.

10. Jeffrey Bell, "Understanding Strong Presidents," *Weekly Standard,* Nov. 18, 2002.

11. Judis and Teixeira, *Emerging Democratic Majority.*

Into the Unknown

Unity and Conflict after September 11, 2001

Jonathan Rieder

We have roamed far and wide over the last fourteen chapters, from the tensions of race to the heated disputes of culture war, from the distinctive dilemmas of Jewish organizations and black intellectuals to the global forces that shape decisions to migrate. Along the way we have encountered gentle polemic and the cool dispassion of social science, analytic journalism in defense of a liberal Third Way and a prophetic sermon in favor of conservative compassion.

Given the range of subjects examined and the levels of analysis engaged, it seems only fitting to pick up the thread of the introduction to ask, Is there some higher unity in all this? What vision of the American state, civil society, and culture emerges from these reflections? Ultimately, what kind of people are we revealed to be? And, given the impact of September 11, how does global threat alter or vindicate the analysis of this volume?

These questions map out the territories of the coda. In the first part I reflect on the composite impression of the United States that can be extracted from the diverse takes offered by this volume. In the second part I consider how September 11 and its aftermath have impinged on the balance of conflict and consensus, division and solidarity, in American life. The third part brings the thematic strands of the first two parts together by suggesting how the forces identified in this volume have conditioned the U.S. response to attack. Finally, the fourth part identifies the conflicts that are likely to emerge in the years ahead over competing visions of domestic politics and the United States' role in the world.

TOWARD CIVIC NATIONALISM

Perhaps it is best to return in closing to our starting point: the mighty fears of fragmentation voiced on the left and the right, by the pundits and by the people. Issuing such warnings has formed something of a cottage industry for decades now. In the summer of 1969 President Richard Nixon warned, "Our fundamental values [are] under bitter and even violent attack. . . . We live in a deeply troubled and profoundly unsettled time. Drugs, crime, campus revolts, racial discord, draft resistance—on every hand we find old standards violated, old values discarded."[1] Taking note of widespread mistrust in the political system and volatile "issue politics" like Vietnam and race that "polarize the electorate sharply," a more cerebral Daniel Bell, the Harvard professor, worried in 1976, "We have then the classic recipe for what political scientists call 'a crisis of the regime.'"[2]

The jeremiads have issued forth ever since, ebbing and flowing with the cadences of conflict, variously fixing concern about breakdown on "the great divide" between the races, the upsurge of the Christian right, even the National Endowment for the Humanities' funding of feminist performance artists. After the 2000 presidential election yielded not just the starkly blue and red electoral map but also the two rival Americas those totemic colors emblazoned, David Brooks wondered in the *Atlantic Monthly*, "These differences are so many and so stark that they lead to some pretty troubling questions. . . . Are Americans any longer a common people? Do we have one national conversation and one national culture? Are we loyal to the same institutions and the same values?"[3]

The cooler tonalities of the authors in this collection indicate a less alarmist sensibility. Underlying their calm is a distinct if loose set of implied axioms about conflict and its role in social life. First, when placed in a larger context, much of the conflict that provokes anxiety appears to be the routine stuff of normal social life and of democracy too. Second, the precise balance of conciliation and conflict has always varied greatly across our history, but the presence of both is part of the mix of American life. Third, integration is often a product of institutional arrangements that permit different kinds of citizens to get along as much

as it is of shared narratives and values. Fourth, fractiousness has often
been a powerful engine of creativity, leading to the incorporation of new
social groups, the discovery of new beliefs and meanings, and the redress
of injustice.

As we consider this rhythm of harmony and dissension, a contradictory dynamic reveals itself across the spheres of cultural dispute, ethnic
and racial relations, and political life. On the one hand, we have confronted organized expressions of conflict that generate much heat and
light. Christian rightists have castigated their enemies as "secular humanists" and sodomites. Some practitioners of identity politics have rejected the identity of "American" as a vile, ersatz concoction, just as some
"Americans" have reviled blacks and immigrants as an alien presence.
And a fiercely ideological claque of House Republicans has demonized
its opponents as beyond the moral pale. In all those instances contention
has gone beyond spirited disagreement to something less savory: transforming opponents into enemies and casting them out from the community of loyal opposition.

On the other hand, we have run up against less contentious dynamics at work in American life, as well as the methodological mistakes that
hinder grasping them. The manifestoes of the partisans of the most vivid
conflicts have not always reflected the sensibilities of the vast majority
of Americans. Indeed, such outbursts have often run counter to those
vernacular leanings. As a result the most spectacular moments of polarization on the surface of American life can easily obscure the underlying
glacial movement toward stability and integration.

Much of the nation has made its peace with the upheavals that have
rearranged sexual life and family relations. As Paul DiMaggio shows in
his chapter on attitudes toward sex education, gender roles, government
support for the arts, and other charged matters, "Americans are far more
united in their opinions on social and cultural issues than talk of culture
wars would lead one to believe; indeed, their views on many issues were
becoming *more* united at precisely the time that scholars and journalists
were warning of growing polarization" (chap. 4).

A similar movement toward integration appears in the realm of ethnic and racial pluralism. In a very brief period Americans have negoti-
ated not just the civil rights revolution but a demographic transition of
immense proportions. In one of those recurrent moments in which the
nation is forced to redefine the meaning of *Americanism,* the United States
has stretched the boundaries of ethnic, religious, and racial belonging to
make room for new people. Despite all the cries about the "balkaniz-

ing" of America, Mary C. Waters points out, surprising numbers of the children of the new immigrants are embracing the language of their new country. In the process, one might add, they are fashioning hybrid identities that have an unmistakably American cast.

Even in the political realm where Third Way and Fourth Way ideologies are rearranging the content of left and right thinking, passions have mainly flowed through established channels. The Christian right, which seemed like a wild populist surge in its early triumphalist phase, ended up entangled in the intricacies of "normal politics," seeking to carve out a niche as one more player in the pluralist mix. Reactionaries in the House continue to try to highjack the policy apparatus, but the discipline of the electoral marketplace exerts its mollifying force, as Democratic victories over conservative ideologues in New Jersey and Virginia after September 11 made clear.

In each of these arenas it is possible to detect if not a crystallizing consensus then at least a center of gravity that is captured by neither the populist conservative apotheosis of the silent majority nor the left demonology of a hidebound Middle America. This center may not fit some ideologue's rendering of "progressive"—it has recurrently exhibited a preference for moderate government—but it is essentially, if modestly, liberal and democratic. To recall once more E. J. Dionne Jr.'s fine rendering, the center consists of a "rich but not necessarily contradictory mix of liberal instincts and conservative values" (chap. 14).

There is nothing mysterious about this "vital center." In good American fashion it has been achieved rather than ordained—and hard won too. The center has come to its moderate state sometimes grudgingly, sometimes kicking; to get it to realize its most generous potential, social movements have had to nudge it, lambast it, and appeal to its sense of fairness. Nonetheless, some of the very sectors—if not individuals then at least their children—that flung themselves into populist-sounding resistance in the late 1960s have come to embrace a good deal of the liberalized regime of race, gender, and culture. Even "the most traditional Americans," Alan Wolfe notes perceptively, "have incorporated into their lives some of the social transformations both positively and negatively associated with the 1960s."[4] The diffusion of a vernacular feminism, characterized by steely demands for equal pay and social respect, offers only one of legion examples of this dynamic.

This context of insurgency and resistance properly historicizes the process of change, just as the notion of social learning—the rhythm of initial rejection and gradual, if selective, assimilation—psychologizes the process. But ultimately this process has been preeminently political: an extension of citizenship and democratic political culture.

As the example of popular feminism suggests, this movement has a "private" aspect, realized in the growth of values of individual rights and personal choice over traditional morality in sexual matters and family life. It is easy to scoff at the most trivial expressions of tolerance in the freak-show spectacles of popular culture. But from the legitimation of abortion to the validation of "alternative sexualities," from respect for children's rights to the constraints placed on male violence against women, Americans have affirmed more than narcissistic individualism. The Jeffersonian stress on "the pursuit of happiness" carries the implication of a folk universalism: mutuality inheres in generalizable claims to recognize the moral autonomy of individuals.

A similar democratic process has been evident in the erosion of older racialist ideologies, liberating human possibility in the process. To borrow Israeli political scientist Yaron Ezrahi's term, the United States has made a big step beyond "Ethno-Democracy."[5] Ezrahi was talking about something distinct to Israel, but he underscored a general dilemma of democracies: how to square democratic ideals and practices with the communal sentiments that reinforce or subvert democracy.

In places like Switzerland and the Netherlands this balancing act takes a rigidly architectural form. In the United States the process has been entangled in the heritage of informality, voluntarism, and individualism. In Garry Wills's words, "Americans have regularly contrasted 'society' and 'government,' and if the theory of *government* has been liberal, the practices of *society* have been decidedly illiberal."[6] But even this way of framing the issue does not go far enough, for illiberal sentiments of a communal sort, from antiblack racism to Protestant supremacism, have shaped the informal practices of government no less than of society. Although the divide between the individualism of our formal tradition and the communal sentiments of our community life invites hypocrisy, the gap between our ideals and practices has often provoked outrage and criticism, thereby reawakening our deepest moral values and their power of persuasion.

Those communal strands have not disappeared, nor have the hardest tasks of incorporation such as residential integration been completed. But despite the rage for identity politics and policies that make race a key criterion in allocation and representation, American life has undergone a profound detribalization. Paul Starr writes, "The restriction of race- and gender-conscious legal remedies, which have never enjoyed majority support, touches only a limited aspect of the larger transformation that has occurred. The new system of 'status relations' penetrates deep into civil society" (chap. 12). "How we talk about and interpret race," concludes Orlando Patterson, "often bears little relation to the progress achieved by ordinary people in their cross-ethnic relations. . . . Afro-Americans have also become full members of . . . the nation's moral community and cultural life."[7]

The realignment of cultural warfare along traditionalist-modernist lines, like the decline of anti-Semitism, further attests to the growing permeability of group boundaries. The gradual political incorporation of Asians, West Indians, and Latinos is further revitalizing democratic practice. Even informal, perhaps trifling, markers such as the infusion of the cuisine of Asians, South Asians, Caribbeans, and Mexicans into the American mix embody the mulatto culture and identities that are being forged.

The United States is moving, if not rushing, toward the "postethnic" ideal described by David A. Hollinger, which "prefers voluntary to prescribed affiliations, appreciates multiple identities, pushes for communities of wide scope, recognizes the constructed character of ethno-racial groups, and accepts the formation of new groups as a part of the normal life of a democratic society."[8] This process implies a more perfect realization of a civic nationalism that considers the nation not as a tribe based on shared race, language, or ethnicity but "as a community of equal, rights-bearing citizens, united in patriotic attachment to a shared set of political practices and values."[9]

Yet the robustness of certain aspects of our democracy cannot obscure a more pessimistic, at least bittersweet, tone that hovers close to the surface of many of the ruminations in *The Fractious Nation?* Many of the authors in this volume recognize that the civic part of this "civic democracy" is not quite civic enough.

I mean more by this than the simple fact that nothing in this book denies the endurance of "fractious tendencies," and even fragmenting ones, although this persistence provides the first bracing qualification of "optimism." At numerous points the authors have gone out of their way to stress that claims about narrowing divides and growing tolerance acquire rigor only in reference to some baseline of comparison. Moreover, Cecilia Muñoz's chapter reminds us how in the 1990s feelings of danger and displacement in Florida, Texas, and California generated anti-immigrant legislation that threatened constitutional community. If that mean-spirited moment has diminished, there is nothing to ensure that it cannot revive. In the nativist surge of right-wing parties in European elections throughout 2002, economic anxiety, street crime, and discontent over immigration brought antidemocratic tendencies unexpectedly to the fore.

Second, the very institutional analysis that vindicates a sunnier view of the civic culture has a profoundly unsettling implication: highly organized cadres can disproportionately affect outcomes. Neither the centrist sensibilities of the electorate nor the extension of norms of ethnic tolerance were able to arrest the power of right-wing House Republicans to push forward draconian immigration legislation in the 1990s. Civic culture, habits of the heart, democratic learning—none of these airy concepts achieves traction independent of such gritty forces as the state of the economy, group struggle, or the alignment of power.

Third, the *civic* in civic democracy should not be romanticized as the apotheosis of the good and just life. Nor should extending rights, including marginal groups, and reinforcing respect be confused with a deep participatory ethic. The somewhat abstract and formal quality of these gains is compatible with "bowling alone," to use Robert Putnam's title, as individuals and groups gain the negative freedom to pursue their own personal and collective needs. One can imagine a more expansive vision of the civic life that is not compatible with the decline of political participation, the influence of corporate wealth in our national political life, or the erosion of debate on critical issues of human suffering and social inequality.

Put somewhat differently, the integrative tendencies at work in the United States—the diffusion of formal rights, the culture of consumption, the informal etiquette of ethnic respect—make for a certain thinness in public life. But this endemic tendency has been reinforced or mitigated by periodic swings in American life between private preoccupation and a more vital sense of public purpose. The recent context has featured various versions of privatization, from school vouchers to faith-based charities, fixation on personal enrichment symbolized by the cult of the stock market, and the absence of urgency about the plight of the nation's most vulnerable citizens.

Mobilizing the will to reduce their suffering requires the revival of moral sympathy. John DiIulio Jr., the first head of President Bush's Office of Faith-Based Charities and a leading exponent of compassionate conservatism, argues that the radically individualistic strains in Republican ideology suffer from a heartless inability to imagine the disprivileged as fellow members of the community (chap. 13). Drawing from the model of his beloved Catholic catechism and the ideal of subsidiarity, he seeks to energize the larger society's sense of connection to ghetto drug addicts, criminals, and teenage single moms. DiIulio quotes St. Matthew, who is quoting Jesus: "I was hungry and you gave me food, I was thirsty and you gave me something to drink. . . . I was in prison and you came to visit me. . . . [J]ust as you did it to one of the least of these who are members of my family, you did it to me." Before all else it is the role of family and community to embody our capacity to care about the "least of these" in a direct and personal form.

As moving as DiIulio's lamentation may be, one has to wonder not about his call for sympathy but about the prophetic rhetorical form through which he expresses it. Can revivalism by itself rouse the spirit? Can federal efforts to inspire faith-based initiatives in civil society of the sort DiIulio promoted when he was in the Bush administration substitute for more coherent federal initiatives? Historically, Theda Skocpol demonstrates in this book, the ethic of care has best been served by reform movements that fortify larger solidarities by linking different classes, regions, and ethnicities through universalistic social policies promoted by the national government. In such cases sentiments of care achieve institutional leverage, and the state becomes both the agent of community at the grandest level and a symbol of our shared obligation to care for all citizens.

It might seem as if the ascension of the Third Way vitiates this past formula for effective social policy. But the logic of the global economy, even as its emphasis on market incentives reshapes the left across the developed world, does not eliminate the need for state engagement; if social justice is to prevail, there is a need to strike a balance between the state, civil society institutions, and the marketplace. "A society that allows the market to infiltrate too far into other institutions," admonishes Anthony Giddens, "will experience a failure of public life."[10] In the United States the persistence of a dispirited ghetto underclass, the crisis of health care for large numbers of citizens, and the uncertain future of a significant portion of the second generation of immigrants call out not just for sympathy but for national action to implement it.

In the end these matters of privilege and inequality underscore the great limitation of the entire debate on "fragmentation": its tendency to reduce debate to matters of communal integration and moral consensus. Collectively, many of the authors in this book suggest at least two things that are wrong with this focus. First, manifestations of "fragmentation" are often inseparable from larger structural forces. The decision to migrate, Douglas Massey makes clear in his chapter, is shaped by vast global forces, and no amount of moralistic breast beating will arrest their power. Second, in the competition for the public's attention, focusing on issues such as exaggerated instances of political correctness distracts from dealing with more pressing needs of homelessness, health care, and poverty.

The imperfect quality of our civility underscores the disparity between the United States' success in forging a national community of ethnic, racial, sexual, and religious difference and our failure to achieve a strong identification with the least privileged members of our nation. Far from an aberration in American life, this tension reprises an ancient friction between utility and virtue, between market and community. Recurrently, the disappointments of one pole of that tension have helped nurture compensatory desires for its opposite. Interestingly enough, the Al Qaeda attack on the United States revealed longings for wholeness that thinner versions of civility could not possibly satisfy.

AFTER SEPTEMBER 11: CIVIC SOLIDARITY VERSUS THE UNITY OF BLOOD

What are we to make of the speed with which the new climate of national solidarity emerged after September 11? In a sense it vindicates the general import of *The Fractious Nation?* Solidarity, which looks strange against a backdrop of presumptive fragmentation, seems less so in the context of this volume's stress on preexisting solidarities, narrowing divides, and integrative forces. At the same time, the passion of our mutual embrace as citizens and the surge of nationalism that accompanied it seem continuous with a longing for a richer form of national communion.

All forms of solidarity, however, are not the same, and the emphasis on continuity seems out of kilter with the radically novel circumstances that prompted the *New York Times* to begin a new daily section called "A Nation Challenged." Moreover, both the positive and negative aspects of the national ideal identified above inhere in its "thinness"; by contrast, the new solidarity is rooted in the emotive experience of shared wounds and is generated by a sharp sense of external threat. Such primordial forms of nationalism, based on an aroused unity against fiendish internal or external enemies, have a deeply compromised history. One can thus easily imagine a more authoritarian aspect to the current unity—not civic nationalism but the nationalism of blood and tribe. This general nervousness is reinforced by the specific history of red scares and

100 percent Americanism that every so often has energized American "patriotism." To assess the dangers of this seeming disappearance of fractiousness, we need to consider in more detail the surge of induced solidarity that came to the fore after September 11.

Following the contested presidential election of 2000, the partisan and ideological cleavages widened by the wounds of the Florida recount finally settled down into something less dire than a full-blown legitimacy crisis. Even Supreme Court justices, court observers discerned, seemed to pull back in subsequent decisions and to vote in somewhat surprising ways, worried they had hurt the Court's aura of impartiality. Complicated by split authority, with Democrats holding sway in the Senate, the intensity of vendetta gave way to policy bickering over the tax cut, the education bill, and prescription drug plans.

The launching of a weirdly diabolical form of Jihad, implemented by Islamic holy warriors who practiced crashing planes on video game flight simulators and drank vodka in Florida lap-dance palaces, smashed this semblance of normal politics in one fell swoop. Beyond the apocalyptic aftershocks and the imminent sense that maybe we had entered the end time, given muted expression by President Bush's sly references to "The Evil One" (an evangelical Christian nickname for Lucifer), it was the prosaic dimensions of the unraveling that loomed most ominously in the aftermath. Actually, it was a sign of the times that drawing fine lines between these two realms became increasingly difficult, at least for the moment. As anthrax contamination ricocheted from Florida tabloid to Majority Leader Tom Daschle's office on Capital Hill and on to random citizens struck down by cross-contamination of letters in mail sorting machines, humdrum routines and apocalyptic musings fused in little frissons of fear before crossing a bridge, ascending an elevator, or opening an envelope.

Here was an assault on one version of the national idea. That continental self-sufficiency had given Americans the privilege of immunity has been a staple of American self-understanding, a feature of the national identity of exceptionalism. In a sense, it provided the ecological condition of our spiritual self-conception as blessed by providence, the city on a hill. But as journalist Mark Lisheron wrote in elegiac response, "An innocence eroding for nearly 30 years was buried as finally and violently Tuesday as the ground floors of the World Trade Center towers. Manhattan was reduced to Beirut, Kabul, Sarajevo. Our streets, our skies, our workplaces and our homes—our lives—were pitched into the global maelstrom. We have lost forever the illusion that the United States could bestride the world with its economic and political power and somehow not be of the world. The world had issued many warnings."[11]

The new reality was greater than a larger world of nations intruding into our national consciousness. The great beyond of macroevents had acquired the insidious power to unsettle everyday life at its pedestrian, Seinfeldian core. As Erving Goffman, reflecting on the routine expectancies that gird everyday life, observed, "One sometimes speaks of an individual as being 'terrorized'" when a sense of alarm does not permit him or her to regard the environment without a high level of attention.[12] This loss of nonchalance had a cost; it required citizens not just to scan the environment but to question it, for terrorism exploits the very "normal appearances" social actors use to reassure themselves that "nothing is happening here" as a masquerade behind which they dissemble their true intentions. "Bedevilments of the environment," wrote Goffman, inject "enough real issues, and each real possibility breeds its own set of unjustly suspected appearances" (283).

Terrorism thus intensifies the possibilities of a "normalcy show," which plays out "with one individual seeking for warnings while concealing his suspicions and the others concealing the threat and opportunity they constitute for him while searching for signs that they are suspected" (282). This challenge to the quintessential American value of going about one's business without worrying about others thus has a normative cost too. "The individual not only anticipates uneventfulness but also feels that he has a moral right to count on it" (240). As a result, as the nation returned to "normalcy," it was a more jittery, watchful normalcy that did not, at least initially, permit the somnolence of inattention.

Normalcy disappeared from less elemental endeavors than constructing a dependable sense of reality, which produced a new set of shared priorities. The great political contention of late August and early September 2001, the Social Security lockbox, began to seem eerily remote. So too did the brave Democratic talk of midterm gains in the 2002 election. In one explosive moment the political divisions of Third Way, Fourth Way, and the other archaic ways gave way to an intense community of agreement, as Bush's approval rating soared. The high figures of support garnered by a previously weak President Bush underlined the same emotional hunger, the reservoir of fellow feeling, the willingness to let bygones be bygones that prevailed elsewhere. "Bush is my president," declared Al Gore, effecting the final mending of a quarrelsome community. Where is the fragmentation in all this? Not inside the body politic but outside, in the shards of flying glass and twisted steel and bodies reduced to their frighteningly dispersed parts.

Citizens' hunger for continuity generated heroic icons. Heroes help us think, and grieve, by giving concrete form to our inchoate longings and abstract values. In the process they bind us together in common rites of appreciation. In a pluralistic society there's no one icon. As a result the impulse to affirm not just social solidarity but also reprieve from existential terror took countless forms. The rebirth of the onetime bristling New York mayor Rudy Giuliani as the heroic avatar of New York grit— his newly found ability to temper command with vulnerability, to speak plainly and bravely to a reeling public—ratified his transformation.

Even more than into the political domain, the semblance of solidarity seeped into the culture. In perfect display of the power of external crisis to bind the nation, the emotive cohesiveness of citizens was a counterpoint to the physical fracture of the World Trade Center and Pentagon. In New York City investment bankers and bond traders physically and mentally hugged police, fire people, and emergency workers, delegations of whom rang the bell to announce the reopening of the stock exchange. Soon after September 11, when a plane full of Dominican immigrants crashed into the Irish neighborhood of the Rockaways, which had given up many firemen to the World Trade Center, members of both communities came to grieve together in a ceremony that mingled Dominican and American flags. Unity was not confined to relations among New Yorkers. Professional baseball and hockey games were postponed and canceled to allow the audience to listen to the president. Pundits even observed that the tragedy had made New Yorkers more a part of the United States. Rescue teams comprising veterans from the heartland of knowing Oklahoma City and the residents of small Virginia hamlets seemed to be declaring, "We are all New Yorkers now."

Across the divide of classes and cultures, the refined and the vulgar, sophisticates and provincials, American flags were hung and draped and paraded in earnest grieving and affirmation. Newspapers ran stories about onetime 1960s radicals who never imagined that one day they would display the stars and stripes. Todd Gitlin, a sociologist and one of those former radicals, hung a flag from the balcony of his Greenwich Village apartment and was quoted as saying, "The flag affirms that you belong to a nation that has been grievously hurt, and you want to show solidarity."[13]

The most poignant commemorative rituals focused on the dead. A spate of racially tinged deaths—Gavin Cato, the little West Indian boy run over and killed by a Hasidic Jewish caravan in Crown Heights, or the countless drive-by shootings of teens during the crack craze of the 1980s and early 1990s—had long accustomed New Yorkers to jerry-rigged shrines of grief-stricken remembrance. Now firehouses across metropolitan New York City crafted their own memorials, and neighbors who had never thought about the daily risk-taking of the protective services stopped by to honor their sacrifices. The *New York Times* captured the mood poignantly in its daily efforts to honor the small acts and ordinary virtues of the dead. Recognizing that these were no ordinary deaths—more precisely, that the social meaning of these deaths was extraordinary—the *Times* foreswore the generic form of the obituary for more novelistic forms of biographical compression: minimalist vignettes that let evocative and emblematic details speak for themselves: "Robert C. McLaughlin Jr. ran with the bulls in Pamplona, visited the killing fields in Cambodia and sailed the South China Sea . . . and later, as vice president for emerging markets at Cantor Fitzgerald, roamed the playing fields of American capitalism. He was a man of adventure and action, a tough guy. He also wrote poetry." As the father of a baby not quite one-half year old, only a few months earlier McLaughlin had exhorted in verse, "Roll over young Nicholas / Roll over and see the light / Of day that awaits you."[14]

The spareness of the quiet elegies intensified their power to move the reader. These details of difference accomplished a paradoxical effect; rather than particularizing, they underscored our common humanity.

It would seem coldly blasé not to be moved by all this drawing together and reaching out toward one another. The nation's newfound appreciation of firemen, who emerged as symbols of moral, as well as physical, courage, reflected a genuine communitarian respect for those willing to sacrifice for the greater good. And the manifest pride of the kin of the passengers on United Air Flight 93 who stormed the terrorists in the cabin and crashed the plane into a Pennsylvania field to avert its Washington, D.C., target cannot be dismissed as mere chest thumping. In affirming this transcendent vision of obligation, Americans clearly embraced a circle of identity greater than their own little communities of faith and tribe. Less clear was the depth and meaning of this change of collective heart.

THE CIVIC CONSTELLATION ENDURES

In putting an end to fractiousness the events of September 11 radically shook the foundations of the nation. Thus it is natural to reach for metaphors of rupture to make sense of our plight. After all, the gap between then and now seems self-evident. In the initial ruminations pundits referred to the attack as a "hinge event." It was said that we had been "irrevocably changed." Parallels were drawn with Pearl Harbor and other moments of critical imprinting that had shifted the course of history.

The imagery of discontinuity raises the possibility that the patterns identified in *The Fractious Nation?* no longer obtain. Certainly it is possible to glimpse in the primordial feelings of solidarity a threat to the more civic form of nationalism that has marked recent decades. The ominous comment of Ari Fleischer, President Bush's press secretary, in response to a remark by political satirist Bill Maher—"It's a terrible thing to say and it's unfortunate. There are reminders to all Americans that they need to watch what they say, watch what they do"—suggested how easily solidarity could slip from warm fellow feeling into something gamier: trimming back on respect for dissent.[15]

The post–September 11 mood also gave new support to the legitimacy of ethnic profiling based on "biological" signs of appearance. Generalized suspiciousness was infused with specifically ethnic and racial content. Most of the hijackers—Arabs, with swarthy complexion, who practiced a strange Wahabbi brand of a not entirely familiar religion—were visibly different. Along with the ability of sleepers to lurk undetected in the open spaces of American life and the seeming inability of the INS to track visa transgressors who slip across the borders, these circumstances intensified the nightmare scenario of some immigration restrictionists: aliens hostile to the American enterprise, Manchurian candidates mixing and mingling among us. Suddenly, the line between anxiety attack and political attack seemed unnervingly blurry.

If even Attorney General John Ashcroft had come to declaim against racial profiling, now ethnic profiling struck increasing numbers of people as common sense: seated on a plane, some liberals asked by way of confession, would you really not look askance at a Middle Easterner with a Muslim name whose screen saver was adorned by a bearded man in Islamic dress? This was the climate in which black Americans voiced a new appreciation for profiling, now that the heat was suddenly off them. In a pointed example of black-white convergence, roughly the same percentage of blacks and whites thought Middle Eastern travelers should be scrutinized more suspiciously than others, Somini Sengupta reported in the *New York Times*. "Black New Yorkers joke among themselves about their own reprieve from racial profiling. Even the language of racial grievance has shifted: Overnight, the cries about driving while black have become flying while brown."[16]

So much for displaced gallows humor. In some corners of the United States ethnic tension transmuted into actual conflict. In the once insular Italian-American neighborhood of Bay Ridge, Brooklyn, home in recent years to increasing numbers of Arab and Asian immigrants, a war veteran took to flying larger and larger American flags after September 11. In seeming recoil the Arab family across the street began to fly the Palestinian flag. The veteran retaliated with a sign that declared, "Fuck Allah." The Arab family summoned the police, who demanded that the veteran remove the sign. The man justified tribal street insult with the rhetoric of formal rationality, citing his "First Amendment [rights]. How dare you tell me what I can do and say in my own home. This is private property. I fought in a war to preserve my right to speak."

Animosity took more physical forms. Muslims were the victims of deprecatory cries of "towel heads" and worse. Schoolyard bullies abused Arab and Muslim children. Sikhs were attacked by confused thugs who couldn't tell them from Arabs and Muslims. Maniac guardians of Americanism rammed their cars into mosques, murdered turbaned Americans, and firebombed convenience stores run by Middle Eastern merchants.

Government abridgements of due process also worried many observers, who cited the fate of Arab and Muslim detainees languishing in limbo or military tribunals that might jettison constitutional values. More generally, the Bush administration has sought to expand the claims of executive power, to restrict access to information, and to control the press. The absorption of the Immigration and Naturalization Service into the Homeland Security Agency, Cecilia Muñoz notes (chap. 7), risks eroding the rights of immigrants, legal residents, and citizens merely suspected of being either. During the winter of 2002 it was reported that Pentagon designers were at work on a supercomputer that could rummage through troves of personal data, from credit card receipts and EZpass scans to phone records and bank transactions. "Total Information Awareness" was the Orwellian title of this effort to enhance the state's capacity to monitor the citizenry and threaten privacy. The very name of the law embodying the Bush administration's response to September 11, the Patriot Act, seemed to provide the president with an immunity from the very criticism that defines a civic version of patriotism.

Yet notwithstanding these troubling developments, in the broader scheme of things the resilience of democratic restraint jumps out more than its violation. The Bush administration, embroiled in the uproar over the Fleischer comment about Maher, was forced to backtrack. Over time it softened the harshest features of military tribunals and decided to try Zacarias Moussaoui, the alleged twentieth hijacker, in an open court. Some federal courts overturned features of the administration's program, and a surge of bipartisan opposition in the House and Senate killed the launch of Total Information Awareness. Even more impressively, no wholesale retreat into undiscriminating xenophobia occurred. So as compelling as it is to focus on the rhetoric of disjuncture, the continuities between the nation before and after September 11 remain profound. There are a number of reasons why this should be so.

First, the imagery of discontinuity implicit in claims such as *September 11 shattered the world we knew* has a suspiciously functionalist character. Marking off a special time by suspending our sense of ordinary life, such declarations help bind us in a shared mission, forge an expansive sense of community, and summon us to existential challenge. They also help us grasp the enormity of the ungraspable. At the same time such metaphors may not best illuminate empirical reality.

Second, old patterns never disappear entirely, even if they are temporarily eclipsed or eventually superseded. This applies to large transformations no less than to cataclysmic events. Even in a postindustrial, knowledge-based society, in which information has become a critical resource, the older powers of capital and land have not utterly dissipated. New cleavages and connections grow up around and over the old ones as well as supplant them.

Third, much of the ritual unity after September 11 was temporary. Perhaps if ongoing bombings heightened insecurity or if anthrax had continued to spread fear and death through the mails, panic would have weakened democratic restraint. But as the passing of time salved its wounds, the nation returned to quarreling. Within weeks right-wing hawks, mistrustful of Colin Powell's caution, sought to press their agenda of attack on Iraq, Sudan, and the Bekaa Valley, and Rush Limbaugh opined that there was no reason not to exploit the emergency to push through on the antimissile shield. After an interval of decency New Jersey reverted to the old habit of enticing lower Manhattan firms to move across the Hudson River. And six months later, as the clarities of bombing the Taliban and Al Qaeda gave way to the elusive complexities of West Bank suicide bombers and West Bank settlements, Bush, vulnerable for abdicating from the Middle East peace process and his own wavering signals, began to see his positive ratings slide.

The fourth reason for continuity lies beyond the passive survival of

old ways or the lapse into normal politics: the pattern of civic nationalism described in *The Fractious Nation?* has become deeply rooted in
America's social fabric, and the Al Qaeda attack did not disrupt that pattern. When all was said and done, the preexisting cultural, social, and
political configuration shaped the nation's response to attack; upheld—
and extended, to some extent—normative boundaries of respectful pluralism; and placed institutional and normative limits on antidemocratic
challenges to civic forms of nationalism. On balance the continuities between the time before and after September 11 were more vivid than the
novel departures.

This civic pattern could be seen in a certain cosmopolitanism that suffused the initial phases of the American war against terrorism. Even before the Al Qaeda attack the most provincial and primordial features of
the United States' relation to global difference were shrinking. The emergence of a world economy, with all the dynamism and fluidity that it in-
spires, has always suggested some variant of globalism as its correlate.
Whether construed as the political face of global capital, as a response
to the geopolitical conditions of a dangerous international order, or as
an idealistic effusion, internationalism is a "natural" adaptation to the
changed environment, in which transfers of technology and information,
currency and people, intensify in volume and speed. To the extent that
both proponents of a Democratic Third Way and a Republican Fourth
Way embrace free trade, open markets, and global exchange, the isola-
tionist and protectionist wings within both parties—and the xenophobic fears of otherness that have often accompanied those stances—have
been weakened.

President Bush's shift into Spanish before a Mexican-American audience during Mexico's president Vicente Fox's visit to the United States
in 2001 reflected the tight link between free trade and conservative multiculturalism. It does not even matter if this "cosmopolitanism" was par-
tially rooted in the particularity of the Texas economy and local Anglo-
Mexican relations. Switching into another culture's language, of course,
may be taken as a marker of sympathetic connection or a humiliating
concession to power. For the right, which has often fumed at Mexicans
and Cubans who refuse to speak English in the United States, Bush's desire to shift codes and speak Spanish to *American* audiences thus marked
an accommodation to the force of transnational pluralism.

September 11 did not rescind the acknowledgment of a world of per-
meable boundaries; it simply underscored the dangers of permeability
and the need to respond to them with force. It also raised the inevitable

question: what would be the fate of civic nationalism as the United States mobilized against an ideologically strange enemy. "Once it is driven on to the world stage by events," admonished Louis Hartz, absolutist Americanism "is inspired willy-nilly to reconstruct the very alien things it tries to avoid and to reconstruct them in its own image." Hartz had in mind the paradox that American isolationism and interventionism both reflected the same American fear of the strange. "An absolute national morality is inspired either to withdraw from 'alien' things or to transform them: it cannot live in comfort constantly by their side."[17]

Absolutist Americanism did not disappear altogether from national life. Hints of the zeal to subdue otherness appeared in Bush's initial talk about launching a "crusade." Throughout 2002 it could be heard regularly in the more florid anti-Muslim rhetoric of the Christian right preachers long associated with the Republican Party. With its echoes of Ronald Reagan's evangelical language of "evil empire," Bush's Manichean formulation of the "axis of evil" evinced the same righteous moralism.

Still, self-righteous absolutism was never the dominant note struck by the nation or the Bush administration. Throughout the war in Afghanistan the United States dispensed with the ethnic mania and jingoistic intoxication that had deformed many previous bouts of intervention. "We have no intention of imposing our culture," President Bush reassured everyone in his 2002 State of the Union Address. He studiously avoided stigmatizing Islam, separating the terrorist squads who perverted the faith from those who were its true exemplars. "No people on Earth yearn to be oppressed, or aspire to servitude, or eagerly await the midnight knock of the secret police . . . [Anyone who doubts that should] look to Islam's own rich history, with its centuries of learning and tolerance and progress." Invoking the universality of the longing for liberty, he underscored, "No nation owns these aspirations."

The wry and reasonable tone adopted by Secretary of Defense Donald Rumsfeld in his press briefings epitomized a similar disavowal of any zealot's intention. Bush's coterie displayed a savvy acceptance of cultural complexity—and limits on its own transformative powers—as it threw itself into a ferocious effort to concoct an algorithm of alliance, mixing Tajiks, the Dari-speaking former constitutional monarch and other "good" Pashtuns, ethnic Uzbeks, Persian speakers in the East, plus assorted tribal warlords. In an ironic reversal Republicans, long critical of political constraints placed by liberals on military victory in Vietnam, restrained the armies of the Northern Alliance, lest they march too quickly into Kabul, thereby upsetting the delicate ethnic balance. Mindful of historical precedents, even military commanders displayed sensitivity to the feelings of Afghanis who might not wish to happen on the United States Army "in country."

It is important to underscore what Bush's "cosmopolitanism" did not entail, for its limitations reveal a distinct parallel with the career of civic conservatism in the domestic sphere. It was a cramped and canny form of cosmopolitanism. Heavily skewed to decorative public relations, liberal tolerance, and the appearance of cultural sensitivity, "cosmopolitanism" remained driven by great power needs of control and security. Both his foray out into the world and his preelection pledge to end Clinton's idealistic experiments in nation building obeyed the same hard-boiled logic of America-First interest. Moreover, globalism extended more to unfettered open markets than to multilateral agreements and institutions to regulate the use of chemical warfare, global warming, and land mines. On those occasions when public opinion and geopolitical logic obliged obeisance to the multilateral imperative, multilateralism was pursued as a means more than as an ultimate end. Finally, Bush's version of globalism was indifferent to larger forces beyond the demonic intentions of evil people that created misfortune around the globe. It did not grasp the limits of the market in redressing global inequality. Nor did Bush own up to the misguided United States policies that contributed to the current miasma, including his father's failure to finish off the Republican Guard in 1991.

One should be careful not to sift foreign affairs too earnestly for clues to American identity; too many expediential forces govern the logic of national self-protection. It thus makes sense that civic nationalism was even more evident in the robustness of the United States' internal cosmopolitanism after September 11.

Even before the attack the limits of the hydraulic analogy that presumed economic or social frustration mechanistically spills over into aggressive demonizing of others were obvious. One version of this model held that removing a sharply clarified external threat, as the end of the cold war did, would redirect the impulse to demonize inward, toward gays, blacks, and other minorities. Something quite different unfolded, as the nation displayed its growing acceptance of ethnic, sexual, and cultural difference. The climate of threat that followed the attack on the Pentagon and World Trade Center did not diminish the resilience of norms of tolerance. When the Reverends Jerry Falwell and Pat Robertson decried the attacks on the World Trade Center as God's retribution for homosexuality and abortion, a chorus of denunciation greeted them. Meanwhile, Laura Bush struck a profeminist note in defense of the rights of Afghani women that gained the approval even of the National Organization for Women.

The vitality of democratic rights in the broader society also appeared in the pragmatism of the debate on detainees, military tribunals, and surveillance. Compared to Attorney General Ashcroft, the public exhibited less a reckless zeal to scrap democratic procedures than a reasonable ambivalence about how precisely to strike the balance in the new climate of correctly perceived threat. Proposals to link airline ticket purchases to national databases, to expand the FBI's ability to extend wiretaps across phones and other media, and to create a national identification card gave credence to nervousness voiced by civil rights advocates and right-wing libertarians. But liberal congressman Barney Frank's alliance with conservative Republicans suspicious of government power produced some basis of dissent from the rush to a more draconian terrorism bill.

Alan Dershowitz's brief for a national identity card with a chip that would match the bearer's fingerprint reflected the pragmatism that sought not to junk all the gains of a rights society but to achieve balance between rights and security. "As a civil libertarian, I am instinctively skeptical of such tradeoffs. But . . . it could be an effective tool for preventing terrorism [that could reduce] . . . other law-enforcement mechanisms especially racial and ethnic profiling that pose even greater dangers to civil liberties." As for some putative right to anonymity, Dershowitz concluded, "I don't believe we can afford to recognize such a right in this age of terrorism. No such right is hinted at in the Constitution."[18]

Beyond the puzzle of defining a judicious response to genuine threats to national security, civic nationalism appeared less ambivalently in official and institutional responses to ethnocentric recriminations. Early in the crisis Mayor Rudy Giuliani sought to construct a nonethnocentric definition of enemies, cautioning against mean reactions to the Arabs and Muslims he embraced as part of the city's rich polyglot mosaic. President Bush went to a Washington, D.C., mosque, where he took off his shoes and preached tolerance. In his speech before Congress Bush declared, "No one should be singled out for unfair treatment or unkind words because of their ethnic background or religious faith."

The White House induction of Ramadan into the pantheon of American religious celebrations offered a telling sign of the stretching of the official civil religion of Judeo-Christianity. According to Elizabeth Bumiller, Maleeha Lodhi, the Pakistani ambassador to the United States, was "dazzled that the White House had a muezzin, a Muslim religious figure, who delivered the prayers" before the ritual meal of iftar that breaks the daily Ramadan fast. Bush, who wished the fifty-two Muslim diplomats "a blessed Ramadan," served fresh dates, with which Muhammad is said to have broken his fast, and vowed, "We're a nation of many faiths."

"The Republican Party wanted God in public life," Jonathan Smaby noted, "but the overriding implication was that God would be Christian. It wasn't entirely clear that all those seeking more religion in public institutions intended to invite Allah to the proceedings." But clearly the Bush administration has been "broadening its vision of God and religion. While the fact has rarely been so visibly affirmed by our national leaders, America has many more kings than Jesus."[19]

A FRACTIOUS FUTURE? DOMESTIC AND
GLOBAL CONTENTION IN THE YEARS AHEAD

As the nation moved beyond the early period of wound and bereavement, even the Trent Lott affair, an inadvertent yet perversely revealing exercise in collective memory, did not challenge the movement toward civil pluralism. The Lott brouhaha erupted on the occasion of the centennial birthday of Senator Strom Thurmond, who had run for president in 1948 promising to stave off race mixing. Goofily, if somewhat obliquely, Lott mused that if the rest of the country had followed Mississippi's lead in voting for the racist Thurmond, "We wouldn't have had all these problems over all these years."[20]

It would be easy to reject the controversy as another instance of media spectacle—the stylized form through which Americans prefer to confront the awkward legacy of race. Once again the nation was privy to a vivid dramaturgy of personal character and sincerity, replete with overheated cries to repent and atone and redemptive appeals for what Lott called "forgiveness and forbearance." "Segregation," he declared at a press conference, "is a stain on our nation's soul." His subsequent appearance on Black Entertainment Television (BET), where he condemned the "wicked[ness]" of racism and confessed that he was part of "immoral leadership in my part of the country," was distinguished from countless other charged moments of racial transgression and apology mainly by its inept groveling. The infinitely pliable Lott told BET newsman Ed Gordon that he now supported a holiday for Martin Luther King Jr. and even affirmative action. The shallowness of Lott's affect and his obsequious mien were emblematic not just of his failure but of the susceptibility of the entire generic form to hollowness and betrayal.

The larger problem with Lott's apology thus transcended questions of authenticity. The personalistic language of sin and redemption did not adequately honor the institutional realities at work. These included the role of racism in building the modern American party system and the Republican Party's continuing reliance on veiled appeals to antidemocratic sentiments. Ronald Reagan may not have been a racist, but when he opened his campaign in Philadelphia, Mississippi, near the Neshoba County killing field of the trinity of civil rights martyrs, segregationists thrilled to his promise of "states rights." Virginia senator Carl Allen, rebutting charges that he flew the Confederate flag, insisted on righting the record: The Confederate flag, he corrected, *hangs* on the wall of his den. Most embarrassing of all, Attorney General Ashcroft, the man in charge of enforcing federal civil rights statutes, had effusively praised the neoracist magazine *Southern Partisan,* as well as its quixotic effort to rehabilitate the president of the Confederacy, Jefferson Davis.

Yet for all its limitations, the Lott drama offered more than fluffy confection. It served as a genuine ritual moment through which "the shape of the devil" was made incarnate and thereby exorcized. If "deviant forms of behavior, by marking the outer edges of group life, give the inner structure its special character,"[21] Lott gave Bush a bonanza chance to consecrate the far boundary. Seizing the offer to clarify the blurry line between ethnic and civic belonging, the president rebuked Lott sternly and cast him beyond the Republican pale. "Any suggestion that the segregated past was acceptable or positive is offensive, and it is wrong. Recent comments by Senator Lott do not reflect the spirit of our country."[22] Reinforcing the pattern of conservative multiculturalism, the watchword of the Republican leadership quickly became *inclusion,* and Republican leaders tripped over themselves to promise rewards to historic black colleges, not quite grasping the irony involved in helping keep blacks in their own separate places.

It scarcely matters that such moral indignation was part of an effort to invent a boundary rather than affirm an established one. Boundary setting almost always has this quality of retrospective conjuring. Still, real consequences will ensue from this moving line of the permissible and forbidden. It will be harder for the Republican Party to wink at the ethnocentric portions of its base. Pilgrimages to Bob Jones University, which into the 1990s translated its fear of racial mongrelization into bans on interracial dating, will carry liability. Waving the Confederate flag, a staple of recent South Carolina Republican primaries and the 2002 Georgia senate race, will be more risky than in the past. Although Bush entered the affirmative action fray by opposing the University of Michigan's point system, his actual court brief pointedly refrained from challenging the *Bakke* formula that specified permissible ways of taking race into account. As various legal commentators pointed out, this was very much like opposing abortion without asking the court to negate *Roe v. Wade.*

There is much here that is less than edifying. Just as the cold calculus of the Latino vote gave birth to the warmth of Republican compassion, the new racial sensitivity of Republicans was less attuned to the hurt feelings of blacks than to the good opinion of white suburban Republicans and independents who bristle at racial meanness. But this is the messy way cultures, and political cultures particularly, work and moral boundaries get defined, through earnest conversion and savvy concession. After all, the political incorporation of the working classes in modern democratic states owed just as much to power and pressure as to persuasion. The result is still an extension of the moral infrastructure of citizenship.

There was something else reassuring about the high camp burlesque of Trent Lott's ablutions, as well as the tawdriness of Enron and World Com and the proliferation of ever more lurid versions of "reality" television and "Girls Gone Wild" videos on late-night cable. It reminded us that September 11 did not put an end to cultural and political life as we have known it. At the same time, the return of Al Qaeda, musings about Islamicists' seizure of Pakistan's nuclear arsenal, brief panics over Arab infiltrators at the Canadian border, the looming war in Iraq, and the frightful bluster of the North Korean dictator Bush liked to call "a pygmy" all hinted at a world spiraling out of control—at least a world escaping the clutch of familiar theories. Given the power of unimagined events to astonish, it may be premature to hazard guesses about the future. Still, it is possible to glimpse two major sources of fractiousness in the years ahead.

The first of these fault lines is domestic. September 11 will continue to complicate the trajectories of civic liberalism and compassionate conservatism and the relationship of each to one another and to the more ancient versions from which each descended. In this context the Republican capture of the Senate is not without danger for the party; Bush's growing power to enact his vision of the United States could split the nation. After all, the detribalization of the right symbolized by Bush's stance on immigration and his response to the Lott affair resolves one aspect of the Republicans' identity quandary only to intensify another: increasingly shorn of its ethnic and racial baggage, reduced down to its philosophic and material essence, conservatism remains torn between the ideals of community and corporation.

The vibrancy of his communitarian rhetoric provides some clues to Bush's response to that choice. His inaugural speech sketched a vision of responsibility, not simply for oneself but a duty to help others: "When we see that wounded traveler on the road to Jericho, we will not pass to the other side." The president's sermonizing at a black church on Martin Luther King Jr.'s birthday in 2003 concretized this ethic of care. "There are still people in our society who hurt. There is still prejudice holding people back. There is still a school system that doesn't elevate every child so they can learn. There is still a need for us to hear the words of Martin Luther King, to make sure the hope of America extends its reach into every neighborhood across this land."[23]

Yet the radical tension between the halcyon Fourth Way rhetoric Bush campaigned on (and continues to utter on ceremonial occasions) and the hard conservative agenda he has plied while governing perhaps better indicates Bush's resolution of the conservative dilemma. Even as he has astutely avoided the most polarizing wedge issues, Bush has signaled a cultural warrior side in his opposition to stem cell research and furtive gambits to define the fetus as a person; in his ardor for abstinence and expunging talk of condoms from government Web sites and social policy; and in federal court nominees whose conservative version of judicial activism is deeply skeptical of the national idea embodied in the doctrine of incorporation and its nationalizing extension of the Bill of Rights to state governments. By waging culture war by other means—on the side, on the sly—Bush has honored the center's moderation in the very effort to evade its attention and wrath.

Bush has offered an equally conservative economics that is at odds with both the idiom of the collective good and popular opinion. The constancy in that stance lies less in the ideological coherence of pristine antistatism than in the indulgence of corporate priorities on taxes, health care, stock market regulation, energy, the environment, and trade. Even the sacrosanct idiom of patriotic unity, let alone national security, did not carry the day against the special wishes of the chemical industry when the two collided over the Chemical Security Act. That bill, authored by Senator Jon Corzine and supported by homeland security chief Tom Ridge, would have subjected chemical plants on which a terrorist attack might produce hundreds of thousands of casualties to the same regula-

tions governing nuclear plants and other prime targets. But after ferocious lobbying by the American Chemistry Council and with the White
House's tacit support, Republicans killed the bill.[24] Similarly, the enactment of compassion faltered mightily in the wake of Bush's other priorities. In fall 2002 the first and former head of faith-based initiatives, John
DiIulio, lamented the "virtual absence as yet of any policy accom-
plishments that might . . . count as the flesh on the bones of so-called
compassionate conservatism." Even the so-called faith bill, The Community Solutions Act, "bore few marks" of compassion.[25] As such practical tests of moral intention hint, the moral imperative of compassion
has often devolved into a sympathetic rhetoric that helps present a moderate, caring self and legitimizes a program of personal enrichment and
social callousness.

The contradiction between such rival images of America will likely fly
apart, although concern with global threat may stave off public restive-
ness, both with Bush's less-than-centrist policies and the disproportionate benefits they allocate to the privileged classes. As E. J. Dionne Jr. argues (chap. 14), it is not impossible that a Fifth Way built around military
mobilization might realign American politics and culture. At the least public attention has been diverted from domestic matters, and our warrior
in chief has deferred the day of reckoning with ominous economic news.
At the same time, Dionne points out, so far terror has altered strategic
possibilities and political priorities more than it has changed the dispositions of the center. Here lie the seeds of serious ideological division in
the years to come, for if anything, September 11 revived the obvious primacy of the national idea. It made clear the need for federal efforts of
all sorts, from homeland defense to public health. Bush suffered defeats
on campaign finance and the Arctic oil reserve and retreated on school
vouchers. The Enron and other corporate scandals lay bare deep populist resentments that had not disappeared from the middle classes simply because they too now had joined the investor classes.

This gap gives Democrats real opportunities. But although their electoral chances may teeter on the empirical shape of the economy and the
contingency of their candidates' charisma, conviction will also determine
their fate. What kind of nation do the Democrats envision? Do they have
the resolve to stand up—*for* a rival vision of America, *against* their own
dependence on wealthy donors. With the exception of Al Sharpton the
Democratic contenders cluster around some variant of the Third Way
creed. They have the advantage of being more in tune with the center of
opinion on health care, abortion, tax cuts, and the environment. To en-

act his dramaturgy of compassion, Bush has to make studied bids to deploy his opponents' rhetoric on prescription drugs and AIDs in Africa. By contrast, the Democrats can argue that no such squirming is required for them; they boast the credibility of not being recent converts who fought Medicare and the civil rights bills at their inception. They also have a standing commitment to a different vision of community, not the spontaneity of disparate little communities of care and individual acts of charity—what Bush calls "acts of compassion that can transform America, one heart and one soul at a time"—but a national state that is the ultimate repository of communal obligation to nurture its citizens.

Already, the civic liberalism of Democrats is vulnerable to venal and parochial tendencies of its own. As with Fourth Way compassion, Third Way respect for civil society and the market can be a marketing device to "take back the center." Second, Democratic attention to *its* fragments, from teachers to trial lawyers, threatens an expansive notion of social membership. Third, aside from Sharpton none of the Democrats has spoken as prophetically as DiIulio has about the ghetto poor. To reduce the moral and emotional distance between the majority and the disprivileged, will Democrats speak as urgently as Bush did in his 2003 State of the Union Address, when he replaced Clinton's therapeutic rhetoric with a more evangelical idiom of recovery? "For so many in our country—the homeless and the fatherless, the addicted—the need is great. Yet there's power, wonder-working power, in the goodness and idealism and faith of the American people." So far, preoccupied with the middle classes, Democratic candidates have been silent. Finally, as the slew of Democrats who voted against the first Gulf War but now embrace the second attests, a more muscular foreign policy can be a stratagem or a craven ritual of masculinity as much as it can be the principled resolve of a liberal nationalism that would extend the duty of the nation-state to the suffering citizens of the world.

The second source of fractiousness ahead lies in global danger, the proper response to which is already creating inchoate divisions among the American people. How to respond is a matter of deep symbolic questions as much as technical ones. *What do we want? What kind of people do we want to be? And what kind of world do we want to be in?*

Bush's answer has been a nationalism that restates the neoisolationist rhetoric of American self-interest—unilateralist in spirit if not execution, suspicious of entanglements, and wary of idealism, yet without the demonizing that marked absolutist Americanism. As in the domestic sphere, external threat has given the commander in chief the slack to finesse the gap between his approach and the public's disquiet. So far unanimity on the imperative of collective survival has blocked serious debate over alternative ways of being in a menacing world. The public has not dwelled too insistently on the failure to finish off the Al Qaeda leadership, although one could imagine the return of the now repressed cry, *Who Lost Tora Bora?* The public has not really scrutinized either Bush's clumsy reversion to the overwrought rhetoric of "axis of evil," redolent of the vestigial tradition of absolutist liberalism, or the impact of this reckless forging of a nonsensical "alliance" of Iran, North Korea, and Iraq on Kim Jong Il's antics.

Still, the public's patience is not infinite. It may be that by the time of this book's appearance, war in Iraq is over or in motion. As of early 2003, however, a goodly portion of the American public was nervous about the direction of Republican foreign policy. Support for war in Iraq plummeted once the proviso was added that the Americans go it alone without allies or multilateral legitimacy. Such nervousness tipped the balance of policy power in December 2002 from renegade unilateralism to the decorative performance of concern for entangling alliances, global opinion, and the United Nations.

Before contention can erupt over foreign policy, however, there must be an alternative, precisely and passionately argued. And the truth is that in whatever other respects Bush's prosecution of the imperial mission remains deficient, he has responded with a resolve that grasps the magnitude of the threats in play and the stakes at peril. Even if the idiom of evil evokes tribal fears of strangeness, even if it expresses the particularistic values of Bush's born-again experience and confirms the increasing sense that he is engaged in a theological showdown with the wicked, it does define the character of the world we live in. It is hard to argue with Bush's simple, but not simplistic, reflection on Saddam Hussein: "[If] electric shock, burning with hot irons, dripping acid on the skin, mutilation with electric drills, cutting out tongues, and rape . . . is not evil, then evil has no meaning." Both the clarity of a bicentric world order defined by superpower competition and the short-lived relief of a post–cold war era have given way to the frightful instability of a single-power hegemony beset by a swirl of regional threats amplified by the dispersal of the technical means of destruction. It behooves those who support a more universalistic notion of American civil religion to specify how they will translate lofty aspirations into a determined response to dangerous enemies.

In such a world, Michael Ignatieff observes, the United States, although maybe a reluctant imperial power, is still an imperial power. But that does not resolve the matter of what sort of imperial power our nation should strive to be. One could argue, following Jennifer Hochschild, that as bystanders with the means to prevent harm we are morally obliged to do so. Surely, as European diffidence in the Balkans attests, at times the United States has been the only nation with the will to intervene on humanitarian grounds.

Woodrow Wilson's image of a redeemer nation, much like his promise "to cleanse," calls up too many bad associations of manifest destiny and *mission civilitrice*; Kennedy's grandiosity—"We shall pay any price, bear any burden"—reminds us that mission can transmute into missionizing hubris. High-flown talk of rights is understandably galling to those who cannot forget oil-driven CIA coups, Central American death squads, and the litany of authoritarian regimes who have been the United States' proxies, henchmen, and "friends." As the United States' task spirals from self-defense to toppling and building regimes to exporting rights to fighting primordial evil, Daniel Bell's warning in "The End of American Exceptionalism," is apt: American righteousness is ever in danger of transmuting into self-righteousness.[26]

But from Carter's version of civil religion—"Because we are free we can never be indifferent to the fate of freedom elsewhere"—to Clinton's more tempered formulation, the idealism of rights enforced by American power remains a powerful beacon. As different as they are, both men, retrieving that moral tradition from the repertoire of American values yet tempering it with humility and historical self-reflection, helped reinvent liberal nationalism; at least they revived its spirit, a necessary step after the disenchantment of Vietnam. Senator Joseph Biden's edgy response to a European journalist at the Davos meeting—in which he first confessed to the astonished reporter that oil really is a key factor in the Iraq debate, then quickly added *at least for the French*—restores perspective: the United States is not the only nation with dirty hands. Similarly, Germany's reluctance on Iraq may serve to restrain the cowboy predilection embodied in Bush's pledge to get Osama Bin Laden "dead or alive," but then again, it is not a bad idea to recall European dithering in the face of Hitler's evil. That the lessons of Munich were learned too well by the generation that gave us Vietnam does not mean one cannot learn them too poorly. Would the world not be a better place if it had taken to heart the lessons condensed in the mantra Never Again and applied them to the Rwanda genocide and not just to ethnic cleansing in the Balkans?

All of this points to the flip side of our imperial role, which Ignatieff notes, too; an imperial power, at times a reluctant one, the United States has also been a strangely idealistic one that embraces the ideal of self-determination. Felicitously, it may be that this deeper idealism, the projection of civic nationalism onto the world stage, may promote our self-interest better than a narrow realpolitik. A little less swagger, not so much amnesia about the United States' complicity in ignoble adventures, and fewer snipes at "Old Europe" might have given more credibility to Bush's last-minute recourse to the tradition of rights as he prepared to strike Baghdad.

As a result one can imagine a convergence of will, duty, interest, and ideals around a rival global stance: against an updated nationalism that avoids entanglements but goes light on the moralistic withdrawal from otherness, an updated universalism that proclaims rights (and partners) but goes light on redemptive crusading. In a sense these two gestalts would represent more tempered, civil versions of their global antecedents of isolationism and interventionism, much as the Third and Fourth Ways represent more temperate versions of their domestic antecedents. To push the isomorphism a bit further, such domestic divisions match global ones, and both express rival moral schema, with their own ways of construing the role of interest and morality in social life, the character of obligation, and the permeability of boundaries of self, community, nation, and humanity.

Who knows what the increasingly menacing future will bring. In any case trying to conjure the future only underscores the limits of the narrative of fragmentation, its ability to direct conversation toward certain topics at the expense of others. Above all, its focus on issues of civic membership and communal integration draws attention away from the matter of unequal life chances in the United States, just as the moralizing rhetoric of "axis of evil" simplifies the complex sources of global alienation and failed states, as well as the United States' historical role in promoting both.

The power of terror to eclipse an array of vital national issues underlines one cost the nation has already incurred. The initial economic repercussions of September 11—airline layoffs and stock market swings; the harm to commerce caused by the anthrax threat to the mail; the disruption of global tourism, travel, and trade; and much more—should also give pause. The strength of the international economy is its weakness: it has never been more tightly coupled and thus vulnerable to shocks. A sustained downturn in American living standards will have long-term implications for the poor, for vulnerable immigrants, for a precarious middle. If coupled with feelings of helplessness and betrayal, economic crisis might inspire a xenophobic search for scapegoats. It is possible that panic could generate new lines of ethnic fracture; quite possibly democratic rights and due process will be swept aside in the precipitous rush to protect ourselves.

At the moment, however, such fearsome scenarios remain more a possibility than a destiny. Our most recent history vindicates a sunnier view. For the most part conflicts stirred by ethnic, racial, and cultural divisions continue to flow through democratic channels of dispute and settlement. The restraints on anti-Muslim and anti-Arab violence affirmed by powerful state institutions attest to the democratic learning that has taken place. There are other grounds for solace, especially those moments of national tribulation during which the end of the American experiment was proclaimed. It may be that the United States has lost a good deal of its self-congratulatory faith in its exceptionalism, its conviction of being a providential nation blessed by God. In the long run that may prove to be a blessing in disguise. This greater sense of humility may temper American arrogance as we navigate a world of dangerous complexity. The stakes have never been higher: not just our most prized values but the nation's very survival.

NOTES

I thank Tom Remington for his astute comments on this chapter.

1. Quoted in Jonathan Schell, *The Time of Illusion: An Historical and Reflective Account of the Nixon Era* (New York: Vintage, 1976), 37.

2. Daniel Bell, "The End of American Exceptionalism," in *The American Commonwealth, 1976,* ed. Nathan Glazer and Irving Kristol (New York: Basic Books, 1976), 220.

3. Quoted in Mark Lisheron, "Before Sept. 11, A Nation Divided," *Austin American-Statesman,* Dec. 30, 2001, D6.

4. Alan Wolfe, *One Nation, After All: What Middle-Class Americans Really Think about God, Country, Family, Racism, Welfare, Immigration, Homosexuality, Work, the Right, the Left, and Each Other* (New York: Viking, 1998), 279.

5. Yaron Ezrahi, "The Clash between Nationalism and Democracy in Contemporary Israel," unpublished manuscript.

6. Garry Wills, *Nixon Agonistes: The Crisis of the Self-Made Man* (1969; reprint, New York: New American Library, 1971), 511.

7. Orlando Patterson, *The Ordeal of Integration: Progress and Resentment in America's "Racial" Crisis* (Washington, D.C.: Civitas, 1997), 2, 17.

8. David A. Hollinger, *Postethnic America: Beyond Multiculturalism* (New York: Basic Books, 1995), 116.

9. Michael Ignatieff, quoted in ibid., 134.

10. Anthony Giddens, *The Third Way and Its Critics* (Cambridge, U.K.: Polity Press, 2000), 51.

11. Mark Lisheron, "From Rubble to Resolve," *Austin American-Statesman,* Sep. 16, 2001, A19.

12. Erving Goffman, *Relations in Public: Microstudies of the Public Order* (New York: Basic Books, 1971), 240.

13. *New York Times,* Sep. 19, 2001, A20.

14. "A Nation Challenged: Portraits of Grief," *New York Times,* Oct. 18, 2001, B13.

15. The host of the television show Politically Incorrect had dared venture the impolitic opinion that Osama Bin Ladin was no coward. "We have been the cowards, lobbing cruise missiles from 2,000 miles away. That's cowardly. Staying in the airplane when it hits the building—say what you want about it, it's not cowardly."

16. Somini Sengupta, *New York Times,* Oct. 10, 2001, B1.

17. Louis Hartz, *The Liberal Tradition in America: An Interpretation of American Political Thought Since the Revolution* (New York: Harcourt, Brace, 1955), 286.

18. Alan A. Dershowitz, "Why Fear National ID Cards," *New York Times,* Oct. 13, 2001, A22.

19. Jonathan E. Smaby, "American Ramadan," *New York Times,* Nov. 18, 2001, sec. 4, 13.

20. Quoted in Michelle Cottle, "Separate Ways," *New Republic,* Dec. 23, 2002, 14.

21. Kai Erikson, *Wayward Puritans* (New York: John Wiley, 1966), 13.

22. *Time Magazine,* Dec. 23, 2002, 25.

23. *New York Times,* Jan. 21, 2003, A16.

24. John Judis, "Poison: The GOP Sacrifices National Security for the Chemical Lobby," *New Republic,* Jan. 27, 2003, 12.

25. John DiIulio to Ron Suskind, Oct. 24, 2002. http://www.esquire.com/features/articles/2002/021202_mfe_diiulio_1.html. The letter was the source of Suskind's story "Why Are These Men Laughing?" *Esquire,* Jan. 2002.

26. Bell, "End of American Exceptionalism" (my paraphrase).

Contributors

RICHARD BERNSTEIN, the author of *Fragile Glory: A Portrait of France and the French* and *Dictatorship of Virtue: Multiculturalism and the Battle for America's Future,* is a book reviewer for the *New York Times* culture section. His most recent book is *Ultimate Journey: Retracing the Path of an Ancient Buddhist Monk Who Crossed Asia in Search of Enlightenment.*

JOHN J. DIIULIO JR. is Frederic Fox Leadership Professor at the University of Pennsylvania and senior fellow at the Manhattan Institute and the Brookings Institution. In 2001 he served as the first director of the White House Office of Faith-Based and Community Initiatives. He is, most recently, the coauthor (with James Q. Wilson) of *American Government: Institutions and Policies* and the coeditor (with E. J. Dionne Jr.) of *What's God Got to Do with the American Experiment?*

PAUL DIMAGGIO is professor of sociology at Princeton University and research director and cofounder of the Princeton University Center for Arts and Cultural Policy Studies. His writings on culture include "Have Americans' Social Attitudes Become More Polarized?" (with Bethany Bryson and John Evans), "The Role of Religion in Public Conflicts over Media and the Arts" (with Wendy Cadge, Lynn Robinson, and Brian Steensland), "Culture and Cognition," and "Enacting Community in Progressive America: Civic Rituals in National Music Week, 1924." He is also coauthor (with Francie Ostrower) of *Race, Ethnicity, and Participation in the Arts.*

E. J. DIONNE JR. is a syndicated columnist at the *Washington Post* and senior fellow in the Governmental Studies Program at the Brookings Institution. He is the author of *Why Americans Hate Politics* and *They Only Look Dead: Why Progressives Will Dominate the Next Political Era.* His edited works include *Com-*

munity Works: The Revival of Civil Society in America; Bush v. Gore: *The Court Cases and the Commentary* (with William Kristol); and *Sacred Places, Civic Purposes: Should Government Help Faith-Based Charity?* (with Ming Hsu Chen).

KEVIN GAINES is an associate professor in the History Department and the Center for Afro-American and African Studies at the University of Michigan. He is the author of *Uplifting the Race: Black Leadership, Politics, and Culture during the Twentieth Century;* and the forthcoming *From Black Power to Civil Rights: African-American Expatriates in Nkrumah's Ghana, 1957–1966.*

JENNIFER HOCHSCHILD is professor of government and a member of the departments of Government and Afro-American Studies at Harvard University. She is the author of *Facing Up to the American Dream: Race, Class, and the Soul of the Nation; The New American Dilemma: Liberal Democracy and School Desegregation;* and *What's Fair? American Beliefs about Distributive Justice.* She is completing a book entitled *The American Dream and the Public Schools* (with Nathan Scovronick).

DOUGLAS S. MASSEY, a former president of the American Sociological Association, is the Dorothy Swaine Thomas Professor of Sociology at the University of Pennsylvania. His coauthored books include *American Apartheid: Segregation and the Making of the Underclass; Return to Aztlan: The Social Process of International Migration from Western Mexico; Worlds in Motion: Understanding International Migration at the End of the Millennium;* and *Beyond Smoke and Mirrors: Mexican Immigration in an Era of Economic Integration.*

MARTHA MINOW is a professor at Harvard Law School. Her books include *Making All the Difference: Inclusion, Exclusion, and American Law; Not Only for Myself: Identity, Politics, and Law; Between Vengeance and Forgiveness: Facing History after Genocide and Mass Violence;* and *Breaking the Cycles of Violence.*

CECILIA MUÑOZ is vice president for the Office of Research, Advocacy, and Legislation, National Council of La Raza (NCLR), where she supervises legislative and advocacy activities on issues of importance to Latinos, including civil rights, employment, poverty, and immigration. In recognition of her work on immigration and civil rights she was awarded a MacArthur Foundation fellowship in 2000.

JONATHAN RIEDER is chair of the Department of Sociology at Barnard College and a member of the graduate faculty at Columbia University. He is the author of *Canarsie: The Jews and Italians of Brooklyn against Liberalism* and the forthcoming *Moral Argument in American Politics: The Social Organization of Righteous Passion.*

THEDA SKOCPOL, the 2002–2003 centennial president of the American Political Science Association, is Victor S. Thomas Professor of Government and Sociology at Harvard University, where she also serves as director of the Center for American Political Studies. Her books include *States and Social Revolutions; Protecting Soldiers and Mothers: Political Origins of Social Policy in the United*

States; The Missing Middle: Working Families and the Future of American Social Policy; and *Diminished Democracy: From Membership to Management in American Civic Life.*

PAUL STARR, professor of sociology at Princeton University and coeditor of the *American Prospect,* is the author of *The Social Transformation of American Medicine* and *The Logic of Health Care Reform.* He has written extensively on privatization, health care, and national politics for the *American Prospect.*

MARY C. WATERS is Harvard College Professor and chair of the Department of Sociology at Harvard University. She is the author of *From Many Strands: Ethnic and Racial Groups in Contemporary America* (with Stanley Lieberson); *Ethnic Options: Choosing Identities in America;* and *Black Identities: West Indian Immigrant Dreams and American Realities.* With Philip Kasinitz and John Mollenkopf she is working on a major study of the immigrant second generation in New York City.

JACK WERTHEIMER is provost and professor of American Jewish History at the Jewish Theological Seminary. He is the author of *A People Divided: Judaism in Contemporary America* and editor of *Jews in the Center: Conservative Synagogues and Their Members.* He is currently writing a book on the transformation of organized Jewish life in the United States during the last half-century.

Index

AARP (American Association of Retired Persons), 192

abortion, 20, 28, 82–83, 90, 95n14, 209

Adarand v. Pena, 207, 210

AFDC (Aid to Families with Dependent Children), 195, 221, 234

affirmative action: benefactors of, 158; black/white agreement on, 166; Bush's stand on, 270; California's reversal on, 207, 231; 1996 campaign issue of, 210–11

Afghanistan war, 246, 265–66

AFL-CIO, 199

African-American intellectuals, 3; anti-integrationist response of, 177–78; corporate marketing of, 173; racial responsibility dilemma of, 3, 170–73, 181n2; with segregation nostalgia, 179–80; Wright's legacy for, 180–81

African Americans: American dream ideology of, 165–66; anti-integration sentiments of, 177–80; anti-Semitism of, 5, 16–17; Bush's pursuit of, 7; class differences of, 158–59; communal injuries to, 69, 76–77n3, 173–74; on criminal justice system, 166, 169n30; on education standards, 166–67; eroded racism against, 11, 31, 38–39, 158, 245–46; on ethnic profiling, 261–62; expanded racial belonging by, 3, 8–9, 18, 37–39, 41;

false perspectives on, 18, 32, 52n34; immigrants' identification with, 125, 126, 127; intellectual community of, 170–72, 181n2; intermarriage statistics on, 122; privatization's appeal to, 213–14; race-blind policies on, 207, 210; of Reconstruction era, 175; transnational identity model of, 172–73; whites' consensus with, 3, 84, 165–66; whites' perceptions versus, 156–58, 167nn2–4. *See also* African-American intellectuals; Afrocentrism

African independence movements, 180

Afrocentrism: as antifeminist/homophobic, 178–79; as anti-integrationist, 177–78; fragmentation linked to, 174–75; intellectuals' alternatives to, 172–73; Schlesinger Jr. on, 175–76; in schools, 60; and Wright legacy, 180–81

Agendas for Public Affairs (NJCRAC), 108

Agnew, Spiro, 23, 45

Agudath Israel movement, 107

AIDS, 27, 108, 156, 167nn3,4, 273

Aid to Families with Dependent Children (AFDC), 195, 221, 234

Alba, Richard D., 121–22

Alien Nation (Brimelow), 70

Allen, Carl, 269

Ameer, Inge-Lise, 18

Text: 10/13 Sabon
Display: Sabon
Indexer: Patricia Deminna
Compositor: Integrated Composition Systems
Printer: Friesens Corporation